Emotion and Meaning in Music

By LEONARD B. MEYER

THE UNIVERSITY OF CHICAGO PRESS

CHICAGO AND LONDON

ISBN: 0-226-52138-9 *(clothbound)*; 0-226-52139-7 *(paperbound)*

Library of Congress Catalog Card Number: 56-9130

THE UNIVERSITY OF CHICAGO PRESS, CHICAGO 60637
The University of Chicago Press, Ltd., London

Preface

The diversity and complexity of twentieth-century modes of thought, together with the clear and pressing need for a more sensitive and comprehensive understanding of how the exchange of attitudes, information, and ideas takes place, has made the analysis of meanings and an examination of the processes by which they are communicated an important focus of interest for many nominally disparate fields of inquiry. Philosophy, psychology, sociology, and anthropology, to name some of those most directly involved, have all become concerned with the problem of meaning: the variety of meanings, their significance and epistemological status, their interrelationships, and manner of communication. Other fields, such as economics, political science, various branches of the humanities, and even the natural sciences, have likewise directed attention to these problems.

The problem of musical meaning and its communication is of particular interest for several reasons. Not only does music use no linguistic signs but, on one level at least, it operates as a closed system, that is, it employs no signs or symbols referring to the non-musical world of objects, concepts, and human desires. Thus the meanings which it imparts differ in important ways from those conveyed by literature, painting, biology, or physics. Unlike a closed, non-referential mathematical system, music is said to communicate emotional and aesthetic meanings as well as purely intellectual ones. This puzzling combination of abstractness with concrete emotional and aesthetic experience can, if understood correctly, perhaps yield useful insights into more general problems of meaning and communication, especially those involving aesthetic experience.

However, before the relationship of music to other kinds of meaning and other modes of communication can be considered, a detailed examination of the meanings of music and the processes by which they are communicated must be made. Thus although it is hoped that the relevance of this study to the larger problems of meaning and communication will be apparent, these matters are not explicitly considered. No attempt, for example, is made to deal with the general logical philosophical status of music—to decide whether music is a language or whether musical stimuli are signs or symbols.

The relationship between music and other realms of aesthetic experience is likewise left for the reader to determine. Where reference has been made to other modes of aesthetic experience, it has been done in order to clarify or bring into sharper relief some point in connection with musical processes rather than to establish a general aesthetic system. On the other hand, one can hardly fail to become aware of the striking similarity of some aspects of musical experience to other types of aesthetic experience, particularly those evoked by literature.

The subject of the present study, though perhaps of more than passing interest from the general viewpoints discussed above, is of vital and paramount importance in the field of music itself.

For if the aesthetics and criticism of music are ever to move out of the realms of whim, fancy, and prejudice, and if the analysis of music is ever to go beyond description which employs a special jargon, then some account of the meaning, content, and communication of music more adequate than at present available must be given. As I. A. Richards puts it, "The two pillars upon which a theory of criticism must rest are an account of value and an account of communication"[1]—and included in an account of

---

1. I. A. Richards, *Principles of Literary Criticism* (New York: Harcourt Brace & Co., 1928), p. 25. Although value judgments are unavoidably implied throughout, the present study is primarily concerned with presenting an account of meaning and communication.

communication is obviously an account of the meanings communicated.

Meaning and communication cannot be separated from the cultural context in which they arise. Apart from the social situation there can be neither meaning nor communication. An understanding of the cultural and stylistic presuppositions of a piece of music is absolutely essential to the analysis of its meaning. It should, however, be noted that the converse of this proposition is also true: namely, that an understanding of the general nature of musical meaning and its communication is essential to an adequate analysis of style and hence to the study of music history and the investigations of comparative musicology as well.

The arguments and debates of aestheticians, the experiments and theories of psychologists, and the speculations of musicologists and composers still continue and are ample indication that the problems of musical meaning and communication are with us today. In fact, the inclusion of music as part of liberal education, the unpatronizing and serious consideration given to non-Western music, and the attempts to include the art of music in studies dealing with cultural history have made the problems even more pressing. It is because of these needs, as well as the more specifically musical ones mentioned earlier, that the author has the temerity to attempt another study in this field.

The book is divided into three main parts. Chapter i considers, first, the nature of emotional and intellectual meanings, their interrelationship, and the conditions which give rise to them, and, second, how in general these conditions are fulfilled in the response to musical stimuli. Chapters ii–v are devoted to a fairly detailed examination of the social and psychological conditions under which meaning arises and communication takes place in response to music. And chapters vi–vii present evidence of various kinds, taken from several cultures and several cultural levels, to support the central hypothesis of the study.

Because this study draws so freely upon work in many diverse fields, it is perhaps important to emphasize that the basic theoretical formulations advanced in it were derived from a study of music rather than, for instance, from a study of aesthetics or psychology. Other fields often furnished exciting and encouraging confirmation for conclusions originally reached through a careful consideration of music and musical processes. Fields outside music have also served to refine concepts or have led to more general formulations. But music was throughout the controlling guide in the formulation of the theory presented here.

The debt which this book owes to other scholars is both so manifest and so vast that only a few of the most important ones can be mentioned. In the field of philosophy the work of Henry D. Aiken, John Dewey, Susanne Langer, and George Mead has been a source of insight and understanding. In the field of psychology I have obviously leaned heavily upon the works of K. Koffka, J. T. MacCurdy, and James Mursell. Though contributing little or nothing to the theoretical formulations made, the work of musicians and musicologists, particularly those working in comparative musicology, has been an important source for most of the evidence presented in the later portions of this book.

Throughout the preparation and writing of this book, I have received valuable advice and encouragement from my colleagues and students. In particular I am indebted to Grosvenor Cooper for his sympathetic understanding of the viewpoint of this study and his many excellent suggestions; to Charles Morris for his cogent criticisms and his precise analysis of many of the problems discussed in the course of this work; to Knox C. Hill, who helped me to edit and cut the text; and to Otto Gombosi, who gave so freely of his wisdom and erudition.

Last but (as tradition hath it) by no means least, I wish to acknowledge the debt I owe to my wife. For it was she who encouraged me when I was depressed; prodded me when I was lazy; ran the household so that I had a maximum of peace and quiet; and at the same time managed to put up with my many moods and perversities. _bastard!_

Table of Contents

Table of Contents

I

Theory

Past Positions as to the Nature of Musical Experience

Composers and performers of all cultures, theorists of diverse schools and styles, aestheticians and critics of many different persuasions are all agreed that music has meaning and that this meaning is somehow communicated to both participants and listeners. This much, at least, we may take for granted. But what constitutes musical meaning and by what processes it is communicated has been the subject of numerous and often heated debates.

The first main difference of opinion exists between those who insist that musical meaning lies exclusively within the context of the work itself, in the perception of the relationships set forth within the musical work of art, and those who contend that, in addition to these abstract, intellectual meanings, music also communicates meanings which in some way refer to the extramusical world of concepts, actions, emotional states, and character. Let us call the former group the "absolutists" and the latter group the "referentialists."

In spite of the persistent wrangling of these two groups, it seems obvious that absolute meanings and referential meanings are not mutually exclusive: that they can and do coexist in one and the same piece of music, just as they do in a poem or a painting. In short, the arguments are the result of a tendency toward philosophical monism rather than a product of any logical opposition between types of meaning.

Because this study deals primarily with those meanings which

1

lie within the closed context of the musical work itself, it is necessary to emphasize that the prominence given to this aspect of
musical meaning does not imply that other kinds of meaning do not
exist or are not important.

On the contrary, the musical theory and practice of many different cultures in many different epochs indicates that music can and
does convey referential meaning. The musical cosmologies of the
Orient in which tempi, pitches, rhythms, and modes are linked to
and express concepts, emotions, and moral qualities; the musical
symbolisms depicting actions, character and emotion, utilized by
many Western composers since the Middle Ages; and evidence
furnished by testing listeners who have learned to understand Western music—all these indicate that music can communicate referential meanings.

Some of those who have doubted that referential meanings are
"real" have based their skepticism upon the fact that such meanings are not "natural" and universal. Of course, such meanings
depend upon learning. But so, too, do purely musical meanings—
a fact that will become very clear in the course of this study.

Others have found the fact that referential meanings are not
specific in their denotation a great difficulty in granting status to
such meanings. Yet such precision is not a characteristic of the
non-musical arts either. The many levels of connotation play a vital
role in our understanding of the meanings communicated by the
literary and plastic arts.

Both the importance of such referential musical meanings and
the difficulties encountered in attempting to base an adequate
aesthetic upon them are discussed in chapter viii. For the present
we must set them aside and simply state that it is not this aspect
of meaning which will primarily concern us in the course of this
study. For an adequate analysis of the problems involved in the
meaning and communication of the referential content of music
would require a separate study of its own.

Let us now make a second point clear, namely, that the distinction just drawn between absolute and referential meanings is
not the same as the distinction between the aesthetic positions
which are commonly called "formalist" and "expressionist." Both

the formalist and the expressionist may be absolutists; that is, both may see the meaning of music as being essentially intramusical (non-referential); but the formalist would contend that the meaning of music lies in the perception and understanding of the musical relationships set forth in the work of art and that meaning in music is primarily intellectual, while the expressionist would argue that these same relationships are in some sense capable of exciting feelings and emotions in the listener.

This point is important because the expressionist position has often been confused with that of the referentialist. For although almost all referentialists are expressionists, believing that music communicates emotional meanings, not all expressionists are referentialists. Thus when formalists, such as Hanslick or Stravinsky, reacting against what they feel to be an overemphasis upon referential meaning, have denied the possibility or relevance of any emotional response to music, they have adopted an untenable position partly because they have confused expressionism and referentialism.

One might, in other words, divide expressionists into two groups: absolute expressionists and referential expressionists. The former group believe that expressive emotional meanings arise in response to music and that these exist without reference to the extramusical world of concepts, actions, and human emotional states, while the latter group would assert that emotional expression is dependent upon an understanding of the referential content of music.

THE PRESENT POSITION AND CRITICISM OF PAST ASSUMPTIONS

The present study is concerned with an examination and analysis of those aspects of meaning which result from the understanding of and response to relationships inherent in the musical progress rather than with any relationships between the musical organization and the extramusical world of concepts, actions, characters, and situations. The position adopted admits both formalist and absolute expressionist viewpoints. For though the referential expressionists and the formalists are concerned with genuinely different aspects of musical experience, the absolute expressionists and the formalists are actually considering the same musical processes and similar human experiences from different, but not incompatible, viewpoints (see p. 39).

Broadly speaking, then, the present investigation seeks to present an analysis of musical meaning and experience in which both the expressionist and the formalist positions will be accounted for and in which the relationship between them will become clear.

Past accounts given by the proponents of each of these positions have suffered from certain important weaknesses. The chief difficulty of those who have adopted the absolutist expressionist position is that they have been unable to account for the processes by which perceived sound patterns become experienced as feelings and emotions. In fact, strange as it may seem, they have generally avoided any discussion of emotional responses whatsoever. These shortcomings have led to a general lack of precision both in their account of musical experience and in their discussions of musical perception.

But, at least, the expressionists have recognized the existence of problems in their position. The formalists, on the other hand, have either found no problems to recognize or have simply turned the other way, seeking to divert attention from their difficulties by attacking referentialism whenever possible. Yet the formalists are faced with a problem very similar to that confronting the expressionists: namely, the difficulty and necessity of explaining the manner in which an abstract, non-referential succession of tones becomes meaningful. In failing to explain in what sense such musical patterns can be said to have meaning, they have also found themselves unable to show the relation of musical meaning to meaning in general.

Finally, this failure to explain the processes by which feelings are aroused and meanings communicated has prevented both groups from seeing that their positions should make them allies rather than opponents. For the same musical processes and similar psychological behavior give rise to both types of meaning; and both must be analyzed if the variety made possible by this aspect of musical experience is to be understood.

Readers familiar with past studies in the aesthetics and psychology of music will perhaps note that much of the earlier work in these fields is not discussed in this study and that many traditional problems are ignored. This neglect stems from the conviction that the assumptions and orientation of this literature have proved sterile and are today untenable. Since this literature has been explicitly and cogently criticized by such writers as Cazden,[1] Farnsworth,[2] and Langer,[3] only a brief comment on these earlier assumptions seems necessary here, in the hope that the position of this book will thereby be clarified.

The psychology of music has, since its beginnings, been plagued by three interrelated errors: hedonism, atomism, and universalism. Hedonism is the confusion of aesthetic experience with the sensuously pleasing. As Susanne Langer writes:

Helmholtz, Wundt, Stumpf, and other psychologists . . . based their inquiries on the assumption that music was a form of *pleasurable sensation*. . . . This gave rise to an aesthetic based on liking and disliking, a hunt for a sensationist definition of beauty. . . . But beyond a description of tested pleasure-displeasure reactions to simple sounds or elementary sound complexes . . . this approach has not taken us. . . .[4]

The attempt to explain and understand music as a succession of separable, discrete sounds and sound complexes is the error of atomism. Even the meager achievement which Mrs. Langer allows to studies of this kind must be still further depreciated. For the tested pleasure-displeasure reactions are not what most of the psychologists tacitly assumed them to be: they are not universals (good for all times and all places) but products of learning and experience.

This is the third error, the error of universalism: the belief that the responses obtained by experiment or otherwise are universal, natural, and necessary. This universalist approach is also related to the time-honored search for a physical, quasi-acoustical explanation of musical experience—the attempt, that is, to account for musical communication in terms of vibrations, ratios of intervals, and the like.

These same errors have also plagued music theory. Attempts to explain the effect of the minor mode of Western music, to cite but one example, in terms of consonance and dissonance or in terms of the harmonic series have resulted in uncontrolled speculations and untenable theories. Even those not thus haunted by the ghost of Pythagoras have contributed little to our understanding of musical and its communication. For, on the whole, music theorists ncerned themselves with the grammar and syntax of music than with its meaning or the affective experiences to which it gives rise.

Today we are, I think, able to take a somewhat more enlightened view of these matters. The easy access which almost all individuals have to great music makes it quite apparent that a Beethoven symphony is not a kind of musical banana split, a matter of purely sensuous enjoyment. The work of the Gestalt psychologists has shown beyond a doubt that understanding is not a matter of perceiving single stimuli, or simple sound combinations in isolation, but is rather a matter of grouping stimuli into patterns and relating these patterns to one another. And finally, the studies of comparative musicologists, bringing to our attention the music of other cultures, have made us increasingly aware that the particular organization developed in Western music is not universal, natural, or God-given.

Evidence as to the Nature and Existence of the Emotional Response to Music

Any discussion of the emotional response to music is faced at the very outset with the fact that very little is known about this response and its relation to the stimulus. Evidence that it exists at all is based largely upon the introspective reports of listeners and the testimony of composers, performers, and critics. Other evidence of the existence of emotional responses to music is based upon the behavior of performers and audiences and upon the physiological changes that accompany musical perception. Although the volume and intercultural character of this evidence compels us to believe that an emotional response to music does take place, it tells us almost nothing about the nature of the response or about the causal connection between the musical stimulus and the affective response it evokes in listeners.

SUBJECTIVE EVIDENCE

From Plato down to the most recent discussions of aesthetics and the meaning of music, philosophers and critics have, with few ex-

from ancient times it has been thought upon

ceptions, affirmed their belief in the ability of music to evoke emotional responses in listeners. Most of the treatises on musical composition and performance stress the importance of the communication of feeling and emotion. Composers have demonstrated in their writings and by the expression marks used in their musical scores their faith in the affective power of music. And finally, listeners, past and present, have reported with remarkable consistency that music does arouse feelings and emotions in them. → EVIDENCE

The first difficulty with this evidence is that, taken at its face value, without benefit of a general theory of emotions as a basis for interpretation, it yields no precise knowledge of the stimulus which created the emotional response. Because music flows through time, listeners and critics have generally been unable to pinpoint the particular musical process which evoked the affective response which they describe. They have been prone, therefore, to characterize a whole passage, section, or composition. In such cases the response must have been made to those elements of the musical organization which tend to be constant, e.g., tempo, general range, dynamic level, instrumentation, and texture. What these elements characterize are those aspects of mental life which are also relatively stable and persistent, namely, moods and associations, rather than the changing and developing affective responses with which this study is concerned.

Much confusion has resulted from the failure to distinguish between emotion felt (or affect) and mood. Few psychologists dealing with music have been as accurate on this point as Weld, who notes that: "The emotional experiences which our observers reported are to be characterized rather as moods than as emotions in the ordinary sense of the term. . . . The emotion is temporary and evanescent; the mood is relatively permanent and stable." [5] As a matter of fact, most of the supposed studies of emotion in music are actually concerned with mood and association.

Taken at face value the introspective data under consideration not only fail to provide accurate knowledge of the stimulus (music) but they cannot even furnish clear and unequivocal information about the responses reported. For several reasons the verbalizations of emotions, particularly those evoked by music, are usually deceptive and misleading.

Emotions are named and distinguished from one another largely in terms of the external circumstances in which the response takes place. Since, aside from the often fortuitous associations which may be aroused, music presents no external circumstances, descriptions of emotions felt while listening to music are usually apocryphal and misleading. If they are to be used at all, they must be analyzed and considered in the light of a general theory of the relation of musical stimuli to emotional responses.

Second, a clear distinction must be maintained between the emotions felt by the composer, listener, or critic—the emotional response itself—and the emotional states denoted by different aspects of the musical stimulus. The depiction of musical moods in conjunction with conventional melodic or harmonic formulas, perhaps specified by the presence of a text, can become signs which designate human emotional states (see pp. 267 f.). Motives of grief or joy, anger or despair, found in the works of baroque composers or the affective and moral qualities attributed to special modes or *rāgas* in Arabian or Indian music are examples of such conventional denotative signs. And it may well be that when a listener reports that he felt this or that emotion, he is describing the emotion which he believes the passage is supposed to indicate, not anything which he himself has experienced.

Finally, even where the report given is of a genuine emotional experience, it is liable to become garbled and perverted in the process of verbalization. For emotional states are much more subtle and varied than are the few crude and standardized words which we use to denote them.

In this connection it would seem that many of the introspections supplied by subjects in the studies made by Vernon Lee, C. S. Myers, Max Schoen, and others contain a large amount of what psychiatrists call "distortion." For example, when a subject in an experiment by Myers reports that while listening to a particular musical selection she had "a restful feeling throughout . . . like one of going downstream while swimming," [6] she is obviously translating unspeakable feelings into symbolic form. The interpretation of such symbols is the task of the psychiatrist, not the music critic. To the music critic such introspections show only that some response, not necessarily a specifically musical one, was present. For it is always possible that the thoughts and reveries thus revealed are without any relation to musical experience. The musical stimuli may have functioned merely as a kind of catalytic agent, enabling the response to take place but playing no controlling part in shaping or determining the experience and figuring nowhere in the end result, except perhaps negatively (see chap. viii).

OBJECTIVE EVIDENCE: BEHAVIOR

The responses of listeners can also be observed and studied objectively. Two general categories of observable responses can be distinguished: (*a*) those responses which take the form of overt changes in behavior and (*b*) those responses which take the form of less readily observable physiological changes. Such objective evidence, though it undoubtedly avoids the difficulties of the verbalization of subjective feelings and emotions, presents other difficulties no less perplexing.

In the first place, emotional responses need not result in overt, observable behavior. As Henry Aiken points out,[7] one of the special characteristics of our responses to aesthetic objects is the very fact that, due to our beliefs as to the nature of aesthetic experience, we tend to suppress overt behavior. Furthermore, as an important adjunct to this point, it should be noted that emotion-felt or affect is most intense precisely in those cases where feeling does not result in or take the form of overt behavior or mental fantasy (see p. 14). This is clear as soon as one considers the tendency of human beings to "work off" or relieve emotional tension in physical effort and bodily behavior. In short, the absence of overt emotional behavior, particularly in response to aesthetic stimuli, is no indication as to either the presence or force of emotional responses.

However, even where overt behavior is present, its interpretation is difficult and problematical. When, on the one hand, overt behavior is the product of particularly powerful emotional tensions, it tends to be diffuse, generalized, or chaotic. Extreme conflict, for example, may result in either motionless rigidity or frenzied activity;

weeping may be the product of either profound grief or extreme joy. Unless we have accurate knowledge of the stimulus situation beforehand, such behavior can tell us little or nothing as to the significance of the response or of its relation to the stimulus.

On the other hand, when emotional behavior does become differentiated it tends to be standardized—to become part of more general patterns of social behavior. Thus although the philosophical aspect of the stimulus situation, the fact that an aesthetic object is being considered, tends toward the suppression of overt behavior, the social aspect of the stimulus situation permits and at times indeed encourages certain standardized types of emotional behavior. This is apparent in the conduct of performers and audiences alike. The jazz performer and his audience, for example, have one mode of socially sanctioned emotional behavior; the concert performer and his audience have another. The difference between the two is more a matter of conventionally determined behavior patterns than it is a matter of musical differences (see p. 21).

Such behavior must be regarded at least in part as a means of communication rather than as a set of natural, reflex reactions. It indicates and designates not only appropriate mental sets but also the proper (i.e., socially acceptable) modes of response. Once this sort of behavior becomes habitual, and it does so very early in life, then it may be activated by the social aspects of the stimulus situation alone, without regard for the stimulus itself. In short, given no theory as to the relation of musical stimuli to affective responses, observed behavior can provide little information as to either the nature of the stimulus, the significance of the response, or the relation between them. For conduct which might to an observer appear to indicate the presence of an emotional response might in point of fact be the result of the subject's day dreams, his observation and imitation of the behavior of others, or his beliefs as to the kind of behavior appropriate and expected in the given social situation.

OBJECTIVE EVIDENCE: PHYSIOLOGICAL RESPONSES

On the physiological level music evokes definite and impressive responses. It "has a marked effect on pulse, respiration and external blood pressure. . . . [It] delays the onset of muscular fatigue . . . [and] has a marked effect upon the psychogalvanic reflex. . . ." [8] In spite of the fact that these changes are the very ones which normally accompany emotional experience, the significance of these data is not completely clear. Two principal difficulties are involved.

To begin with, no relation can be found between the character or pattern of the musical selection evoking the response and the particular physiological changes which take place. These changes appear to be completely independent of any particular style, form, medium, or general character. The same responses will take place whether the music is fast or slow, exciting or soothing, instrumental or vocal, classical or jazz.

Because tonal stimulation is a constant factor of all musical stimuli, Mursell is led to conclude that the power of "tone as such" must be the cause of the physiological changes observed. [9]

There is, however, another constant involved in the perception of music; namely, the mental attitude of the audience. The listener brings to the act of perception definite beliefs in the affective power of music. Even before the first sound is heard, these beliefs activate dispositions to respond in an emotional way, bringing expectant ideo-motor sets into play. And it seems more reasonable to suppose that the physiological changes observed are a response to the listener's mental set rather than to assume that tone as such can, in some mysterious and unexplained way, bring these changes about directly. For while the relationship between mental sets and physiological changes has been demonstrated beyond doubt, the effect of "tone as such" has not (see pp. 74 f.).

This does not imply that the presence of a physiological environment, which is a necessary condition for the arousal of emotion, is not a significant fact. The existence of this necessary condition increases the likelihood that emotional responses do take place—a fact which some critics have sought to deny. What this analysis indicates is that not only are these physiological adjustments pre-emotional, as Mursell would admit, but they are also pre-musical.

Furthermore, even the conclusions just reached about the significance of the physiological data are probably an exaggeration, if not from a psychological point of view, at least, from a logical one. For such adjustments not only accompany affective responses, but they are also concomitants of clearly non-emotional responses.

In the light of present knowledge it seems clear that though physiological adjustments are probably necessary adjuncts of affective responses they cannot be shown to be sufficient causes for such responses and have, in fact, been able to throw very little light upon the relationship between affective responses and the stimuli which produce them. The situation is concisely summarized by Rapaport:

(*a*) On the basis of the material surveyed nothing can be definitely stated as to the relation to "emotion felt" of physiological processes concomitant with emotions. Proof has not been offered to show that the usually described physiological processes are *always* present when emotion is felt. (*b*) Nothing is known about the physiological processes *underlying* emotional experience. However, sufficient proof has been adduced that neither the James-Lange theory nor the hypothalmic theory explains the origin of "emotion felt." (*c*) The investigations into the physiology and the neural correlates of emotional expression are of importance; their relation to the psychic process designated as "emotion felt" is the crucial point of every theory of emotions. However, the knowledge concerning this relation is so scant that investigations into the influence of emotions on other physiological processes will have to be based rather on what is known about the psychology of emotions.[10]

There is one basic problem with all the objective data discussed: namely, that even when affective experiences result in objective adjustments, whether behavioral or physiological, what can be observed is not the emotion-felt, the affect, but only its adjuncts and concomitants, which in the case of behavior tend to become standardized and in the case of physiological changes are not specific to emotion. What we wish to consider, however, is that which is most vital and essential in emotional experience: the feeling-tone accompanying emotional experience, that is, the affect.

Here we face a dilemma. On the one hand, the response with which we are concerned is profoundly and permanently subjective and hence of necessity concealed from the scrutiny of even the most scrupulous observers; and, on the other hand, we have found that the subjective data available, taken by themselves, provide no definite and unequivocal information about the musical stimulus, the

affective response, or the relation between them. This di[...]
be resolved only if the subjective data available, includ[...]
sponses of the readers and the author of this study, can be[...]
sifted, and studied in the light of a general hypothesis as to the
nature of affective experience and the processes by which musical
stimuli might arouse such experience.

Such a hypothesis is provided by the psychological theory of
emotions. For although much work undoubtedly remains to be done
in the field of emotional theory, there appears to be general agreement among psychologists and psychiatrists at least as to the conditions under which emotional responses arise and as to the relationship between the affective stimulus and the affective response.

The Psychological Theory of Emotions

Since the physiological changes which accompany emotional experience, whatever their importance, do not provide a basis for
differentiating affective from non-affective states, the differentia
must be sought in the realm of mental activity.

However, not all mental responses are affective. We speak of
dispassionate observation, calm deliberation, and cool calculation.
These are non-emotional states of mind.

If we then ask what distinguishes non-emotional states from emotional ones, it is clear that the difference does not lie in the stimulus
alone. The same stimulus may excite emotion in one person but not
in another. Nor does the difference lie in the responding individual.
The same individual may respond emotionally to a given stimulus
in one situation but not in another. The difference lies in the relationship between the stimulus and the responding individual.

This relationship must first of all be such that the stimulus produces a tendency in the organism to think or act in a particular way.
An object or situation which evokes no tendency, to which the
organism is indifferent, can only result in a non-emotional state of
mind.

But even when a tendency is aroused, emotion may not result. If,
for example, a habitual smoker wants a cigarette and, reaching into
his pocket, finds one, there will be no affective response. If the

tendency is satisfied without delay, no emotional response will take place. If, however, the man finds no cigarette in his pocket, discovers that there are none in the house, and then remembers that the stores are closed and he cannot purchase any, he will very likely begin to respond in an emotional way. He will feel restless, excited, then irritated, and finally angry.

This brings us to the central thesis of the psychological theory of emotions. Namely: Emotion or affect is aroused when a tendency to respond is arrested or inhibited.

SUPPORTING THEORIES

In 1894 John Dewey set forth what has since become known as the conflict theory of emotions.[11]

In an article entitled "The Conflict Theory of Emotion," [12] Angier shows that this general position has been adopted, in more or less modified form, by many psychologists of widely different viewpoints. For instance, the behaviorists, who emphasize the excitement and confusion which disrupt behavior as important characteristics of emotional conduct, would seem to be describing objectively what others view as the result of inner conflict. But the difficulty with examining emotions from the point of view of behaviorism is that, as we have seen, emotion may be felt without becoming manifest as overt behavior.

MacCurdy, whose own attitude is psychoanalytical, points out that it is precisely "when instinctive reactions are stimulated that do not gain expression either in conduct, emotional expression, or fantasy, that affect is most intense. It is the prevention of the expression of instinct either in behavior or conscious thought that leads to intense affect. In other words the energy of the organism, activating an instinct process, must be blocked by repression before poignant feeling is excited." [13] MacCurdy's analysis involves three separate phases: (*a*) the arousal of nervous energy in connection with the instinct or tendency; [14] (*b*) the propensity for this energy to become manifest as behavior or conscious thought once the tendency is blocked; and (*c*) the manifestation of the energy as emotion-felt or affect if behavior and conscious thought are also inhibited. Of course, if the stimulation is so powerful that the total energy cannot be absorbed by either behavior or affect alone, both will result.[15]

It is obvious that a shift of emphasis has taken place in the statement of the theory of emotions. Dewey and his followers tended to stress the conflict or opposition of tendencies as being the cause of emotional response. MacCurdy and most of the more recent workers in the field believe that it is the blocking or inhibiting of a tendency which arouses affect. Actually the concept of conflict through the opposition of simultaneously aroused conflicting tendencies may be regarded as a special and more complicated case of the arrest of tendency.

This point was made in Paulhan's brilliant work, which in 1887, almost ten years before Dewey's formulation, set forth a highly sophisticated theory of emotions. "If we ascend in the hierarchy of human needs and deal with desires of a higher order, we still find that they only give rise to affective phenomena when the tendency awakened undergoes inhibition." [16]

However, more complex phenomena are possible as the result of "the simultaneous or almost simultaneous coming into play of systems which tend toward opposite or different actions and which cannot both culminate in action at the same time; always provided that the psychical systems brought into play do not differ too widely in intensity. . . ." [17] Such a situation results, according to Paulhan, in an emotion or affect characterized by confusion and lack of clarity.

In other words, in one case a tendency is inhibited not by another opposed tendency but simply by the fact that for some reason, whether physical or mental, it cannot reach completion. This is the situation of the inveterate smoker in the example given earlier. In the other case two tendencies which cannot both reach fruition at the same time are brought into play almost simultaneously. If they are about equal in strength, each tendency will block the completion of the other. The result is not only affect, as a product of inhibition, but doubt, confusion, and uncertainty as well.

These latter concomitants of conflict are of importance because they may themselves become the basis for further tendencies. For to the human mind such states of doubt and confusion are abhorrent;

and, when confronted with them, the mind attempts to resolve them into clarity and certainty, even if this means abandoning all other previously activated tendencies.

Thus confusion and lack of clarity, growing out of conflicting tendencies, may themselves become stimuli producing further tendencies—tendencies toward clarification—which may become independent of the originally conflicting tendencies. Such tendencies need not be definite in the sense that the ultimate resolution of the doubt and confusion is specified. Some resolution of the confusion may be more important than this or that particular solution, assuming that the final result is not in conflict with other aspects of the stimulus situation or other mental sets.

Furthermore, it should be noted that uncertainty and lack of clarity may be products not only of conflicting tendencies but also of a situation which itself is structurally confused and ambiguous. This is of capital importance because it indicates that a situation which is structurally weak and doubtful in organization may directly create tendencies toward clarification. Delay in such a generalized tendency toward clarification may also give rise to affect.

Although the main tenets of the psychological theory of emotions have been widely accepted, there have, needless to say, been criticisms of the theory. In the main these have come from those who have sought, as yet without success, to account for, describe, and distinguish emotions in purely physiological terms. The theory of emotions, it is objected, does not tell us what an emotion is; it does not tell us precisely what takes place in the body to make us feel.

This objection, though valid, is irrelevant for our purposes. For just as the physicist long defined magnetism in terms of the laws of its operation and was able to deal with the phenomena without knowing the nature of the magnetic states so, too, the psychologist can define emotion in terms of the laws governing its operation, without stipulating precisely what, in physiological terms, constitutes feeling—what makes affect felt.

THE DIFFERENTIATION OF AFFECT

Thus far we have considered emotion as though it were a general, undifferentiated response, a feeling whose character and quality were always more or less the same. While there is a good deal of evidence for this view, it is nevertheless clear that in common speech and everyday experience we do recognize a variety of emotional states—love, fear, anger, jealousy, and the like.[18] The whole problem of whether undifferentiated feelings, affects per se, exist, of their relation to differentiated emotional experience, and of the basis for such differentiation is of importance in the present study. For while music theorists and aestheticians have found it difficult to explain how music designates particular emotions, they have found it almost impossible to account for the existence of less specific affective experience.

Were the evidence to show that each affect or type of affect had its own peculiar physiological composition, then obviously undifferentiated feeling would be out of the question. However, Woodworth's summary of the work in this field makes it clear that this is not the case.[19]

The evidence in the case of "emotional (affective) behavior" (the term which will henceforth be used to designate the overt and observable aspects of emotional conduct) is more complex. Much emotional behavior, though habitual and hence seemingly automatic and natural, is actually learned. Because this aspect of behavior serves in the main as a means of communication, it will be called "designative (denotative) behavior." To this category belong most of the postural sets, facial expressions, and motor responses accompanying emotional behavior. Though designative behavior is definitely and clearly differentiated, the differentiation is not a necessary one and indicates nothing as to the possible differentiation of the affect itself.

Other aspects of affective behavior, such as skeletal and muscular adjustments, have been said to be automatic, natural concomitants of the affective response. These will be called "emotional reactions." Supposing that such automatic reactions do exist, a fact that has been debated, it has not been definitely shown that they are differentiated as between types of affective experience.

However, even if it were demonstrated that emotional reactions were differentiated, this would not necessarily prove or even indicate that the affects which they accompany are also differentiated. For the reaction is a response made to the total emotion-provoking situation and not necessarily a product of affect itself. In other words, it may well be that such automatic behavior is called forth by the peculiar nature of the objective situation rather than by the operation of the law of affect itself. Were this the case, such a reaction would be independent of affect and might indeed take place, as does designative emotional behavior, in the absence of affect.

The suppositions that behavior reactions are essentially undifferentiated, becoming characteristic only in certain stimulus situations, and that affect itself is basically undifferentiated are given added plausibility when one considers the following:

a) The more intense emotional behavior is, and presumably therefore the more intense the affective stimulation, the less the control exerted by the ego over behavior and the greater the probability that the behavior is automatic and natural.

b) The more intense affective behavior is, the less differentiated such behavior tends to be. In general, the total inhibition of powerful tendencies produces diffuse and characterless activity. For example, extreme conflict may result in either complete immobility or in frenzied activity, while weeping may accompany deepest grief, tremendous joy, or probably any particularly intense emotion.

c) Thus the more automatic affective behavior is, the less differentiated it tends to be.

It seems reasonable then to conclude that automatic reflex reactions not only fail to provide reasons for believing that affect itself is differentiated but the evidence seems to point to just the opposite conclusion.

Finally, our own introspective experience and the reports of the experiences of others testify to the existence of undifferentiated emotions. It is affect as such which Cassirer is discussing when he writes that "Art gives us the motions of the human soul in all their depth and variety. But the form, the measure and rhythm, of these motions is not comparable to any single state of emotion. What we feel in art is not a simple or single emotional quality. It is the dynamic process of life itself." [20]

The conclusion that affect itself is undifferentiated does not mean that affective experience is a kind of disembodied generality. For the affective experience, as distinguished from affect per se, includes an awareness and cognition of a stimulus situation which always involves particular responding individuals and specific stimuli.

Not only do we become aware of and know our own emotions in terms of a particular stimulus situation but we interpret and characterize the behavior of others in these terms. "When an organism is in a situation which results in a disturbed or wrought-up condition, then the situation plus the reaction gives us the name or word which characterizes the whole as a specific emotion. The reaction itself is not sufficient to differentiate the emotion, the character of the situation is involved in this differentiation." [21]

Thus while affects and emotions are in themselves undifferentiated, affective experience is differentiated because it involves awareness and cognition of a stimulus situation which itself is necessarily differentiated. The affective states for which we have names are grouped and named because of similarities of the stimulus situation, not because the affects of different groups are per se different. Love and fear are not different affects, but they are different affective experiences.

Awareness of the nature of the stimulus situation also seems to be the real basis for the distinction which Hebb draws between "pleasant" and "unpleasant" emotions. According to the present analysis, there are no pleasant or unpleasant emotions. There are only pleasant or unpleasant emotional experiences. This is of importance in understanding the distinction made by Hebb.

According to Hebb, the difference between pleasant and unpleasant emotions lies in the fact that pleasant emotions (or, in our terminology, pleasant emotional experiences) are always resolved. They depend "on first arousing apprehension, then dispelling it." [22] But were this actually the case we could only know whether an emotion were pleasant or unpleasant after it was over. Yet, surely, we know more than this while we are experiencing affect. The pleasantness of an emotion seems to lie not so much in the fact of resolution itself as in the belief in resolution—the knowledge, whether true or false, that there will be a resolution. It is not, as Hebb seems to assert when he cites as pleasurable the "mildly frustrating or the mildly fear-provoking," [23] the control actually exercised over a situation which distinguishes pleasant from unpleasant emotions. It is the control which is believed to exist over the situation.

The sensation of falling through space, unconditioned by any belief or knowledge as to the ultimate outcome, will, for instance, arouse highly unpleasant emotions. Yet a similar fall experienced as a parachute jump in an amusement park may, because of our belief in the presence of control and in the nature of the resolution, prove most pleasurable.

The foregoing analysis is of genuine importance in the present study because it explains and accounts for the existence and nature of the intangible, non-referential affective states experienced in response to music. For in so far as the stimulus situation, the music, is non-referential (in the sense that it pictures, describes, or symbolizes none of the actions, persons, passions, and concepts ordinarily associated with human experience), there is no reason to expect that our emotional experience of it should be referential. The affective experience made in response to music is specific and differentiated, but it is so in terms of the musical stimulus situation rather than in terms of extramusical stimuli.[24]

In the light of this discussion it is evident that, though it is wrong to assert, as some have done, that emotions exist which are *sui generis* musical or aesthetic, it is possible to contend that there are emotional experiences which are so.[25] By the same token, however, any number of emotional experiences can be grouped together so long as their stimulus situations are in some respects similar. Musical affective experiences, for example, might be differentiated into operatic, orchestral, baroque, and so forth. But the most significant distinction would still lie in the fact that musical stimuli, and hence musical affective experiences, are non-referential.

EMOTIONAL DESIGNATION

Although emotional behavior is frequently characterless and diffuse, often it is differentiated and intelligible. Even without knowledge of the stimulus situation, motor behavior, facial expression, tone of voice, and manner of speaking can tell us not only that an individual is responding in an emotional way but also something of the character of his feelings or, more accurately, of the character of his affective experience.

Differentiated behavior, as we have seen, is not an automatic or a necessary concomitant of affect itself or even of affective experience. The more automatic behavior is, the less likely it is to be differentiated. Differentiation involves control, and control implies purpose.

The purpose of emotionally differentiated behavior is communication. The individual responding, having an affective experience or simulating one, seeks to make others aware of his experience through a series of non-verbal behavioral signs. Because the gestures and signs which differentiate such behavior are purposeful, this mode of behavior will be called "emotional designation" or "designative behavior." [26]

Such signs not only act as cues for appropriate behavior in the social situation but are probably, at least in part, aimed at making other individuals respond in an empathetic way. As the saying goes: Misery loves company. And so do other emotional states. Not only do we dislike physical isolation, but we want to share our emotional life with others. And, indeed, such sharing does take place. For an observer, recalling a situation in his own experience similar to the one signified by the behavior of another, may respond to the re-membered situation in an affective way. Though designative affective behavior may, through constant use, become habitual and automatic so that it is almost invariably called up as part of the total emotional response, it is not basically a necessary concomitant of the response but one brought into play as a result of a desire to communicate.

Designative behavior is differentiated largely by custom and tradition. It varies from culture to culture and among different groups within a single culture. This does not mean that there are no features of such behavior which are natural and widespread. In all probability there are. However, three points should be kept in mind: (1) There is no real evidence to show that there is only one single natural mode of behavior relevant to a given stimulus situation. When alternative modes of behavior are possible, cultural selection probably determines the composition of any particular pattern of affective designation. (2) Whatever natural tendencies toward a particular pattern of behavior exist may be altered or suppressed by the demands of the larger behavior patterns of the culture. (3) Even where natural behavior is retained in the pattern of emotional behavior, it inevitably becomes codified and standardized for the sake of more efficient communication.

Above all, we understand and make appropriate responses to designative behavior as a total behavior pattern, not just to some features of it, whether natural or otherwise. As a total pattern designative behavior is a cultural phenomenon, not a natural one. It is, in the final analysis, learned.

This is important as it takes most of the sting out of the criticism that music which attempts to designate emotional states depends for its effect upon the learning of conventional signs and symbols. For this fact is. not peculiar to music but is characteristic of all emotional designation. If one excludes such designation as a legitimate means of musical communication, one must by the same token exclude it as a means of human communication in general.[27]

The Theory of Emotions Related to Musical Experience

AN ASSUMPTION

An examination of the psychological theory of emotions was made because the evidence furnished by the introspections of musicians, aestheticians, and listeners and the objective data gathered from the observation of behavior and the study of the physiological responses to musical stimuli did not yield reliable information about the musical stimulus or the affective responses made to it. Implicit in this examination was an assumption which must now be made explicit: Though the stimulus situation may vary indefinitely, the conditions which evoke affect are general and are, therefore, applicable to music. In other words, it was assumed that the law of affect, which states that emotion is evoked when a tendency to respond is inhibited, is a general proposition relevant to human psychology in all realms of experience.

This assumption does not, however, imply or stipulate that musical affective experiences are the same as the affective experiences made in response to other stimulus situations. Musical experience differs from non-musical or, more specifically, non-aesthetic experience in three important ways.

First, as we have seen, affective experience includes an awareness and knowledge of the stimulus situation. This being so, the affective experience of music will differ from other types of affective experience, particularly in so far as musical stimuli are non-referential.

Second, in everyday experience the tensions created by the inhibition of tendencies often go unresolved. They are merely dissipated in the press of irrelevant events. In this sense daily experience is meaningless and accidental. In art inhibition of tendency becomes meaningful because the relationship between the tendency and its necessary resolution is made explicit and apparent. Tendencies do not simply cease to exist: they are resolved, they conclude.[28]

Third, in life the factors which keep a tendency from reaching completion may be different in kind from those which activated the tendency in the first place. The stimulus activating a tendency may, for example, be a physical or psychic need of the organism, while the inhibiting factors may simply be a series of external circumstances which keep the organism from satisfying the need. This is the situation in the case of the habitual smoker who can find no cigarette. Or the situation may be reversed; that is, a tendency activated by an external stimulus may be inhibited by the psychic processes of the organism.

Furthermore, in everyday experience the resolutions of the tensions brought into play by inhibition may be irrelevant to the tendencies themselves. Tensions arising from psychic needs may be "worked off" in sheer physical activity which is without meaningful relation to the original stimulus or to the tendency itself.

In music, on the other hand, the same stimulus, the music, activates tendencies, inhibits them, and provides meaningful and relevant resolutions.

TENDENCY AND EXPECTATION IN MUSIC

The assumption that the same basic psychological processes underlie all affective responses, whether the stimulus be musical or of some other kind, has been implicit in much musical theory and in the speculations of many aestheticians. But this does not in itself increase our understanding of the nature of musical experience and of the musical processes which form it. It does not explain the nature of the relationships which exist between the stimulus, the listener's perceptions and mental processes, and his responses. To do this it is necessary to demonstrate precisely how musical stimuli do, in fact, arouse and inhibit tendencies and thereby give rise to emotions.

What is meant by a tendency to respond? A "tendency" or, as MacCurdy uses the term, an "instinct" "is a pattern reaction that operates, or tends to operate, when activated, in an automatic way." [29] A pattern reaction consists of a set or series of regularly coincident mental or motor responses which, once brought into play as part of the response to a given stimulus, follow a previously ordered course, unless inhibited or blocked in some way. The order established by a pattern reaction is both temporal and structural; that is, the series involves not only the relation of the parts of the total pattern to each other but also their timing. Thus a series may be disturbed either because the succession of the parts of the pattern is upset or because the timing of the series is upset or both.

The term "tendency," as used in this study, comprises all automatic response patterns, whether natural or learned. Since habit is "a mechanism of action, physiologically ingrained, which operates spontaneously and automatically," [30] the term "tendency" also "includes habit reactions and, inevitably, acquired concepts and meanings." [31]

The tendency to respond may be either conscious or unconscious. If the pattern reaction runs its normal course to completion, then the whole process may be completely unconscious. Countless reaction patterns, of which the responding individual is unaware, are initiated and completed each hour. The more automatic behavior becomes, the less conscious it is. The tendency to respond becomes conscious where inhibition of some sort is present, when the normal course of the reaction pattern is disturbed or its final completion is inhibited. Such conscious and self-conscious tendencies are often thought of and referred to as "expectations."

In a broader sense all tendencies, even those which never reach the level of consciousness, are expectations. For since a tendency is a kind of chain reaction in which a present stimulus leads through a series of adjustments to a more or less specified consequent, the consequent is always implied in the tendency, once the tendency has been brought into play. Thus while our conscious minds do not actively expect a consequent unless the pattern reaction is disturbed, our habits and tendencies are expectant in the sense that each seeks out or "expects" the consequents relevant and appropriate to itself. Though he may never become aware of his expectations as he reaches in his pocket for a pack of cigarettes, the behavior of the habitual smoker shows that he does expect or, perhaps more accurately, his habits expect for him.

If tendencies are pattern reactions that are expectant in the broad sense, including unconscious as well as conscious anticipations, then it is not difficult to see how music is able to evoke tendencies. For it has been generally acknowledged that music arouses expectations, some conscious and others unconscious, which may or may not be directly and immediately satisfied.

> . . . the pleasure . . . arises from the perception of the artist's play with forms and conventions which are ingrained as *habits* of perception both in the artist and his audience. Without such habits . . . there would be no awareness whatever of the artist's fulfillment of and subtle departures from established forms. . . . But the pleasure which we derive from style is not an intellectual interest in detecting similarities and differences, but an immediate aesthetic delight in perception which results from the arousal and suspension or fulfillment of expectations which are the products of many previous encounters with works of art.[32]

EXPECTATION, SUSPENSE, AND THE UNEXPECTED

Sometimes a very specific consequent is expected. In Western music of the eighteenth century, for example, we expect a specific chord, namely, the tonic (C major), to follow this sequence of

EXAMPLE 1

harmonies (see Example 1). Furthermore, the consequent chord is expected to arrive at a particular time, i.e., on the first beat of the next measure.

Of course, the consequent which is actually forthcoming, though it must be possible within the style, need not be the one which was specifically expected. Nor is it necessary that the consequent arrive at the expected time. It may arrive too soon or it may be delayed. But no matter which of these forms the consequent actually takes, the crucial point to be noted is that the ultimate and particular effect of the total pattern is clearly conditioned by the specificity of the original expectation.

At other times expectation is more general; that is, though our expectations may be definite, in the sense of being marked, they are non-specific, in that we are not sure precisely how they will be fulfilled. The antecedent stimulus situation may be such that several consequents may be almost equally probable. For instance, after a melodic fragment has been repeated several times, we begin to expect a change and also the completion of the fragment. A change is expected because we believe that the composer is not so illogical as to repeat the figure indefinitely and because we look forward to the completion of the incomplete figure. But precisely what the change will be or how the completion will be accomplished cannot perhaps be anticipated. The introductions to many movements written in the eighteenth or nineteenth centuries create expectation in this way, e.g., the opening measures of Beethoven's Ninth Symphony or the opening measures of the "March to the Gallows" from Berlioz's *Symphonie Fantastique*.

Expectation may also result because the stimulus situation is doubtful or ambiguous. If the musical patterns are less clear than expected, if there is confusion as to the relationship between melody and accompaniment, or if our expectations are continually mistaken or inhibited, then doubt and uncertainty as to the general significance, function, and outcome of the passage will result. As we have already seen (see pp. 15 ff.), the mind rejects and reacts against such uncomfortable states and, if they are more than momentary, looks forward to and expects a return to the certainty of regularity and clarity. This is particularly striking in the responses made to works of art where, because of a firm belief in the purposefulness and integrity of the artist, we expect that order will in the end triumph, and precision will replace ambiguity.

However, the manner in which clarification and order will be restored may not be predicted or envisaged. Expectation is not specific; the state is one of suspense. In fact, if doubt and uncertainty are strong enough, almost any resolution, within the realm of probability, which returns us to certainty will be acceptable, though no doubt some resolutions will, given the style, seem more natural than others.

The inclusion of suspense arising out of uncertainty may, at first sight, appear to be an extension and amplification of the concept of arrest and inhibition of a tendency. But when the matter is considered more carefully, it will be seen that every inhibition or delay creates uncertainty or suspense, if only briefly, because in the moment of delay we become aware of the possibility of alternative modes of continuation. The difference is one of scale and duration, not of kind. Both arouse uncertainties and anxieties as to coming events.

Suspense is essentially a product of ignorance as to the future course of events. This ignorance may arise either because the present course of events, though in a sense understandable in itself, presents several alternative and equally probable consequents or because the present course of events is itself so unusual and upsetting that, since it cannot be understood, no predictions as to the future can be made.

From the outset ignorance arouses strong mental tendencies toward clarification which are immediately affective. If ignorance persists in spite of all, then the individual is thrown into a state of doubt and uncertainty (see pp. 15–16). He commences to sense his lack of control over the situation, his inability to act on the basis of the knowledge which he supposed that he possessed. In short, he begins to feel apprehensive, even fearful, though there is no object for his fear. Ignorance and its concomitant feelings of impotence breed apprehension and anxiety, even in music. But ignorance also gives rise to more sanguine feelings; for since the outcome cannot be envisaged, it may be pleasant. These feelings are themselves tendencies (the avoidance of painful apprehension and the expectation of a propitious conclusion) which become focused upon an expected resolution of the unpleasant stimulus situation.

The longer doubt and uncertainty persist, the greater the feeling of suspense will tend to be. The stimulus situation creating doubt and uncertainty must, of course, be progressively intensified if suspense is to be maintained or increased. For as we become accustomed to a given stimulus situation, even an unpleasant one, its effectiveness tends to diminish. Moreover, without a change in the stimulus situation in the direction of complication and uncertainty, those vital anticipatory feelings (that a break must come, that doubt and perplexity must give way to knowledge) which make us expect (both apprehensively and hopefully) would be lost.

The greater the buildup of suspense, of tension, the greater the emotional release upon resolution. This observation points up the fact that in aesthetic experience emotional pattern must be considered not only in terms of tension itself but also in terms of the progression from tension to release. And the experience of suspense is aesthetically valueless unless it is followed by a release which is understandable in the given context.

Musical experiences of suspense are very similar to those experienced in real life. Both in life and in music the emotions thus arising have essentially the same stimulus situation: the situation of ignorance, the awareness of the individual's impotence and inability to act where the future course of events is unknown. Because these musical experiences are so very similar to those existing in the drama and in life itself, they are often felt to be particularly powerful and effective.

Musical suspense seems to have direct analogies in experience in general; it makes us feel something of the insignificance and powerlessness of man in the face of the inscrutable workings of destiny. The low, foreboding rumble of distant thunder on an oppressive summer afternoon, its growing intensity as it approaches, the crescendo of the gradually rising wind, the ominous darkening of the sky, all give rise to an emotional experience in which expectation is fraught with powerful uncertainty—the primordial and poignant uncertainty of human existence in the face of the inexorable forces of nature. With mixed feelings of hope and apprehension in the presence of the unknown, we anxiously await the breaking of the storm, the discovery of what unrelenting fate has decreed.

Similarly in music the state of suspense involves an awareness of the powerlessness of man in the face of the unknown.

What is expected in this state of suspense may not be specified, but this does not mean that any consequent is possible. Our expectations are inevitably circumscribed by the possibilities and probabilities of the style of the composition in question. The consequent must, given the circumstances, be possible within what Aiken has called "an ordering system of beliefs and attitudes." [33]

Although the consequent in any musical sequence must, in this sense, be possible, it may nevertheless be unexpected. But the unexpected should not be confused with the surprising. For when expectation is aroused, the unexpected is always considered to be a possibility, and, though it remains the less expected of several alternatives, it is not a complete surprise. Conditions of active expectation (especially general expectation and suspense) are not the most favorable to surprise. For the listener is on guard, anticipating a new and possibly unexpected consequent. Surprise is most intense where no special expectation is active, where, because there has been no inhibition of a tendency, continuity is expected.

As soon as the unexpected, or for that matter the surprising, is experienced, the listener attempts to fit it into the general system of beliefs relevant to the style of the work. This requires a very rapid re-evaluation of either the stimulus situation itself or its cause— the events antecedent to the stimulus. Or it may require a review of the whole system of beliefs that the listener supposed appropriate and relevant to the work. If this mental synthesis does not take place immediately, three things may happen: (1) The mind may suspend judgment, so to speak, trusting that what follows will clarify the meaning of the unexpected consequent. (2) If no clarification takes place, the mind may reject the whole stimulus and irritation will set in.[34] (3) The unexpected consequent may be seen as a purposeful blunder. Whether the listener responds in the first or third manner will depend partly upon the character of the piece, its mood or designative content. The third response might well be made to music whose character was comic or satirical. Beckmesser's music in Wagner's *Die Meistersinger* would probably elicit this type of interpretive understanding.[85] In a piece whose character admitted no such purposeful blunders, the second response would probably be elicited.

CONSCIOUS AND UNCONSCIOUS EXPECTATIONS

In the light of these observations it is clear that an expectation is not a blind, unthinking conditioned reflex. Expectation frequently involves a high order of mental activity. The fulfilment of a habit response, in art as well as in daily life, requires judgment and cognition both of the stimulus itself and of the situation in which it acts. The stimulus as a physical thing becomes a stimulus in the world of behavior only in so far as the mind of the perceiver is able to relate it, on the one hand, to the habit responses which the perceiver has developed and, on the other hand, to the particular stimulus situation. This is clear as soon as one considers that the same physical stimulus may call forth different tendencies in different stylistic contexts or in different situations within one and the same stylistic context. For example, a modal cadential progression will arouse one set of expectations in the musical style of the sixteenth century and quite another in the style of the nineteenth century. Likewise the same musical progression will evoke one set of expectations at the beginning of a piece and another at the end.

Expectation then is a product of the habit responses developed in connection with particular musical styles and of the modes of human perception, cognition, and response—the psychological laws of mental life.[36]

The mental activity involved in the perception of and response to music need not, however, be conscious. ". . . the intellectual satisfaction which the listener derives from continually following and anticipating the composer's intentions—now, to see his expectations fulfilled, and now, to see himself agreeably mistaken . . . this intellectual flux and reflux, this perpetual giving and receiving takes place unconsciously, and with the rapidity of lightning flashes." [37] So long as expectations are satisfied without delay, so long as tendencies are uninhibited, though intelligence is clearly and necessarily involved in the perception and understanding of the stimulus situation, the response will probably remain unconscious.

Mental activity tends to become conscious when reflection and deliberation are involved in the completion of the response pattern, that is, when automatic behavior is disturbed because a tendency has been inhibited. "Impulsion forever boosted on its forward way would run its course thoughtless, and dead to emotion. . . . The only way it can become aware of its nature and its goal is by obstacles surmounted and means employed." [38]

But even when a habit response is inhibited, conscious awareness of the mental activity involved in the perception of and response to the stimulus situation is by no means inevitable. Intellectual experience (the conscious awareness of one's own expectations or, objectively, of the tendencies of the music), as distinguished from intellectual activity, is largely a product of the listener's own attitude toward his responses and hence toward the stimuli and mental activities which bring them into existence. That is to say, some listeners, whether because of training or natural psychological inclination, are disposed to rationalize their responses, to make experience self-conscious; others are not so disposed. If intellectual activity is allowed to remain unconscious, then the mental tensions and the deliberations involved when a tendency is inhibited are experienced as feeling or affect rather than as conscious cognition (see pp. 38 f.).

Having shown that music arouses tendencies and thus fulfils the conditions necessary for the arousal of affect (see p. 22) and having demonstrated how this is accomplished, we can now state one of the basic hypotheses of this study. Namely: Affect or emotion-felt is aroused when an expectation—a tendency to respond—activated by the musical stimulus situation, is temporarily inhibited or permanently blocked.

As noted earlier (see pp. 22–23) in musical experience the same stimulus, the music, activates tendencies, inhibits them, and provides meaningful and relevant resolutions for them. This is of particular importance from a methodological standpoint. For it means that granted listeners who have developed reaction patterns appropriate to the work in question, the structure of the affective response to a piece of music can be studied by examining the music itself.

Once those sound successions common to a culture, a style, or a particular work have been ascertained, then, if the customary succession is presented and completed without delay, it can be assumed that, since no tendency would have been inhibited, the listener would not respond in an affective way. If, on the other hand, the sound succession fails to follow its customary course, or if it involves obscurity or ambiguity, then it can be assumed that the listener's tendencies would be inhibited or otherwise upset and that the tensions arising in this process would be experienced as affect, provided that they were not rationalized as conscious intellectual experience.

In other words, the customary or expected progression of sounds can be considered as a norm, which from a stylistic point of view it is; and alteration in the expected progression can be considered as a deviation. Hence deviations can be regarded as emotional or affective stimuli.

The importance of this "objective" point of view of musical experience is clear. It means that once the norms of a style have been ascertained, the study and analysis of the affective content of a particular work in that style can be made without continual and explicit reference to the responses of the listener or critic. That is, subjective content can be discussed objectively.[39]

The Meaning of Music

THE PROBLEM OF MEANING IN MUSIC

The meaning of music has of late been the subject of much confused argument and controversy. The controversy has stemmed largely from disagreements as to what music communicates, while the confusion has resulted for the most part from a lack of clarity as to the nature and definition of meaning itself.

The debates as to what music communicates have centered around the question of whether music can designate, depict, or otherwise communicate referential concepts, images, experiences, and emo-

tional states. This is the old argument between the absol
the referentialists (see pp. 1 f.).

Because it has not appeared problematical to them, the referentialists have not as a rule explicitly considered the problem of musical meaning. Musical meaning according to the referentialists lies in the relationship between a musical symbol or sign and the extramusical thing which it designates.

Since our concern in this study is not primarily with the referential meaning of music, suffice it to say that the disagreement between the referentialists and the absolutists is, as was pointed out at the beginning of this chapter, the result of a tendency toward philosophical monism rather than the result of any logical incompatibility. Both designative and non-designative meanings arise out of musical experience, just as they do in other types of aesthetic experience.

The absolutists have contended that the meaning of music lies specifically, and some would assert exclusively, in the musical processes themselves. For them musical meaning is non-designative. But in what sense these processes are meaningful, in what sense a succession or sequence of non-referential musical stimuli can be said to give rise to meaning, they have been unable to state with either clarity or precision. They have also failed to relate musical meaning to other kinds of meaning—to meaning in general. This failure has led some critics to assert that musical meaning is a thing apart, different in some unexplained way from all other kinds of meaning. This is simply an evasion of the real issue. For it is obvious that if the term "meaning" is to have any signification at all as applied to music, then it must have the same signification as when applied to other kinds of experience.

Without reviewing all the untenable positions to which writers have tenaciously adhered, it seems fair to say that much of the confusion and uncertainty as to the nature of non-referential musical meaning has resulted from two fallacies. On the one hand, there has been a tendency to locate meaning exclusively in one aspect of the communicative process; on the other hand, there has been a propensity to regard all meanings arising in human communication as designative, as involving symbolism of some sort.

Since these difficulties can be best resolved in the light of a general definition of meaning, let us begin with such a definition: ". . . anything acquires meaning if it is connected with, or indicates, or refers to, something beyond itself, so that its full nature points to and is revealed in that connection." [40]

Meaning is thus not a property of things. It cannot be located in the stimulus alone. The same stimulus may have many different meanings. To a geologist a large rock may indicate that at one time a glacier began to recede at a given spot; to a farmer the same rock may point to the necessity of having the field cleared for plowing; and to the sculptor the rock may indicate the possibility of artistic creation. A rock, a word, or motion in and of itself, merely as a stimulus, is meaningless.

Thus it is pointless to ask what the intrinsic meaning of a single tone or a series of tones is. Purely as physical existences they are meaningless. They become meaningful only in so far as they point to, indicate, or imply something beyond themselves.

Nor can meaning be located exclusively in the objects, events, or experiences which the stimulus indicates, refers to, or implies. The meaning of the rock is the product of the relationship between the stimulus and the thing it points to or indicates.

Though the perception of a relationship can only arise as the result of some individual's mental behavior, the relationship itself is not to be located in the mind of the perceiver. The meanings observed are not subjective. Thus the relationships existing between the tones themselves or those existing between the tones and the things they designate or connote, though a product of cultural experience, are real connections existing objectively in culture.[41] They are not arbitrary connections imposed by the capricious mind of the particular listener.

Meaning, then, is not in either the stimulus, or what it points to, or the observer. Rather it arises out of what both Cohen and Mead have called the "triadic" relationship between (1) an object or stimulus; (2) that to which the stimulus points—that which is its consequent; and (3) the conscious observer.

Discussions of the meaning of music have also been muddled by the failure to state explicitly what musical stimuli indicate or point to. A stimulus may indicate events or consequences which are different from itself in kind, as when a word designates or points to an object or action which is not itself a word. Or a stimulus may indicate or imply events or consequences which are of the same kind as the stimulus itself, as when a dim light on the eastern horizon heralds the coming of day. Here both the antecedent stimulus and the consequent event are natural phenomena. The former type of meaning may be called designative, the latter embodied.

Because most of the meanings which arise in human communication are of the designative type, employing linguistic signs or the iconic signs of the plastic arts, numerous critics have failed to realize that this is not necessarily or exclusively the case. This mistake has led even avowed absolutists to allow designation to slip in through the secret door of semantic chicanery.[42]

But even more important than designative meaning is what we have called embodied meaning. From this point of view what a musical stimulus or a series of stimuli indicate and point to are not extramusical concepts and objects but other musical events which are about to happen. That is, one musical event (be it a tone, a phrase, or a whole section) has meaning because it points to and makes us expect another musical event. This is what music means from the viewpoint of the absolutist.

MUSIC AND MEANING

Embodied musical meaning is, in short, a product of expectation. If, on the basis of past experience, a present stimulus leads us to expect a more or less definite consequent musical event, then that stimulus has meaning.[43]

From this it follows that a stimulus or gesture which does not point to or arouse expectations of a subsequent musical event or consequent is meaningless. Because expectation is largely a product of stylistic experience, music in a style with which we are totally unfamiliar is meaningless.[44]

However, once the aesthetic attitude has been brought into play, very few gestures actually appear to be meaningless so long as the listener has some experience with the style of the work in question. For so long as a stimulus is possible within any known style, the listener will do his best to relate it to the style, to understand its meaning.

In and of themselves, for example, the opening chords of Beethoven's Third Symphony have no particular musical stylistic tendency. They establish no pattern of motion, arouse no tensions toward a particular fulfilment. Yet as part of the total aesthetic cultural act of attention they are meaningful. For since they are the first chords of a piece, we not only expect more music but our expectations are circumscribed by the limitations of the style which we believe the piece to be in and by the psychological demand for a more palpable pattern (see chaps ii–v).

Thus the phrase "past experience," used in the definition of meaning given above, must be understood in a broad sense. It includes the immediate past of the particular stimulus or gesture; that which has already taken place in this particular work to condition the listener's opinion of the stimulus and hence his expectations as to the impending, consequent event. In the example given above, the past was silence. But this fact of the past is just as potent in conditioning expectation as a whole section of past events.[45] The phrase "past experience" also refers to the more remote, but ever present, past experience of similar musical stimuli and similar musical situations in other works. That is it refers to those past experiences which constitute our sense and knowledge of style. The phrase also comprehends the dispositions and beliefs which the listener brings to the musical experience (see pp. 73 ff.) as well as the laws of mental behavior which govern his organization of stimuli into patterns and the expectations aroused on the basis of those patterns (see chaps. iii and iv).

The words "consequent musical event" must be understood to include: (1) those consequents which are envisaged or expected; (2) the events which do, in fact, follow the stimulus, whether they were the ones envisaged or not; and (3) the more distant ramifications or events which, because the total series of gestures is presumed to be causally connected, are considered as being the later consequences of the stimulus in question. Seen in this light, the meaning of the stimulus is not confined to or limited by the initial triadic relationship out of which it arises. As the later stages of the musical process establish new relationships with the stimulus, new meanings arise. These later meanings coexist in memory with the earlier ones and, combining with them, constitute the meaning of the work as a total experience.

In this development three stages of meaning may be distinguished.

"Hypothetical meanings" are those which arise during the act of expectation. Since what is envisaged is a product of the probability relationships which exist as part of style (see pp. 45 ff., 54 ff.), and since these probability relationships always involve the possibility of alternative consequences, a given stimulus invariably gives rise to several alternative hypothetical meanings. One consequent may, of course, be so much more probable than any other that the listener, though aware of the possibility of less likely consequences, is really set and ready only for the most probable. In such a case hypothetical meaning is without ambiguity. In other cases several consequents may be almost equally probable, and, since the listener is in doubt as to which alternative will actually materialize, meaning is ambiguous, though not necessarily less forceful and marked (see pp. 51 ff.).[46]

Though the consequent which is actually forthcoming must be possible within the style, it may or may not be one of those which was most probable. Or it may arrive only after a delay or a deceptive diversion through alternative consequences. But whether our expectations are confirmed or not, a new stage of meaning is reached when the consequent becomes actualized as a concrete musical event.

"Evident meanings" are those which are attributed to the antecedent gesture when the consequent becomes a physico-psychic fact and when the relationship between the antecedent and consequent is perceived. Since the consequent of a stimulus itself becomes a stimulus with consequents, evident meaning also includes the later stages of musical development which are presumed to be the products of a chain of causality. Thus in the following sequence, where a stimulus (S) leads to a consequent (C), which is also a stimulus that indicates and is actualized in further consequents,

$$S_1 \ldots \ldots C_1 S_2 \ldots \ldots C_2 S_3 \ldots \ldots \text{ etc.}$$

evident meaning arises not only out of the relationship between S_1 and C_1 but also out of the relationships between S_1 and all subsequent consequences, in so far as these are considered to issue from S_1. It is also important to realize that the motion $S_1 \ldots \ldots C_1$ may itself become a gesture that gives rise to envisaged and actual consequents and hence becomes a term or gesture on another level of triadic relationships. In other words, both evident and hypothetical meanings come into being and exist on several architectonic levels.

Evident meaning is colored and conditioned by hypothetical meaning. For the actual relationship between the gesture and its consequent is always considered in the light of the expected relationship. In a sense the listener even revises his opinion of the hypothetical meaning when the stimulus does not move to the expected consequent.

"Determinate meanings" are those meanings which arise out of the relationships existing between hypothetical meaning, evident meaning, and the later stages of the musical development. In other words, determinate meaning arises only after the experience of the work is timeless in memory, only when all the meanings which the stimulus has had in the particular experience are realized and their relationships to one another comprehended as fully as possible.

THE OBJECTIFICATION OF MEANING

A distinction must be drawn between the understanding of musical meaning which involves the awareness of the tendencies, resistances, tensions, and fulfilments embodied in a work and the self-conscious objectification of that meaning in the mind of the individual listener. The former may be said to involve a meaningful experience, the latter involves knowing what that meaning is, considering it as an objective thing in consciousness.

The operation of intelligence in listening to music need never become self-conscious. We are continually behaving in an intelligent way, comprehending meanings and acting upon our perceptions, cognitions, and evaluations without ever making the meanings themselves the objects of our scrutiny—without ever becoming self-conscious about what experience means. What Bertrand Russell says about understanding language also applies to the understanding of music: "Understanding language is . . . like understanding cricket: it is a matter of habits acquired in oneself and rightly presumed in others." [47]

Meanings become objectified only under conditions of self-consciousness and when reflection takes place. "One attains self-consciousness only as he takes, or finds himself stimulated to take, the attitude of the other." [48] Though training may make for a generally self-conscious attitude, one is stimulated to take the attitude of the other when the normal habits of response are disturbed in some way; when one is driven to ask one's self: What does this mean, what is the intention of this passage? Reflection is likewise brought into play where some tendency is delayed, some pattern of habitual behavior disturbed. So long as behavior is automatic and habitual there is no urge for it to become self-conscious, though it may become so. If meaning is to become objectified at all, it will as a rule become so when difficulties are encountered that make normal, automatic behavior impossible. In other words, given a mind disposed toward objectification, meaning will become the focus of attention, an object of conscious consideration, when a tendency or habit reaction is delayed or inhibited.

MEANING AND AFFECT

It thus appears that the same processes which were said to give rise to affect are now said to give rise to the objectification of embodied meaning.

But this is a dilemma only so long as the traditional dichotomy between reason and emotion and the parent polarity between mind and body are adopted. Once it is recognized that affective experience is just as dependent upon intelligent cognition as conscious intellection, that both involve perception, taking account of, envisaging, and so forth, then thinking and feeling need not be viewed as polar opposites but as different manifestations of a single psychological process.

There is no diametric opposition, no inseparable gulf, between the affective and the intellectual responses made to music. Though they are psychologically differentiated as responses, both depend upon the same perceptive processes, the same stylistic habits, the same modes of mental organization; and the same musical processes give rise to and shape both types of experience. Seen in this light, the formalist's conception of musical experience and the expressionist's conception of it appear as complementary rather than contradictory positions. They are considering not different processes but different ways of experiencing the same process.

Whether a piece of music gives rise to affective experience or to intellectual experience depends upon the disposition and training of the listener. To some minds the disembodied feeling of affective experience is uncanny and unpleasant and a process of rationalization is undertaken in which the musical processes are objectified as conscious meaning. Belief also probably plays an important role in determining the character of the response. Those who have been taught to believe that musical experience is primarily emotional and who are therefore disposed to respond affectively will probably do so. Those listeners who have learned to understand music in technical terms will tend to make musical processes an object of conscious consideration. This probably accounts for the fact that most trained critics and aestheticians favor the formalist position. Thus while the trained musician consciously waits for the expected resolution of a dominant seventh chord the untrained, but practiced, listener feels the delay as affect.

MUSIC AND COMMUNICATION

Meanings and affects may, however, arise without communication taking place. Individual A observes another individual B wink and interprets the wink as a friendly gesture. It has meaning for A who observes it. But if the wink was not intentional—if, for instance, B simply has a nervous tic—then no communication has taken place, for to B the act had no meaning. Communication, as Mead has pointed out, takes place only where the gesture made has the same meaning for the individual who makes it that it has for the individual who responds to it.[49]

It is this internalization of gestures, what Mead calls "taking the attitude of the other"[50] (the audience), which enables the creative artist, the composer, to communicate with listeners. It is because the composer is also a listener that he is able to control his inspiration with reference to the listener.[51] For instance, the composer knows how the listener will respond to a deceptive cadence and controls the later stages of the composition with reference to that supposed response. The performer too is continually "taking the attitude of the other"—of the listener. As Leopold Mozart puts it, the performer "must play everything in such a way that he will himself be moved by it." [52]

It is precisely because he is continually taking the attitude of the listener that the composer becomes aware and conscious of his own self, his ego, in the process of creation. In this process of differentiation between himself as composer and himself as audience, the composer becomes self-conscious and objective.[53]

But though the listener participates in the musical process, assuming the role which the composer envisaged for him, and though he must, in some sense, create his own experience, yet he need not take the attitude of the composer in order to do so. He need not ask: How will someone else respond to this stimulus? Nor is he obliged to objectify his own responses, to ask, How am I responding? Unlike the composer, the listener may and frequently does "lose himself in the music"; and, in following and responding to the sound gestures made by the composer, the listener may become oblivious of his own ego, which has literally become one with that of the music.

We must, then, be wary of easy and high-sounding statements to the effect that "we cannot understand a work of art without, to a certain degree, repeating and reconstructing the creative process by which it has come into being." [54] Certainly the listener must respond to the work of art as the artist intended, and the listener's experience of the work must be similar to that which the composer envisaged for him. But this is a different thing from experiencing the "creative process which brought it into being."

However, the listener may take the attitude of the composer. He may be self-conscious in the act of listening. Those trained in music, and perhaps those trained in the other arts as well, tend, because of the critical attitudes which they have developed in connection with their own artistic efforts, to become self-conscious and objective in all their aesthetic experiences. And it is no doubt partly for this reason that, as noted above, trained musicians tend to objectify meaning, to consider it as an object of conscious cognition (see also p. 70 n. 24).

Finally, and perhaps most important of all, this analysis of communication emphasizes the absolute necessity of a common universe of discourse in art. For without a set of gestures common to the social group, and without common habit responses to those gestures, no communication whatsoever would be possible. Communication depends upon, presupposes, and arises out of the universe of discourse which in the aesthetics of music is called style.

II

Expectation and Learning

In the preceding chapter the inhibition of a tendency to respond or, on the conscious level, the frustration of expectation was found to be the basis of the affective and the intellectual aesthetic response to music. If this hypothesis is correct, then an analysis of the process of expectation is clearly a prerequisite for the understanding of how musical meaning, whether affective or aesthetic, arises in any particular instance. Such an analysis is also necessary if the evidence used in support of the hypothesis, evidence which relates specific musical processes to stipulations of affectivity and aesthetic pleasure, is to be interpreted in a meaningful way.

A general distinction must be drawn at the outset between those expectations that arise out of the nature of human mental processes —the modes in which the mind perceives, groups, and organizes the data presented by the senses—and those expectations that are based upon learning in the broadest sense of the term. In the actual perception of music there is, of course, an intimate and subtle interaction between the two types of expectation.

Paradoxical though it may seem, the expectations based upon learning are, in a sense, prior to the natural modes of thought. For we perceive and think in terms of a specific musical language just as we think in terms of a specific vocabulary and grammar; and the possibilities presented to us by a particular musical vocabulary and grammar condition the operation of our mental processes and hence of the expectations which are entertained on the basis of

43

those processes. The mind, for example, expects structural gaps to be filled; but what constitutes such a gap depends upon what constitutes completeness within a particular musical style system. Musical language, like verbal language, is heuristic in the sense "that its forms predetermine for us certain modes of observation and interpretation." [1] Thus the expectations which result from the nature of human mental processes are always conditioned by the possibilities and probabilities inherent in the materials and their organization as presented in a particular musical style.

In this chapter the relationship between expectation and learning will be examined. The manner in which the mind groups and organizes the data presented to it by the senses, the structure of the thinking process as conditioned by the learned response sequences, and the manner in which this process gives rise to expectation will be the subject of chapters iii, iv, and v.

The study of expectation which follows makes no pretense to completeness: first, because a complete and systematic study of the process of expectation would be a formidable task, requiring a separate monograph of its own; [2] second, because a detailed account of expectation would have to be preceded by a great deal of experimental work in the field of pattern and figure perception in music; and third, because such a study would entail a detailed description and sensitive appreciation of the stylistic context within which the process of expectation was being studied.

This necessity for stylistic understanding has determined the choice of examples in the following chapters. In order not to further complicate the already difficult and delicate task of discussing expectation, no attempt is made in this and the following three chapters to prove that the processes examined do, in fact, have affective aesthetic meaning; that is, no commentaries from outside sources, from composers, critics, theorists, and the like, as to the affective aesthetic nature of the various examples are introduced. Since the general reader is more likely to have developed sensitive habit responses to the music of Western Europe of the past three hundred years than to any other part of the literature of music, the examples in these chapters have been chosen from the music of this period.

In chapters vi and vii, where comments on the examples by composers, performers, theorists, and critics are introduced in evidence, both the examples and the commentaries have been taken from a wide variety of cultures, styles, and epochs.

Style: Formal Considerations

Musical styles are more or less complex systems of sound relationships understood and used in common by a group of individuals. The relationships obtaining within such a style system are such that: (*a*) only some sounds or "unitary sound combinations" are possible; (*b*) those sounds possible within the system may be plurisituational within defined limits; (*c*) the sounds possible within the system can be combined only in certain ways to form compound terms; (*d*) the conditions stated in (*a*), (*b*), and (*c*) are subject to the probability relationships obtaining within the system; [3] (*e*) the probability relationships prevailing within the system are a function of context within a particular work as well as within the style system generally. The occurrence of any sound or group of sounds, simultaneously or in sequence, will be more or less probable depending upon the structure of the system and the context in which the sounds occur.

SOUND TERMS AND SOUND STIMULI

A sound or group of sounds (whether simultaneous, successive, or both) that indicate, imply, or lead the listener to expect a more or less probable consequent event are a musical gesture or "sound term" within a particular style system. The actual physical stimulus which is the necessary but not sufficient condition for the sound term will be called the "sound stimulus." The same sound stimulus may give rise to different sound terms in different style systems or within one and the same system. This is analogous to the fact that the same word (sound stimulus) may have different meanings (may become different sound terms, implying different consequents) in different languages or within one and the same language. The word "gauche," for example, has different, though related, meanings in English and French, while words such as "cross," "ground," or "interest" have different meanings within one and the same language. In other words, a sound stimulus does not become a sound term until it becomes realized as part of a system of sound relationships and until its particular function within that system is made apparent.

On the other hand, although it is clear that a sound stimulus cannot become a sound term apart from the context of a particular style system, it must be remembered that, since the listener is part of a culture that he takes for granted, a single isolated sound stimulus will tend to be interpreted as part of the prevalent style system of the culture, i.e., as a sound term. Thus a dominant seventh chord, for example, even though not incorporated into a specific context, is for the Western listener still a sound term, since the sound stimulus is heard within the prevalent style of Western music.

As we shall see, almost all studies in comparative musicology emphasize that the same sound stimulus often has different meanings, is a different sound term, in different musical cultures and styles and that seeming similarities are often very deceptive. Fox Strangways, for instance, points out that a piece of Indian music which sounds to Western ears as though it were in C major actually has quite a different "tonic" and, consequently, quite a different group of tendencies and probability relationships for the knowledgeable Hindu listener.[4]

Within a single culture or even within one piece of music the same sound stimulus may give rise to several different sound terms. This is easily seen in the tonal system of Western music of the past two hundred years. From a harmonic point of view, for example, a chord (sound stimulus) may have different functions in different keys. A chord which is a tonic in one key (which bears certain more or less definite probability relationships to other harmonic possibilities) may be a dominant in another key, and so forth. Within one and the same tonality a particular sound stimulus may give rise to a sound term at one time and not at another. For whether a sound stimulus becomes a sound term depends upon its function in the particular passage. At one time the sound stimulus may imply and indicate consequents and be considered as being structural, as being a sound term; at another time the same stimulus, though it is part of a sound term which has implications, is not itself a sound term—does not in and of itself give rise to meaning.

Since musical structures are architectonic, a particular sound stimulus which was considered to be a sound term or musical gesture on one architectonic level will, when considered as part of a larger more extended sound term, no longer function or be understood as a sound term in its own right.[5] In other words, the sound stimulus which was formerly a sound term can also be viewed as a part of a larger structure in which it does not form independent probability relations with other sound terms. In short, the same sound stimulus may be a sound term on one architectonic level and not on another.

The various levels of architectonic signification are, of course, interdependent. Just as there can be no chapters without meaningful relationships between paragraphs, or paragraphs without meaningful relationships between sentences, so the significance of the longer parts of a musical work depends upon the existence of meaningful relationships between the shorter ones. There could be no musical sections if one period did not in some way imply and lead to consequent periods, and there could be no periods if the phrases which form them did not follow one another in an understandable and meaningful way. The existence and coherence of higher, more extensive architectonic levels is dependent upon the meaningful relationships established on lower architectonic levels. This is not to say that the meaning of higher architectonic levels is merely the sum of the meanings of the sound terms included in them, any more than a chapter is the sum of the paragraphs, sentences, and words contained in it.

While the meaning of a musical work as a whole, as a single sound term, is not simply the sum of the meanings of its parts, neither is the entire meaning of the work solely that of its highest architectonic level. The lower levels are both means to an end and ends in themselves. The entire meaning of a work, as distinguished from the meaning of the work as a single sound term, includes both the meanings of the several parts and the meaning of the work as a single sound term or gesture. Both must be considered in any analysis of meaning.

As observed in chapter i, meaning is not static and immutable but an evolving, changing attribution of a gesture or sound term. The meaning of sound terms on all architectonic levels, even the highest one, exhibits growth and change. And the entire comprehensive meaning of a given musical work includes the hypothetical, evident, and determinate meanings of the multitude of sound terms that are contained in it as well as the relationships existing between these sound terms.

Often the hypothetical meaning of a sound term is very different from its evident meaning, and its evident meaning is conditioned and modified by this difference. The C-minor Fugue from the first book of the *Well-tempered Clavier* furnishes an excellent instance of such a change in the meaning of a sound term (measures 9–11, Example 2). In measure 9 a sequence through the cycle of fifths

EXAMPLE 2

with imitations between the soprano and alto is begun. The sequence continues through measure 10 and apparently into measure 11, where the motive marked *x* is at first understood as part of the sequence; that is, we suppose that the soprano will move to D in the following bar. However, once the whole of measure 11 and the beginning of measure 12 have been heard, we realize that the hypothetical meaning attributed to *x* was wrong, that it is not really part of the sequence but the beginning of the fugue theme, in short, that its evident meaning is quite different from its hypothetical meaning. It is very clear that Bach intends us to make this "mistake." For he could easily have made it clear that the fugue subject begins at this point by stopping the sequential progression in the left hand at the beginning of measure 11. Notice that our cognition of the evident meaning includes our conception of the hypothetical meaning; the sound term is not only evidently the beginning of the fugue subject, but it is the beginning about which we were originally mistaken. Furthermore, it is not only our opinion of the significance of *x* that is revised in measure 11 but our opinion as to the significance of the whole episode, which now appears to have this musical "pun" as one of its meanings.

The fact that as we listen to music we are constantly revising our opinions of what has happened in the past in the light of present events is important because it means that we are continually altering our expectations. It means, furthermore, that repetition, though it may exist physically, never exists psychologically. Thus, though it may seem a truism, it is of some moment to recognize that the repetition, say, of the exposition section of a sonata-form movement or that of the first-theme group in the recapitulation has quite a different meaning from that communicated by the original statement.

It is also important to realize that the more complete a series becomes, the more specific become the hypothetical meanings attributed to parts of the series. The relationships obtaining between two tones provide the listener with less basis for specific expectation than the relationships between five, six, or ten tones. Similarly the repetition or seeming repetition of a part arouses more specific expectations than the first statement of the part. The less complete the part, the more probable that we shall have to revise our opinion of some or all of its terms. To put it another way, the less complete the part, the weaker the probability relations between those terms already established and any future parts.

Here perhaps an illustrative analogy might be helpful. Suppose that we are presented with the number series

$$2 . 3 . 5$$

The continuation of the series is in doubt. It might continue with the number 10 if the series were arrived at through over-all summation, or it might continue with the number 8. In the latter case the series might continue in at least two ways, depending upon whether the number 8 was obtained by progressively augmenting the amount of increase between successive numbers ($2 + 1 = 3$, $3 + 2 = 5$, $5 + 3 = 8$), in which case the next number would be twelve ($8 + 4 = 12$), or whether the series was obtained by adding its two final numbers $(2 + 3 = 5, 3 + 5 = 8)$, in which case the next term would be 13 $(5 + 8 = 13)$. As the series unfolds, our expectations as to subsequent terms become more and more specific. This is exactly what happens as a musical sound term unfolds.

It follows from this that, since departures from or delays in the normally expected course of musical events will be most effective where that course is most specifically and precisely envisaged, deviations will be most effective where the pattern is most complete. And presuming that such affective deviants would occur where they would be most effective, we should expect to find them where the pattern is most complete. This expectation is borne out by the practice of musicians. "Observe especially that embellishments are best applied to those places where a melody is taking shape, as it were, or where its partial, if not complete, meaning or sense has been revealed. Hence with regard to the latter case, they are found chiefly at half or full closes, caesurae, and *fermate*." [6] Sachs attributes the fact that a "new tone generally ventures to appear only toward the end of the phrase, when the nucleus has been well established," [7] to the power of tradition. But the explanation would also seem to lie in the fact that such new tones, which are palpably deviations, delaying the arrival of expected, traditional consequents, are probably introduced for the sake of expression and affect. They are brought in at the end of the phrase, when it has already taken shape, because it is at this point, where the subsequent terms of the series are most specifically envisaged, that they will have the greatest effect.

Thus the effect of any particular deviant is a function of its position in the series. A deviant which might have only a slight effect at the beginning of a series, where expectation entertains a greater number of alternatives of approximately equal probability, may have a powerful effect toward the end of the series, where expectation is more particular and where the probability of expectation is liable to be greater. Of course, if a series is being repeated, then any point in the series will arouse definite expectations based upon the earlier version of the series; and a variation in the series will be most effective.

AMBIGUITY

A sound term can have different meanings at different times, but this does not prove that the term, or the hypothetical meaning which it first has, is ambiguous. For ambiguity is a state of mind in the listener, not simply a case of double meanings. If we are certain in our minds as to the meaning of a sound term when it first appears, then it is not ambiguous at that time. And if we are not in doubt when the same sound term is understood in a new way, when we know its evident meaning, then it is still not ambiguous. Thus in the Bach Fugue, discussed previously, we are at first quite sure that the motive sounded on E-flat is a continuation of the established sequence; but as soon as the expected sequence is not forthcoming, we revise our opinion and are certain, as we hear more music, that what we heard and are hearing is the fugue subject itself rather than a fragment of it.

But even a sound term which does imply several alternative modes of continuation may seem clear and unambiguous. For the expected consequents need not be mutually exclusive. They may be realized successively. Often a well-shaped melody, for instance, implies several alternative goals. And the realization of one mode of continuation does not preclude the subsequent realization of another (see p. 100). What is important is that the implications be definite and clear.

There are, however, sound terms that are decidedly ambiguous.[8] Ambiguity arises either because the progressions involved in a passage are so consistently irregular and unexpected that the listener begins to doubt the relevance and efficacy of his own expectations or because the shapes of the sound terms are so weak and uniform that there is only a minimal basis for expectation. The feeling is one of suspense and ambiguity. Both these aspects of ambiguity are more fully discussed in chapter v.

Ambiguity is important because it gives rise to particularly strong tensions and powerful expectations. For the human mind, ever searching for the certainty and control which comes with the ability to envisage and predict, avoids and abhors such doubtful and confused states and expects subsequent clarification (see pp. 16, 26).

There would seem to be various degrees of ambiguity. A sound stimulus becomes a sound term by entering into probability relationships with other sound terms within the style. These probability relationships are of different degrees. For example, it is quite probable that the tone which comes after an upward skip of a minor sixth will descend, while the probability of which tone will come after a skip of a major third is more doubtful. The more equal the probability of different alternative consequents, the more likely that the musical progression will seem ambiguous.

The fact that as we listen to music we not only interpret present stimuli on the basis of past events but also view past events and expect future ones on the basis of present stimuli means that a process at first felt to be ambiguous may later be seen as less so. Similarly processes at first considered unambiguous may later be seen as involving or leading toward ambiguity. In other words, ambiguity depends upon the structural architectonic viewpoint taken toward the stimulus series in question. A passage or section which on the level of the phrase or period appears to the mind as ambiguous and doubtful will, as a rule, seem unambiguous when considered from the viewpoint of the total section. To put the matter paradoxically: the unambiguous meaning of the whole may be a product of the ambiguity of the part.

STATIC VERSUS DYNAMIC CONCEPTIONS OF MUSICAL PROCESS

The preceding discussion points up the dangers of concentrating too much attention upon the structure of the musical work as a single sound term interpreted as a stable whole. The disciples of Schenker have not been sufficiently aware of this danger. Too much emphasis upon the highest architectonic level not only tends to minimize the importance of meanings as they arise and evolve on other architectonic levels but it also leads to a static interpretation of the musical process.

The very conception of "chord prolongation," so important to their view of musical growth, is a semantic confession that the musical process is, in spite of their explicit statements to the contrary, basically seen as static. If what occurs after a given structural harmony "prolongs" it, the implication is that the music is heard more in relation to the past than in relation to what is still to come. And while the past of any sound term is of great importance, it is of importance mainly because our expectations as to impending events are based upon our experience and remembrance of the past.

If, for example, the introduction to the first movement of Beethoven's Piano Sonata, Op. 81a is regarded as an extended prolongation of the opening E-flat major harmony, the main point of the introduction is, it seems to me, missed. For the passage is heard just the other way around: the opening progression leads us to expect a cadence in E-flat, and the whole introduction consists, in a sense, in delaying the arrival of such a cadence until after the allegro has already begun. The meaning of the passage and its affective power derives from this inhibited tendency toward a perfect cadence in E-flat. All this is missed if the introduction is considered as a prolongation of E-flat major. At best, we understand the introduction as a prolongation only after it is finished.

Felix Salzer's condemnation of the concept of modulation [9] is symptomatic of this essentially static view of musical meaning. It is true that, when we consider the evident and determinate meaning of the whole work, modulations can be regarded as passing intensifications of the main key. But this view ignores that the entire meaning of the work includes the meanings of the several parts and the various architectonic levels.

While we are experiencing music, we hear modulations and changes of key; we experience shifts in tonal center. Merely because some of these changes cannot be directly and immediately related to the key of the work as a whole does not mean that they are not felt and lack signification; nor does it mean that they cannot be understood. To extend an analogy, borrowed from Salzer himself, harmonic excursions can be understood in just the same way as departures from the straight narrative line in a novel—the complications of the plot—can be understood.

Only when the piece of music is complete, when it is timeless in memory, does Salzer's picture of music exist. And even then the picture is incomplete, since it ignores the experience of the work in time, which is part of our picture of the work as a whole.

Theories of music which imply that melodic similarity results in musical unity of necessity adopt a more or less mechanistic conception of what constitutes aesthetic unity. Unity is not a matter of employing a single tonality or a single melodic kernel as the basis of all the themes of a piece.

What is required if the elements of a work of art are to be compounded into an aesthetic whole is the presence of an ordering system of beliefs and attitudes which make them mutually relevant to one another; and, conversely, the materials handled in a work of art and the emotions which they express, may vary indefinitely without endangering the integrity of the whole so long as they are held together by a controlling system of expectations.[10]

The criticisms of the disciples of Schenker should by no means be understood as a wholesale condemnation. The method and many of the concepts which Schenker and others have developed can be a great value in the analysis of music, and their influence upon this study is obvious. The criticisms are directed merely against those aspects of the theory that tend to treat a musical composition as a thing instead of as a process which gives rise to a dynamic experience.

PROBABILITY

We have stated that styles in music are basically complex systems of probability relationships in which the meaning of any term or series of terms depends upon its relationships with all other terms possible within the style system. A glance at almost any book on the theory of music (whether Zarlino's or Rameau's) or the examination of any discussion or description of style (whether oriental, occidental or primitive) will indicate, either directly or by implication, that this is the case. For example, the following table (only the beginning of which is cited) given by Walter Piston [11] is actually nothing more than a statement of the system of probability which we know as tonal harmony:

TABLE OF USUAL ROOT PROGRESSIONS

I is followed by IV or V, sometimes by VI, less often II or III.
II is followed by V, sometimes VI, less often I, III, or IV.
III is followed by VI, sometimes IV, less often II or V.
IV is followed by V, sometimes I or II, less often III or II.
V is followed by I, sometimes VI or IV, less often III or II.

Laws of melodic progression, such as the Lipps-Meyer law, are essentially statements of probability relationships stated in a quasi-mathematical formulation relevant to particular style systems.

Stylistic descriptions are also expositions of the probability relations that prevail within the system under investigation. When, for example, Fox Strangways gives the scale of *Rag Pilu*[12] as in Example 3, he is indicating by his notation certain probability

EXAMPLE 3 *

relationships within the tonal materials available. He is telling us, for example, that C is likely to be the final tone, that the melody will tend to center about the tone E-flat, that the tones D-flat, E, F-sharp, A-flat and B-natural will be tones which tend to move toward the more stable tones in the system, and so forth. The relationships obtaining within this particular part of the total style system are further specified by written exposition: ". . . Pilu, for instance, has an E and an E-flat with a D and an F on either side of them; but in a given passage either E or E-flat will occur, but not both as a rule."[13] Notice, too, that certain temporal relationships are also implicit in this material; that is, that the tones written as underlined whole tones are likely to be sustained longer than the tones not so marked and that those not underlined are likely to be held longer than those written as quarter notes, etc.

Statistical style studies, such as those made by Frances Densmore in her work on American Indian music, also indicate that probability is one of the central facts of style. Tables listing the number of ascending and descending intervals, the number of accidentals, or the number of times a certain interval is employed in ascent or descent, for instance, are all statements about probability. This conclusion is emphasized by the fact that the figures are given in percentages.[14]

The difficulty with statistical style studies is threefold. First, there are, as we shall see in chapter iii, certain natural probabilities, such

* By permission of The Clarendon Press, Oxford.

as the fact that a process once established tends to continue in the same manner, which need not become musically actualized in a majority of cases in order to become probable within a style system. Although this might be overcome by positing certain "natural" probabilities, it is always possible that what is natural, even in this psychological sense, may become culturally overlaid and hence inoperative. Statistics cannot tell us whether or not this is the case. Second, in styles which are not static the probability relations are constantly changing, albeit slowly and subtly. This is simply another way of saying that, in a sense, each particular piece is also a particular style system. Third, it is clear that one style system may presume a knowledge of other styles which do not become overtly realized in a statistical sense. Thus, although the full cadence and diatonic melodic motion are not prevalent in the style of Wagner, for example, Wagner's style nevertheless presupposes these as basic norms. It seems to this writer that in stylistic study and analysis there is no substitute for a sensitive response to the style.[15] This can be achieved only through practice in listening and better still in performance.

Finally, we may note that in many theoretical systems the importance of probability relationships is made clear in the way in which the tones of the system are named. Thus the normative tones, those toward which other tones will probably move, have been given the basic names, while the other tones have been given names related to these, often in terms of their probable motions. In Western music, for example, the stable tones are named the tonic, mediant, and dominant, while the subsidiary tones are named in relation to these, for instance, leading tone (leading to the tonic) and supertonic. In the music of China non-structural tones take the name of the structural tone to which they move together with the word *pièn,* meaning "on the way to" or "becoming." Probability relationships are likewise implicit in the names given to several of the structural tones in the theory of Hindu music, e.g., *amsa, samvadi,* etc.

FORM, PROBABILITY, AND EXPECTATION

The architectonic nature of most larger musical structures has been mentioned. Although the probability relationships of the smaller units are also appropriate to the organization of larger structures, it is clear that the larger groups and sections exhibit certain special modes of organization and combination, certain special probability relationships, which exist in addition to, though not in conflict with, the probability relationships of the smaller parts. In other words, forms are special aspects of style, alternative probability groups, each of which exhibits its own special probability relationships within the total stylistic context. Like the perception of and response to the more generally continuous aspects of style, the understanding of form is learned, not innate.

The concept of a form involves abstraction and generalization. Our feeling of what a sonata form or a theme and variations is does not derive from our experience of this or that particular sonata or theme and variations but from our experience of a host of works in such forms. Out of this experience the class concepts which we label as this or that form are developed. The genesis of class concepts in which forms, under the influence of mental tendencies, become normalized will be further discussed in chapter iii. Here it is sufficient to point out that once a work is recognized as being a type for which an abstract, normative class concept has been evolved, then that "ideal type" becomes the basis for expectations.

At first glance the formation of class concepts seems to distinguish the probability relationships developed in connection with form from those established in connection with the more continuous aspects of style discussed earlier. In the case of style it might seem as though habit responses and probabilities are established by exact repetition, while in the case of form exact repetition is unknown. However, the development of all stylistic response sequences involves abstraction; and every occurrence of a given tonal sequence or rhythmic succession is a particular, for it becomes significant and meaningful only in its context, which is of necessity particular. Thus our conception of a plagal cadence is just as much an abstraction as is our conception of, for instance, a concerto grosso.

We have, let us say, a concept of what a fugue is. The concept is not of this or that particular fugue but is based upon our experience of a multitude of fugues. As we listen to a particular fugue we compare its special progress with the progress expected on the basis of our normalized concept of a fugue. Those progressions which seem irregular and unexpected relative to the generalized fugue of our imagination are then the deviants (the delays and resistances) which arouse the affective aesthetic response.

Such ideal types are not, however, fixed and rigid. They are flexible from two separate points of view. Our class concept of a form is constantly being modified by new experiences of that form. Each time, for example, we hear a new work that can be related to our concept of sonata form or perceive a work already heard from a new point of view, our generalized conception of sonata form is modified, if only slightly. It is partly this continual modification of formal conceptions (and, incidentally, general stylistic ones as well) which enables us to rehear a work many times. For as the norm with which we compare the particular has changed since a previous hearing, the expectations which are entertained on the basis of the norm will also have changed, and the new hearing will involve new perceptions and new meanings. Norms, furthermore, are flexible, in the sense that each of the various possible antecedents usually has several alternative consequents, some of which may be equally normative, i.e., equally probable. Of course, as noted earlier, as the work progresses the alternatives become fewer and the sequence becomes more determined.

Not only are there class concepts of forms in general but these concepts are always modified by a particular style. That is, we not only have an abstract conception of fugue in general but we also have an ideal type fugue in the style of Bach as distinguished from one by Brahms or Hindemith. A whole hierarchy of forms is maintained in the mind, from the generalizations resulting from several performances of the same work and those arising from stylistic experience to those based on the concept of form in general.

Thus it is not only important to know, in a general way, what the style of a piece of music is so that the responses brought into play will be the relevant ones, but it is also important to know what formal procedures are being employed. For our opinions as to form modify and condition our expectations. We bring different sets of expectations to a Schubert impromptu than to a sonata movement by the same composer. Moreover, as noted above, nominally similar forms which differ in style are often quite different in form as well.

Hence form is always specified with reference to style, just as style should be particularized with reference to form. The experienced listener will, for example, bring a very different set of habit responses into play if he is about to hear a sonata movement by Stravinsky from those which will be activated if he is about to hear a sonata by Schubert. This does not mean that the experience of the Schubert sonata does not play a part in the perception of the one by Stravinsky. In so far as the general concept of sonata is brought to bear on the listener's experience, it is clear that having heard a sonata by Schubert does influence our perception of Stravinsky. Likewise our experience of sonatas by Stravinsky or another modern composer, by modifying our class concept of sonata, will influence, though to a lesser extent, our experience of Schubert's sonatas.

Furthermore, information about the form and style of a work is important because, as we shall see later in this chapter, it conditions not only what we look for, and hence what we perceive, but also the speed of our perceptions and our responses.

Of course, we need not be told what we are going to hear. An experienced listener can place a work as to form and style on the basis of musical clues, such as harmony, melody, texture, instrumental style, and the like. Nor is it necessary that we should be able to name the composer or the style. What is vital is that we recognize, in the sense of bringing appropriate habit responses into play, the style and form early enough in the course of listening so that important initial relationships are not missed.

A distinction was drawn earlier between active and latent expectation, and active expectation was found to be a product of a delay or deviation in the normal sequence of events. It would seem that the situation with regard to form is somewhat more complex. In form we are, in a sense, constantly expecting. Under certain conditions we expect change, under others continuity, and under still others repetition; until, finally, we expect the conclusion of the piece. Thus in a very general way expectation is always ahead of the music, creating a background of diffuse tension against which particular delays articulate the affective curve and create meaning. Formal expectation is constantly active on several architectonic levels as a sort of generalized aesthetic tension which is shaped and particularized in the course of listening.

Revision of opinion, stressed earlier in the discussion of probability, is also important in the perception of form. Here, too, the listener often finds it necessary to revise his opinions of the significance of what has passed and his expectations of what is still to come in the light of an unexpected present. Thus the meaning and significance of the slow introduction to a sonata form movement will depend in part upon later developments which may take place in the allegro. The significance of the slow introduction to Beethoven's Piano Sonata, Op. 111 is quite different from that of the introduction to his String Quartet, Op. 130. The Sonata creates strong tension and suspense relative to the impending allegro which, because of what we know about sonata form in the classical style, is expected. The Quartet creates much less tension but serves as a source for many later developments as well as a factor in the articulation of events within the allegro proper. These differences become clearer and more specific as each work unfolds.

Style and Social Process

Musical meaning and significance, like other kinds of significant gestures and symbols, arise out of and presuppose the social processes of experience which constitute the musical universes of discourse. The perception of and response to the probability relationships obtaining within any style system are not naïve reflex reactions. Nor are the probability relationships universals having some kind of "natural," physical meaning. The response to music as well as its perception depend upon learned habit responses. The style systems to which these responses are made are, in the last analysis, artificial constructs developed by musicians within a specific culture.

The very fact that there are many different musical style systems, both in different cultures and even within a single culture, demonstrates that styles are constructed by musicians in a particular time and place and that they are not based upon universal, natural relationships inherent in the tonal material itself. And if the experience

of music is not based upon natural, universal responses, it must be
based upon responses which are acquired through learning.

LEARNING AND STYLE

The norms and deviants of a style upon which expectation and
consequently meaning are based are to be found in the habit responses of listeners who have learned to understand these relationships (also see p. 83).

> We speak of "traditions," "styles of art," "meanings" and so on, as if these
> things had a kind of independent reality of their own which are eternally
> attached to works of art. But traditions and meanings are kept alive only
> through the dispositions and habits which form the subjective contexts of
> countless individuals. . . . There can be no aesthetic response whatever
> apart from the responses of individual men which gives it meaning.[16]

These dispositions and habits are learned by constant practice in
listening and performing, practice which should, and usually does,
begin in early childhood. Objective knowledge and conceptual
understanding do not provide the automatic, instinctive perceptions
and responses which will enable the listener to understand the
swift, subtle, changeable course of the musical stream. To paraphrase Bertrand Russell (see p. 39): Understanding music is not a
matter of dictionary definitions, of knowing this, that, or the other
rule of musical syntax and grammar, rather it is a matter of habits
correctly acquired in one's self and properly presumed in the particular work.

It is not enough, for example, for the listener to know that in
Western music of the past three hundred years a particular sound
term, the dominant seventh chord, creates an expectation that another particular sound term, the tonic chord, will be forthcoming.
The expectation must have the status of an instinctive mental and
motor response, a felt urgency, before its meaning can be truly comprehended. The story of the young composer who got out of his bed
and ran to the piano to resolve a dominant seventh chord which
someone else had left unresolved is a good instance of this power
of felt urgency—of ingrained habit.

"I emphatically repeat," writes Hugo Riemann, "that practice and

good will are required for the understanding of a great and complicated musical work of art." [17] This practice is both mental and
motor. The relation between thinking and motor responses will be
discussed in some detail later in this chapter. The distinction between mental habits and motor habits is a difficult one; however,
both play an important part in the learning of musical styles. There
is probably a time in the development of children when motor
learning plays a particularly important role in the development of
response patterns. And, hence, early instruction in musical performance is important, not only because of the immediate pleasure in
performance which it gives, but also because it instills into the child
the proper habit responses, which are the life stream of musical
perception and communication.

THE PLURALITY OF STYLES

As Russell observes, not only must habits be properly acquired in
us but they must also be properly presumed in others; that is, our
trained habits of discrimination and response must be relevant to
the particular style of music to be heard. For the habits acquired
are not universal but are acquired in connection with a particular
style and are relevant to that particular style.

Music is not a "universal language." The languages and dialects
of music are many. They vary from culture to culture, from epoch
to epoch within the same culture, and even within a single epoch
and culture. An American must learn to understand Japanese music
just as he must learn to understand the spoken language of Japan.
An individual familiar with the tradition of modern European music
must practice playing and listening to the music of the Middle Ages
just as he must practice reading and speaking the language of
Chaucer. Even within one and the same culture and epoch it is the
exception rather than the rule when a musical style is understood
by all members of the culture. Witness the fact that in our own
culture the devotees of "serious" music have great difficulty in
understanding the meaning and significance of jazz and vice versa.

Yet, while recognizing the diversity of musical languages, we
must also admit that these languages have important characteristics
in common. The most important of these, and the one to which

least attention has been paid, is the syntactical nature of different musical styles. The organization of sound terms into a system of probability relationships, the limitations imposed upon the combining of sounds, and so forth are all common characteristics of musical language. It is to these that comparative musicology must turn if it is to make further progress in studying the music of different cultures. In this respect musical languages are like spoken or written languages which also exhibit common structural principles.

But different musical languages may also have certain sounds in common. Certain musical relationships appear to be well-nigh universal. In almost all cultures, for example, the octave and the fifth or fourth are treated as stable, focal tones toward which other terms of the system tend to move. Similarly many systems have organized tonal progressions, scales, though the relationships between these sound stimuli will vary greatly from system to system.

In so far as different styles have traits in common, the listener familiar with the music of one can perhaps "get the gist" of music to which he is not accustomed to respond; just as one can at times "get the drift" of a play or poem heard in a foreign language that has some words in common with one's native tongue. It is important, however, to note that the unpracticed listener is also very likely to make mistakes by reading into oriental or primitive music implications relevant only to the style system of recent Western music.

Because harmonies are used constantly in our music, they have permeated our musical consciousness to such an extent that the Western listener by necessity experiences music as harmonic—whether harmonies are actually present, are merely implied (as in the folk-songs of Western Europe from the last few centuries), or are entirely missing, as in most Primitive music. Only by prolonged training and familiarity is the investigator able to acquire the ability to experience monolinear music as such. Harmonic habits condition not only our mode of experiencing music, but also the nature of our musical concepts.[18]

In general it seems wise and prudent to treat all aspects of a style system as learned and culturally determined. First, because it seems likely that even the so-called "natural" stylistic traits are actually learned, just as certain phonemes are common to a language family but are nevertheless learned. And second, because the distinction between natural and learned characteristics is unnecessary. If the natural traits persist in a given style system, they can be studied as though they were learned, culturally determined elements just as easily as they can be as natural ones. While if natural traits are not operative within the given style, then they need not be considered, except perhaps from a genetic point of view, i.e., we may ask why they are not operative.[19]

PATTERNS OF STYLE CHANGE

Thus far we have been dealing largely with style systems, by which term something analogous to language has been meant. Where style systems are similar in important ways, we may say that they belong to the same style-system family, just as the Indo-European languages have certain basic traits in common because they stem from a common root language. By style, as distinguished from style system, is meant the more particular variants and modifications of a style system made at different epochs within a culture or by different composers within the same epoch. Thus Bach and Beethoven represent different styles within a single style system, while Mozart and Machaut employ different style systems.

Styles and style systems are not permanent, fixed, and rigid. Within cultures which do not impose strong social sanctions upon art, changes in style have been the rule rather than the exception. One style gradually replaces another, attains its own particular fruition, declines and is replaced by another style. The process is gradual and, since not all aspects of the system are necessarily changed, it is often impossible to mark off the historical limits of a style. We must be content to point out its ultimate fruition and its general limits. This has also been the case, though less frequently, with style systems.

It has been customary to relate such changes to social, political, and cultural changes—to explain the history of styles and style systems in terms of general, non-musical history. No doubt such extrastylistic events are of great importance as necessary causes in the history of style and style systems. This appears to be particularly true in the case of the radical changes which occur when one style system replaces another, e.g., the stylistic cultural changes which took place during the period of Western history known as the Renaissance.

Yet the explanations furnished by reference to political, social, and cultural history tell only part of the story. For stylistic changes and developments are continually taking place which appear to be largely independent of such extramusical events. Although an important interaction takes place between the political, social, and intellectual forces at work in a given epoch, on the one hand, and stylistic developments, on the other, there is also a strong tendency for a style to develop in its own way. If this is the case, then the causes of these changes must be looked for in the nature of aesthetic experience, since both for the composer and listener style is simply the vehicle for such an experience.

A discussion of the causes of such purely aesthetic stylistic development is important, not only as part of a general discussion of style, but also because the hypothesis of this study derives additional weight and support from the fact that it is able to account for processes which have as a rule been described rather than explained. To put it in another way, one of the logical consequences of the present hypothesis would be that a tendency toward intraaesthetic change would be the rule, a deduction which is confirmed by the facts of music history. For in any style the deviants as well as the norms are finite in number; and it is both possible and likely that a deviant through constant employment may become so fixed, so common in its recurrence in particular situations, that the probability relationships of the system become modified by this recurrence. Consequently a sound term which was once a definite deviant may become more or less normative within the style and thus lose its potential for expression.

In other words, deviation, originating as expression, may after a time become normative, and when this occurs it is necessary either to invent new deviations for the sake of aesthetic effect or to point up those already in use. This means that once a style is established there is a constant tendency toward the addition of new deviants and toward pointing up, through emphasis or exaggeration, those deviants already present. In short, the nature of aesthetic communication tends to make for the eventual destruction of any given style.

This process of stylistic genesis can be seen not only in the history of Western music but also in much oriental and primitive music.

In Western music we may take as an example the changing use of the vibrato in string playing. Originally in the eighteenth century the vibrato was an expressive device whose use was confined to specific passages. Gradually it became a fairly constant feature in string playing, thus losing some of its expressive effect. At present the ordinary vibrato is a norm of string playing from which there are two types of deviation: first, the use of an unusually rapid, and sometimes "wide," vibrato and, second, the use of no vibrato at all. It is particularly interesting to note that this latter alternative is becoming more and more prevalent in the rendition of expressive passages. Several contemporary scores specifically stipulate "no vibrato," e.g., Bartók's String Quartet No. 4, third movement, or Berg's Violin Concerto. What was once an affective aesthetic deviant has, through constant employment, become normative, and what was once considered normative has become a valuable expressive device.

We can see a similar change of function in the employment of modal cadences which, though normative in the Middle Ages and Renaissance, become expressive deviants in the style of some composers of the late nineteenth and twentieth centuries. Similarly the authentic cadence, a norm in classical and early romantic music, sometimes appears to be a deviant in the style of the late nineteenth century. There is a striking example of this in *Ein Heldenleben* by Strauss. Just before number 77 (Eulenberg, miniature score) there is a perfectly regular cadential progression, II-I$^6_4$ -V, in E-flat major, which in a piece written a hundred years earlier would lead us to expect the tonic chord. Here, however, it leads us to expect almost anything but the tonic; and when the tonic does come, it is definitely felt to be a deviant.

From Herzog's description of the development of Pueblo musical style, it seems clear that the same process takes place in primitive music: the deviants become normative within the style and provide the basis for further deviation.

If one of the two sections is a pentachord—which often results from the extension of a tetrachord—this wider section is frequently found in the lower position. . . . On the fringes of such sections decorative tones appear; in time these become standardized and strengthened, and this new growth finally results in extended forms. . . .

Tonal growth has progressed to such a degree of saturation that the original structure—probably pentatonic—often becomes grown over and obscured. Sharp accentuation and other features of the singing technic give rise to a greater number of secondary tones which in turn provide material for further melodic growth.[20]

A similar development seems to have taken place in the case of Byzantine melodic style. At first deviation and expression was a matter of combining brief melodic formulas in different and surprising ways, thus producing new hymn melodies. However,

The immense number of hymns introduced into the service made it necessary for the ecclesiastical authorities to prohibit the addition of new hymns to the repertory, and the artistic activity of the monks from that time onwards was concentrated upon the embellishment of the music, which, in the following centuries, and even after the fall of the Empire, became increasingly rich and elaborate, until the originally simple structure of Byzantine melodies was transformed into an ornamented style and the words of the text made unrecognizable by extended coloraturas.[21]

Here we have an excellent example of the relation between sociopolitical conditions and stylistic development. For the pressure exerted by the authorities of the Byzantine Church, though it influenced the course of stylistic development, did so largely in a negative way; certain possibilities of deviation were excluded, but there was no stipulation as to the future course of stylistic change. This is particularly interesting because under rather similar conditions the composers of the Western Church eventually turned to other methods of deviation, e.g., the vertical embellishment called organum.

The fact that the socio-cultural situation in which an art flourishes limits, at least in a negative way, the modes of deviation is perhaps most clearly seen in the case of folk music. Because the true tradition of folk music is aural rather than written, deviation is a matter of improvisations made upon a learned basic structure and shape. Sometimes this shape may be purely melodic, while in others it is harmonic as well:

Hot jazz melody is improvisatory, but its structure is held to a coherent formal pattern which restrains it from complete chaos. This coherent pattern is provided by the harmonic sequences of the underlying accompaniment. . . . It is the simple harmonic phrase . . . that provides the unifying principle in hot jazz improvisation. . . . This phrase is repeated over and over again, with occasional interpolations, perhaps, of other similar chordic sequences, forming a sort of 'ostinato' on which the melodic and rhythmic variations are built. At each variation of the harmonic phrase a new melodic and rhythmic superstructure is improvised by the hot player.[22]

In the case of folk music, including jazz, the basic, normative patterns are fixed by custom and tradition, but the degree and manner of deviation may change, bringing new styles into existence. Thus, for example, Dixie Land jazz and Bebop are both based upon essentially the same basic pattern, but their manner and style of deviation differ.

Suppose that a device which was once a deviant in a given style becomes fixed in its relationships and constant in use. Does this mean that it necessarily ceases to be aesthetically effective, that it becomes a norm? The answer appears to be negative. Though a deviation may no longer actually function to inhibit a tendency, it may still function expressively as a sign. Whether a deviation becomes a norm or a sign of expression would seem to depend largely upon the context in which it is employed. If it is associated in practice with real deviants, it will probably continue to function in an affective way. If, on the other hand, it becomes associated with clearly normative progressions, then it will tend to become normative within the style.

Even where a deviant does not become an expressive sign it need not necessarily become a norm. If the expressive value of a relationship becomes weakened through standardization, several alternatives present themselves: (1) The degree of deviation can at times be increased as, for example, it was in the elaboration of *coloratura* passages in late Byzantine melodies. (2) New deviant devices can be introduced into the style as alternatives, weakening the probability relationships between the former deviant and its consequents. That is, if A to D (a former deviant) is becoming a normative (probable) relationship, the introduction of D_1, as an alternative, will of necessity weaken the probability that A will be followed by D and hence renew, as it were, the deviant quality of D. (3) New deviants can be used to replace those which are becoming normalized. The introduction of modal relationships into the harmonic style of the late nineteenth century was an instance of this. (4) Old relationships can be revitalized through changes in other aspects of style and through new and different uses for fixed relationships. Harmonic style underwent such a revitalization in the second half of the eighteenth century. The essential structure of the harmonic scheme which flourished during the later baroque was maintained, but its use in the organization of the total structure of the work was new.

Several instances in which norms became deviants have been noted. Actually, however, this is neither a necessary nor a common occurrence. If norms do become deviants, the change of function does not as a rule take place immediately but rather after a considerable lapse of time and the establishment of a new style system.

STYLE CHANGES AND THE COMPOSER

Styles are made, modified, and developed by composers and performers, both as individuals and as groups. The tendency toward stylistic change results not only from the musician's conscious aesthetic intent but also from the fact that the composer and performer, by their very nature as creators and makers, regard the traditions and styles which they inherit from their predecessors as a challenge—as a more or less fixed, recalcitrant material, whose resistance to change and modification the true artist delights in overcoming and conquering. Stravinsky, for example, writes that "as I am by nature always tempted by anything needing prolonged effort, and prone to persist in overcoming difficulties . . . the prospect . . . greatly attracted me." [23] In his experimenting and playing with his inheritance the artist often taxes his own ingenuity and imagination to the utmost and, like a virtuoso on the high wire, tries to see how far he can go in creating new aesthetic problems, or how he can solve old problems in new and significant ways. How far, in short, he can deviate without losing his aesthetic balance.

The creation and overcoming of difficulties, an apparently intellectual process, and the modification and remolding of style for the sake of affective aesthetic responses are but two facets of a single process. And once again we are reminded of the groundlessness of the traditional dichotomy between emotions and intellect.

This analysis of the relation between artistic creation and deviation explains in part the process of stylistic change. It also enables us to introduce as evidence in the ensuing chapters the statements of composers, performers, and critics referring to the creative experience of the artist rather than to affective experience itself. For if the conquest of difficulties and the affective aesthetic processes can usually [24] be equated, then a passage designated by a writer as involving the delight in conquering difficulties can also be considered as potentially affective or aesthetic. It must then be shown that the passage in question does, in fact, involve delay in expectation or, in other words, deviation.

The relation of artistic creation to play must be mentioned. Many references are made in the literature of music to the playfulness of a particular passage or to the delight taken by musicians in play. It seems very probable that this too is a way of referring to the conquest of self-imposed difficulties. Karl Groos frequently emphasizes that this is an essential feature of all play; that, in his own words, "play leads up from what is easy to more difficult tasks, since only deliberate conquest can produce the feeling of pleasure in success." [25]

This delight in the conquest of difficulties, in aesthetic play with the recalcitrant mass of traditional materials, is important in performance as well as composition, particularly where the performer is free to, or supposed to, improvise upon either a written score, as in the seventeenth and eighteenth centuries of the Western tradition, or upon a tune handed down by oral tradition, as in much of the music of the Orient and in folk music. But even the performer with a fully notated score, if he is truly creative, is engaged in this process of deviation for the sake of expressive play (see p. 199).

The degree and extent of deviation and the rapidity of stylistic change depend upon the extramusical forces at work in the historical situation, the specifically musical situation, and the personality of the composer. If Bach wrought fewer changes in the style he inherited than Beethoven did, it was not necessarily because he took less delight in playful deviation and the overcoming of difficulties but rather because of the cultural and social situation in which he found himself and because of his personality, which was in part a product of that situation. Hence we must modify the statement made at the outset of this section by saying that creative musicians in their search for new facets of expression and in their play with their inheritance tend to change style, but this tendency is conditioned by the exigencies of extrastylistic forces.

This exposition of the relation of the creative artist to a tradition which, on the one hand, he wants to preserve (for without it no expression is possible) and within which, on the other hand, he seeks to deviate and create anew, throws into sharp relief the differences between traditional, academic, and decadent art. The traditional artist is one who understands the relationship of norms to deviants and who works within this relationship. For him both norms and deviants are valued for the sake of the meaning and significance to which their interrelation gives rise. The academic artist, extolling what he thinks to be tradition, views norms as ends in themselves. He codifies not only the norms but also the deviations, giving these the status of norms. Failing to understand the necessity for flexibility in deviation, his art becomes fixed and sterile. Decadent art, in contrast with this, is art in which traditional modes of deviation are exaggerated to extremes and where these deviations are, so to speak, pursued for their own sake. Here the artist tends to destroy, through exaggeration, the very tradition upon which his expression depends. The difficulty in this case is that it is often doubtful whether we are witnessing the destruction of an old style or the creation of a new one. Certainly the line is very hard to draw, and it seems possible that what appears as decadent from the point of view of one style may appear as creative from the point of view of another.

CYCLIC CHANGE AND STYLE

Implicit in this whole discussion is the conclusion that the process of stylistic change is a cyclic one. There must first be a period during which norms and their related deviants become established. This cannot be accomplished by theorists or by decree; the new norms and their related deviants must gradually become part of the habit responses of composers, performers, and listeners alike. Such a period is usually marked by a plurality of styles. The situation will tend to be uncertain and ambiguous. There will be conservatives who adhere to the old style and there will be avant-gardists who are attempting to build the new style. Both groups will be very conscious of technique, and the partisans of the new style will be especially conservative, in the sense that they will tend to impose very strict limitations upon themselves. Cultural tension and conflict will give rise to schools, pamphleteers, and apologists. The increased concern with music theory, with the grammar and syntax of style, will produce a host of theoretical and aesthetic treatises.

Following this there is a period in which the new style becomes established and accepted. There is a tendency toward singleness of style. In contrast to the first period, which was largely concerned with the establishment of norms, we now find an equal concern for deviant and norm. The musical situation is relatively stable and all energy is turned to the production of music. Theoretical and partisan writings about music become infrequent.

In the course of time, however, some of the deviations developed become almost clichés, and composers search for new means of expression and new difficulties to conquer. The whole system of probabilities gradually breaks down under the weight of an increased number and degree of deviations and the end of the style is in view.

Such a cyclical view of the process of music history seems, whether we like it or not, to be a part of the facts of aesthetic process. This process does not, of course, result in any rigid determinism. For the rate of change, the kind of change, and even the fact of change, all are conditioned by the social, political, and cultural climate in which the process must take place. And though these extramusical factors may, and often do, obscure the cyclical processes which mark the genesis of style systems and idioms yet the tendency toward cyclical change seems to be confirmed by the facts of music history.

The probabilities of style and form, the norms upon which expectations rest, differ from culture to culture and style to style. What remains constant in the flux of music history is not any particular organization of the materials of sound. The patterns of style are fixed by neither God nor nature but are made, modified, and discarded by musicians. What remains constant is the nature of human responses and the principles of pattern perception, the ways in which the mind, operating within the framework of a learned style, selects and organizes the sense data presented to it. But before these perceptual processes are brought into play, before the music begins to sound, the listener prepares to attend.

The Preparatory Set

Like other intentional activities listening to music is preceded by a number of mental and physical adjustments, performed consciously or unconsciously, which serve to facilitate and condition the subsequent responses made to the expected stimulus. These adjustments are known as a "preparatory set." The specific adjustments made are products of (1) the listener's beliefs about aesthetic experience in general and musical experience in particular, (2) the experience and knowledge previously acquired in listening to and studying about music, and (3) information gathered on the particular occasion in question.[26]

AESTHETIC BELIEF

The listener brings to music not only specifically musical experiences, associations, and dispositions but also important beliefs as to the nature and significance of aesthetic experience in general and the expected musical experience in particular.

The belief that we are dealing with an aesthetic object leads to what Henry Aiken has called the idea of "framing," that is, the belief that an aesthetic object is a special kind of stimulus to which we do not respond by overt action. The fact that the response to aesthetic experience is not overt has, as we have already seen, very important consequences in conditioning our responses; for the repression of overt behavior is a vital factor in the development of affect.

The idea of framing does not, however, detract from the feeling of reality which is so important in aesthetic experience. "The mechanism of denial can operate; a firm belief in the 'reality of play' can coexist with a certainty that it is play only. Here lie the roots of aesthetic illusion." [27] Furthermore, the ability of the mind to believe, to enter into the special nature of the aesthetic situation, in part makes possible the fact that a single work can be heard many times. For here, too, the mechanism of denial operates in such a way that the listener holds his knowledge of the final aesthetic outcome in suspense and believes in the reality of all the expectations, surprises, and delays set forth in the work, even though he may have experienced them in an earlier hearing.

Nor should the role played by the belief in the seriousness, significance, and power of aesthetic experience be overlooked. [28] For the attention given to a work of art is a direct product of the belief in the significance and vitality of aesthetic experience. And attention not only focuses our minds upon the musical work but also modifies perception itself, since "when the organism is active, at a high degree of vigilance . . . it will produce good articulation; when it is passive, in a low state of vigilance, it will produce uniformity." [29]

It seems quite probable, moreover, that it is the belief in the power and importance of aesthetic experience, the belief that we are going to have such an experience, that is responsible for the fact, noted earlier (p. 11), that "tone as such has a very powerful emotional influence. It sets up organic conditions which are involved in strong feeling. . . ." [30] It is very doubtful whether an individual engaged in the chores of everyday life will respond in this way to the tone of a violin played by a child practicing his scales or to the sound of the chimes of a particular radio station. The changes in pulse, respiration, metabolism, and psychogalvanic reflex, which Mursell attributes to "tone as such," do not appear to accompany all acts of attention, though attention is an important factor in their arousal. Rather believing in the aesthetic affective significance of musical experience, we expect to have such an experience, and our bodies, responding to this mental set, prepare themselves for the experience. This supposition is supported by evidence indicating that the act of attention, of which listening to music is a special type, is often accompanied by physical adjustments, including those of the central nervous system. There is also evidence that affect is related to motor attitudes which, as will be shown below, form an important part of the total preparatory set.[31]

The situation is further complicated by the fact that the belief that we are about to have an experience may itself give rise to special tensions which are relieved only when the music begins to sound and the more specifically aesthetic tensions begin to prevail. The atmosphere of the concert hall, hushed and quiet before the music starts, is charged with the tension of expectancy. The behavior of the audience is usually an indication of this tension. They are not calm and relaxed but strained and excited, their mental tensions often finding relief in bodily behavior, e.g., coughing, whispering, and so forth.[32]

BELIEF AND THE PRESUMPTION OF LOGIC

Related to the belief in the power and significance of aesthetic experience is the belief in the seriousness, purposefulness, and "logic" of the creative artist and the work he produces. The presumption that nothing in art happens without a reason and that any given cause should be sufficient and necessary for what takes place is a fundamental condition for the experience of art. Though seeming accident is a delight, we believe that real accident is foreign to good art. Without this basic belief the listener would have no reason for suspending judgment, revising opinion, and searching for relationships; the divergent, the less probable, the ambiguous would have no meaning. There would be no progression, only change. Without faith in the purposefulness and rationality of art, listeners would abandon their attempts to understand, to reconcile deviants to what has gone before, or to look for their *raison d'être* in what is still to come.

The term "serious" as applied to art does not, then, mean heavy or world-shaking as opposed to comic or light but rather that the relationships set forth in the art work are significant, logical relationships and hence to be taken seriously. To put it paradoxically, a rollicking rondo by Haydn is less capricious, is more serious, than some of the stately symphonies by Mahler.

Because of the tremendous importance of belief in the response to art, the most devastating criticism that can be leveled against a work is not that it is crude or displeasing but that it is not aesthetically purposeful and meaningful. Statements that compositions in the twelve-tone technique are conceived within an essentially mathematical framework, implying that they are not honestly felt or aesthetically conceived by the composer, have done more to make the music of this school unpopular and hated than all the accusations of cacophony and ugliness put together. It seems probable that audiences object to the dissonance in this music, not because it is unpleasant, but because they believe that it is the product of calculation rather than an aesthetic affective conception. These criticisms have weakened belief in the logic and seriousness of the music, and listeners have consequently abandoned their attempts to understand.[33] The power of most journalistic criticism derives not so much from its ability to influence judgment as from its power to enhance or weaken belief.

Much of the information supplied in the program notes for a symphony concert, the popular biographies of composers, or the run-of-the-mill music appreciation course is aimed, albeit unconsciously, primarily at enhancing belief. The story of the composer's "life and hard times," the circumstances under which a particular composition was written, the testimonials to the greatness of the work to be heard, and so forth do not help us to appreciate (to understand) the work directly, only our own proper habit responses can do this, rather they aid appreciation by strengthening belief and creating a willing attitude (see pp. 61–62).

Just as criticism can enhance belief (and hence the disposition to respond) through praise or negate belief (and the disposition to respond) through blame, so too the composition of the audience and its attitude toward the performers and the compositions to be heard can play an important part in coloring belief. A half-empty concert hall with an unenthusiastic audience or even a full hall with an inattentive audience will tend to minimize belief and probably the responses of a good many members of the audience, while a full house with a devoted audience will tend to enhance belief.[34]

Obviously fashions, "right opinion," as set by the social group which constitutes a particular segment of the total audience, also influence belief in important ways. And it would seem that such socially determined beliefs and tastes are becoming increasingly effective in conditioning the responses of what David Riesman has called the "other directed" man of our society.[35]

Learned Habits and the Preparatory Set

The preparatory sets which arise as a result of our beliefs as to the nature of musical experience are not specific to any particular musical style or form. The disposition to respond is general, i.e., mental attitudes and bodily tensions which arise are relevant to musical experience per se.

Together with these general beliefs about aesthetic experience the practiced listener also brings with him, as we have seen, a wealth of more specific dispositions or ideo-motor sets based upon past experience in listening and knowledge acquired either systematically or by chance. Once the listener knows, either precisely or in terms of general style characteristics, what kind of music he is going to hear, this information conditions his perceptions, modifies his opinion of what is heard, and qualifies his later responses.

The information which brings the preparatory sets into play need not be verbal. It may consist of visual signs, such as the presence of a particular instrumental group, or the gestures of performers, the kind of audience, and so forth.

THE INFLUENCE OF KNOWLEDGE AND EXPERIENCE
ON PERCEPTION

What we know and hence expect influences what we perceive, that is, the way in which the mind groups and organizes the sense data presented to it. Knowledge as to the style and form brings about an increased clearness and acuteness in perception; "for attention, adding energy to the particular field part, will increase its articulation, if it is not articulated as well as it might be." [36] This direction of attention toward a particular aspect of the musical structure and texture is also important because "where the center of our interest lies, there, *ceteris paribus*, a figure is likely to arise." [37] Thus, for instance, if a piece were known to be built upon a ground bass, attention, focusing upon this aspect of the musical structure, would tend to "bring the bass out," even though other voices might tend to obscure its progress. Similarly if we know that a particular movement is a theme and variations, we are intent on following the theme, and hence those variations in which the quality of the figure has been much weakened will seem better structured than they might seem otherwise. From a negative point of view this "search attitude" is important because small differences, which may be very important in the understanding of a work, may pass unnoticed if one is not set to perceive them. It is often the preparatory set which brings this readiness to perceive into play.

Knowledge and experience often color or modify our opinion about what is heard. If, for example, we see a large orchestra on the concert stage, we immediately become aware of its potential sound. Consequently an opening solo for a single instrument, e.g., the flute solo at the beginning of Debussy's *Afternoon of a Faun,* will have quite a different effect, will be heard differently, than it would be were it the opening music of a sonata for unaccompanied flute. Furthermore, our expectations of what will follow, partly based upon our belief that the musicians are not gathered upon the stage by chance, are colored by the presence of the orchestra; the longer the solo passage continues, the stronger is the presumption that the orchestra will enter.

To take another example, if one is listening to a bell tolling the hour and knows, say, that it is ten o'clock, then the tenth stroke will probably be perceived as accented and longer than the others, although, in point of fact, all strokes were equal in intensity and duration. In like manner Ortmann's experiments show that what is considered to be the end of a melody or rhythm depends not only upon certain natural tendencies of closing inflection and upon cadential formulas learned by experience but also upon which tone in the series—fourth, fifth, seventh, etc.—the subjects were told would be the final one.[38]

The practiced listener can recognize the style and often the form of a composition without being given information beforehand. But even for him knowledge which brings the preparatory set into play is sometimes important because it conditions not only what is perceived but also the speed of perception and hence of response. An expected stimulus will be perceived and understood more rapidly than would otherwise be the case.[39]

Motor Attitudes and Motor Responses

Like other acts of attention, listening to music is accompanied by physiological and motor adjustments. The physiological changes, as we have seen, appear to be products of the belief and expectation that we are going to have an affective aesthetic experience. They are quite general and are probably not differentiated as between different kinds of aesthetic objects. Nor do they undergo changes that can be traced to changes in the stimulus conditions—the music. Motor attitudes and responses involve the voluntary muscle systems, and, aside from a general tensing of the muscles related to all feelings of effort, of which listening to music is a special kind, they are more or less specific to particular styles and forms and tend to change with changes in the stimulus conditions.

Anticipatory motor attitudes form part of the preparatory set. They are brought into play on the basis of: (*a*) information as to composer, style, or form which leads the listener to expect a repetition of past motor experiences evoked by the particular type of work; (*b*) program notes or other statements as to tempo, volume, mode, mood, and so forth that supply information as to the appropriate motor attitude; and (*c*) visual clues provided by performers in the form of gestures and postures, which lead the listener to assume a like attitude, though these need not be manifest in the listener's overt behavior. Whether based upon experience or current clues, the listener's anticipatory motor behavior will be different if he is about to hear a Strauss waltz from what it will be if he expects to hear a Bach cantata or a Schoenberg string quartet. Such adjustments may also be made to a particular movement of a work or even special parts within a given movement. The motor preparation for the hearing of a minuet or scherzo of a classical symphony will usually be very different, whether we know the particular work or not, from that assumed toward the playing of the slow movement or the finale.

Motor attitudes not only form part of the preparatory set but also play a part in the perception and response sequences made to the changing progress of the musical form. Changes in rhythm, dynamics, tempo, and the like will bring about appropriate changes in motor attitude. For this reason the present discussion of motor attitudes is not confined to their function in the preparatory set.

The importance of the listener's motor behavior has been implied or directly stated by composers and psychologists alike. C. P. E. Bach, for example, tells us that:

A musician cannot move others unless he too is moved . . . for the revealing of his humour will stimulate a like humour in the listener. . . . Those who maintain that all of this can be accomplished without gesture will retract their words when, owing to their own insensibility, they find themselves obliged to sit like a statue before their instrument. Ugly grimaces are, of course, inappropriate and harmful; but fitting expressions help the listener to understand our meaning.[40]

Although espousing a very different aesthetic position, Stravinsky also emphasizes the importance of motor adjustments in the understanding of music. "The sight of the gestures and movements of the various parts of the body producing the music is fundamentally necessary if it is to be grasped in all its fullness." [41]

At first sight there would appear to be a distinction between a response to the gesture or motor behavior of a performer and a response to one's own aural experience. In point of fact, however, the distinction is apparent rather than real. For the motor behavior of the performer, in so far as it is related to the musical continuum at all, arises out of his own musical perceptions and is therefore behavior that the listener might have performed directly. That is, the empathetic response to another's behavior, which is itself a response to a stimulus perceived by both persons, generally serves to initiate or enforce behavior that might have taken place as a direct response to the stimulus. That the player's gestures must be made only in response to the music is also stressed by Stravinsky, who observes that only "if the player's movements are evoked solely by the exigencies of the music" will they "facilitate one's auditory perceptions." [42]

Although motor attitudes both anticipate and accompany the response to music, the precise role played by motor behavior in the perception and understanding of music is both problematic and complex.

On the one hand, it seems clear that almost all motor behavior is basically a product of mental activity rather than a kind of direct response made to the stimulus as such. For aside from the obvious fact that muscles cannot perceive, that there seems to be no direct path from the receptors to the voluntary muscle systems, motor responses are not, as a rule, made to separate, discrete sounds but to patterns and groupings of sounds. The more order and regularity the mind is able to impose upon the stimuli presented to it by the senses, the more likely it is that motor behavior will arise. Such grouping and patterning of sounds is patently a result of mental activity.

In the field of rhythmic experience, where motor responses have been most systematically studied and their importance most emphatically stressed, James Mursell, after a careful and thorough review of the literature, while admitting the importance of motor behavior, decides *that the ultimate foundation of rhythm is to be found in mental activity.* [43] Curt Sachs, writing from a very different viewpoint, arrives at the same conclusion, quoting Brelet to the effect that: "Rhythm comes from the mind not the body." [44]

On the other hand, the facts indicate that somehow motor behavior does play an important part in facilitating and enforcing the musical aesthetic experience. How this takes place need not detain us here. However, it does seem significant to recognize that motor behavior often plays an important part in making the listener aware, whether consciously or unconsciously, of the structure and progress of the music. Some listeners become aware of the tendencies of music partly in terms of their own bodily behavior. Such listeners might be said to objectify and give concrete reference to music, to perceive it through their own motor responses. And perhaps this in part accounts for the emphasis which has been placed upon motor responses.

What does seem clear is that since motor behavior is a product of and runs concurrent with mental behavior, it requires no special, independent analysis; for the experience of motor attitudes is not structurally differentiated in any way from the mental responses made in listening but rather exhibits a one to one correspondence with them.

One point, however, remains. It has been fairly well established that a regular, periodic motor pattern, once begun by and in congruence with a mentally perceived pattern, tends to continue, to perpetuate itself. Does this mean that motor behavior can become independent of the perception of new stimuli? In concrete terms: Will the motor response made to, say, a rhythm in triple meter continue and persist after the meter has changed to four-four? The answer would seem to be that it can and often will.

Yet, even here, the separation between mental and motor responses, if one exists, creates no great difficulties. For, as we shall see in the following chapter, the tendency of a motor action to perpetuate itself has its "mental" counterpart in the Gestalt concepts of the laws of continuity and completion, which recognize a similar tendency in the habits of the mind (see pp. 92 f.). The question which might be raised, and one that we will not attempt to answer, is this: To what extent are the laws of continuity and completion themselves a product of the tendency of voluntary motor behavior to perpetuate itself and follow the line of least resistance? In other words, is the tendency of the eye to continue its motion in a given way or the "mental ear" to continue its motions to some extent a product of the natural tendencies of motor behavior?

In conclusion we may say that there appears to be nothing autonomous and independent about the motor response to music. Everything which occurs as a motor response can be accounted for in terms of mental activity and, since the converse of this is not true, music is best examined in terms of mental behavior. We do not by this statement intend to minimize the importance of motor responses. Their ability to give force and urgency to musical experience is evidently of great importance.

III

Principles of Pattern Perception: The Law
of Good Continuation

General Considerations

Our whole intelligent process seems to lie in the attention which is selective of certain types of stimuli. Other stimuli which are bombarding the system are in some fashion shunted off. . . . Our attention is an organizing process as well as a selective one. . . . The organism goes out and determines what it is going to respond to, and organizes that world.[1]

The organization which the mind imposes upon the separate stimuli which are constantly "bombarding the system" is not an accidental or an arbitrary one. The mind in its selection and organization of discrete stimuli into figures and groupings appears to obey certain general laws. These not only account, in part, for the way in which the mind organizes musical stimuli but also explain how some of the expectations which the mind entertains on the basis of such groupings arise.

LEARNING AND PERCEPTION

Many of these mental laws, formulated upon a wealth of empirical data, were first discerned by a group of psychologists who later became known as the Gestalt school and whose theories were incorporated into a system now known as Gestalt psychology. It is important to distinguish between the experimental findings made in connection with Gestalt theory and the theory itself, because the distinction makes clear that it is possible to accept the empirical data, the laws, discovered by Gestalt psychologists without adopting the hypothetical explanations furnished by the theory.

For Gestalt theory in reacting against the sensationist concept of perception and the association theory of learning leaned too far in another direction. It attributed almost all grouping to the "spontaneous organization of simple shapes" and tended to minimize or deny the role of learning in the perception and organization of figures. Since the present analysis of expectation has continually stressed the importance of learning in the selection and organization of sense data, it is necessary to emphasize that it is employing Gestalt terminology and utilizing the data supplied by its experiments but that it is not adopting its theoretical explanation of perception.

This is not the place for a critique of Gestalt theory. In his book, *The Organization of Behavior,* Hebb examines the Gestalt theory of learning in some detail and advances convincing evidence of its shortcomings. He shows that "animal experiments and human clinical data alike indicate that the perception of simple diagrams as distinctive wholes is not immediately given but slowly acquired through learning." [2] According to Hebb, "the fundamental difficulty with configuration theory, broadly speaking, is that it leaves too little room for the factor of experience." [3]

It is possible that the laws of the mind may in some circumstances be independent of cultural conditioning. Where human communication is involved, however, though the laws still operate, they do so within a socio-cultural context where attitude, belief, and learning qualify their operation. That this is so can easily be seen from the following example. The symbols

R S E T E L T

appear at first to be discrete, individual stimuli. If so instructed, the mind can group these symbols, but it does so with difficulty and the result is somewhat arbitrary. If these stimuli are arranged thus:

T T R L S E E

the similarity and symmetry of the grouping appear immediately (TT, RLS, EE). The grouping could be changed if the factor of proximity were altered:

T   TR   L   SE   E

though even here similarity will play some part in the organization of the patterns so that TR may be seen as a subgroup of *TTR* and

SE as a subgroup of *SEE* with *L* as an isolated middle term. In all these cases the natural laws of grouping are functioning, though even here the ability to discriminate easily between the symbols is probably a product of learning.

Notice, however, that these same

LETTERS

immediately form a convincing and satisfactory Gestalt, which has as its basis of organization not a natural mode of grouping but one learned through experience. Were it not for the fact that this is a word in our language and our beliefs as to the nature of letters in general, our grouping of these stimuli would be quite different. In other words, though, as we shall see, the mind organizes and groups the stimuli it perceives into the simplest possible shapes or the most satisfactory and complete figures possible, what is, in fact, the most satisfactory organization in any given case is a product of cultural experience.

DIFFICULTIES IN THE APPLICATION OF GESTALT CONCEPTS

The vital role occupied by learning in conditioning the operation of Gestalt laws and concepts indicates at the outset that any generalized Gestalt account of musical perception is out of the question. Each style system and style will form figures in a different way, depending upon the melodic materials drawn upon, their interrelationships, the norms of rhythmic organization, the attitudes toward texture, and so forth.

For instance, in a culture or style system where the tonal materials are arranged in two disjunct tetrachords:

$$\text{E F A} \overline{\text{B C E}}$$

the fragment in Example 4 would be grouped differently from what it would be were it interpreted within the context of the minor mode of Western tonal music.[4] Furthermore, just as tonal relations will always be modified by rhythmic structure so basic structural tonal

EXAMPLE 4

groupings play an important part in rhythmic perception. The fact that we hear the opening notes of the Finale of Mozart's Symphony No. 40 as a unitary, upbeat group is partly a result of our having learned to regard the triad as a single figure. Yet even this statement must be conditional, for the unity of the triad or any other traditionally developed tonal set depends for its unity upon other factors, such as rhythm, tempo, instrumentation, and so forth.

Nor does it seem that, even within the confined limits of a particular style, a precise and systematic account of musical perception solely in Gestalt terms is possible. Even given additional empirical data about aural perception, certain basic difficulties in the application of Gestalt principles to any specific musical process would still remain.

These difficulties do not derive from any basic weakness in Gestalt laws per se but from the fact that the number, interdependence, and subtlety of the variables involved in musical perception make the establishment of a system of analytical rules of thumb impossible.

Although there is ample reason for believing that the laws developed by Gestalt psychologists, largely in connection with visual experience, are applicable in a general way to aural perception,[5] they cannot be made the basis of a thoroughgoing system for the analysis of musical perception and experience. This perception, as we have already affirmed, must depend on the sensitive responses of experienced listeners. Nor is the development of the present analysis contingent upon the discovery of further laws of aural perception. The laws already established can lead us to, and form the basis for, a general understanding of the natural modes of expectation as they function within the cultural context.

Basic Concepts and Formulations

THE LAW OF PRÄGNANZ

The fundamental axiom of Gestalt theory is the law of Prägnanz, which states that "psychological organization will always be as 'good' as the prevailing conditions allow. In this definition the term 'good' is undefined. It embraces such properties as regularity, symmetry, simplicity and others which we shall meet in the course of our discussion." [6] It is of utmost importance to realize that this law does not mean that psychological organization will always be satisfactory. On the contrary, in many instances the figures perceived, the relation of figure to ground, or the relation of figures to each other will be less than satisfactory, either in and of themselves or in relation to the stylistic context in which they appear or both.

It is this lack of satisfaction with the psychological organization that gives rise to what we have referred to as the natural modes of expectation. For the mind is constantly striving toward completeness and stability of shapes. This tendency of the mind toward regularity and simplicity of organization is shown, among other things, by the fact that "a system left to itself will, in its approach to a time independent state, lose asymmetries and become more regular." [7] The mind when left to operate on its own, as it does in the case of remembered patterns and organizations, will improve those figures which are not as "good" as they might be. This tendency of the mind to improve the psychological organization, to discriminate between satisfactory patterns and those which require improvement, has been confirmed by striking empirical evidence. [8]

The converse of this is also true: Good organization, stable shapes, will resist change and will tend to remain constant even in changes of the stimulus conditions. For example, a theme or motive which is well formed will be perceived as an identity, as the same theme, in spite of changes in instrumentation, range, dynamics, or harmonization. "A thing is a particularly well integrated part of the total field. The stronger its integration, the stronger the forces which hold it together, the more constant will it be in changes of stimulation. . . ." [9] The better the psychological organization, the less likely is it that expectation will be aroused.

THINKING, MEMORY, AND EXPECTATION

Without thought and memory there could be no musical experience. Because they are the foundation for expectation, an understanding of the way in which thought and memory operate throws light both upon the mechanism of expectation itself and upon the relation of prior experience to expectation.

Max Wertheimer, one of the most important members of the Gestalt school, describes the thinking process in the following way:

Generally speaking, there is first a situation
S_1, the situation in which the actual thought process starts, and then,
   after a number of steps,
S_2, in which the process ends, the problem is solved.
Let us consider the nature of situation 1 and situation 2 by comparing
them, and let us consider what goes on between, how and why. Clearly
the process is a transition, a change from S_1 into S_2. S_1 as compared to S_2,
is structurally incomplete, involves a gap or a structural trouble, whereas
S_2 is in these respects structurally better, the gap is filled adequately, the
structural trouble had disappeared; it is sensibly complete as against S_1.

When the problem is realized, S_1 contains structural strains and stresses
that are resolved in S_2. The thesis is that the very character of the steps,
of the operations, of the changes between S_1 and S_2 springs from the
nature of the vectors set up in these structural troubles in the direction
of helping the situation, of straightening it out structurally.

. . . often the process does not start with S_1 and end with S_2, but that in
$$\ldots\ldots\ldots S_1 \ldots\ldots\ldots S_2 \ldots\ldots\ldots,$$
S_1 already is part of a development; that, moreover, S_2, the very solution,
does not represent an end but that by its very nature leads to further
dynamic consequences.[10]

The relation of this description of thinking and problem solving to
the aesthetic process is self-evident. Problem solving and the aesthetic process are essentially one and the same thing except for this
proviso: that in aesthetic thinking, the relationship between structural troubles and their resolutions are intelligible and resolvable.
It is also evident that thinking, the overcoming of difficulties, and
expectation are one process. Finally, the place of affect in this process is not difficult to discover. If expectation results from, say, a
definite structural gap, the delay in completion of the thought
process will result in affect unless the process is rationalized on the
conscious level. Alternatively a confused and doubtful situation,
resulting in a generalized expectation of clarification, will give rise
to feelings of suspense and affective responses.

Expectation depends in very important ways upon memory processes. As we listen to a particular musical work we organize our
experience and hence our expectations both in terms of the past of
that particular work, which begins after the first stimulus has been
heard and is consequently "past," and in terms of our memories of
earlier relevant musical experiences.

Memory is not simply a recording machine in which past events and experiences are stored in an immutable way. The traces left in the memory by experience are constantly changing. These changes may be grouped into three classes: normalization, emphasizing or pointing, and autonomous changes.

Normalizing occurs when the reproductions [of remembered figures made by a subject] approach successively a familiar form; pointing, when a particular feature of the pattern, which strikes the observer as such when he perceives it, becomes more and more exaggerated; autonomous changes, lastly, are such as derive from neither of the two other sources but are inherent in the trace pattern itself, a result of its own intrinsic stresses.[11]

All such changes take place in the remembering of music. Since, however, music is an art which is essentially without external referents, these processes occur within a more or less closed system, and memory operates either between different musical experiences or between different parts of the same experience.

The fact, already noted, that a system left to itself "will, in its approach to a time independent state, lose asymmetries and become more regular"[12] applies alike to parts of a piece and to the whole musical work. The law of Prägnanz functions within the memory process, which tends to complete what was incomplete, to regularize what was irregular, and so forth. Moreover, those shapes which are not well figured and which the memory is unable to "straighten out," complete, or make symmetrical will tend to be forgotten.[13]

In other words, an unstable memory trace will first tend toward stability; and, if this is impossible, it will tend to disintegrate. This aspect of the memory process would seem to account for the fact that the well-organized processes of themes and melodies are better remembered than the more or less irregular parts of a musical work; e.g., the melodies of the first or second theme group of a sonata exposition are better remembered than the irregular and often quasi-chaotic processes of the development section.

As we have seen, even those figures which are remembered are changed in the process. This means that we tend to remember themes as being simpler than they really are and that we remember forms as "ideal types" rather than as particular things. For as recollections of similar types, whether of parts or wholes, become regularized in the memory, they tend to be grouped into classes, thus forming the norms which are the basis of stylistic perception and expectation. In other words, traces "produced by similar excitations do not remain independent of each other but form larger trace systems which influence newly formed traces in definite ways." [14] This process of normalization is connected to what Koffka has called the "averaging effect"—an effect whereby similar figure processes become formed into a single class concept. Of course, such concepts or trace systems are not really averages; but ". . . we possess within our store of traces many systems which, through a process of condensation and assimilation form the basis for 'class' perceptions, for the 'normal' and 'unusual.' " [15]

Normalization plays an important part in facilitating the rehearing of musical compositions. As noted earlier, the norms developed in the memory are not rigidly fixed but change with the addition of each new memory trace; to the extent that the norms have changed, a rehearing of a work is a new hearing, yielding new insights. Those factors which are the immediate cause of affect and aesthetic response, the deviations, are the very ones that either become regularized and averaged or forgotten. For this reason they tend to surprise us, to remain deviants even after many hearings of a work.

It may, at this point, be objected that after all we do not really forget the asymmetrical parts of a piece of music. We can, for example, recognize a symphony by hearing a few measures of its development section, presumably the portion of the piece which will most likely be forgotten or changed in the memory process. The objection is not cogent because there is a great difference between recognition and recall. For instance, we may be able to recognize a portion of a musical work, even to the point of recognizing each tone as it is presented, without recalling it, in the sense of being able to predict the succession of tones correctly. But since the ability to envisage accurately, to predict, is just what distinguishes norms from deviants, the deviants would still seem unusual. The very fact that when the deviants are presented we say to ourselves "Oh, yes, now I remember" is a clear indication that they were not really, or only vaguely, expected.

Memory tends to improve shapes in the direction of regularity, symmetry, and completion. But this does not mean that completed tasks or shapes are better remembered than ones which are not complete. Where incomplete figures set up real tensions toward completion, where shapes are well articulated so that the manner of their completion is clear, they are better remembered than complete ones.[16]

Finally, memory, activated by knowledge and information, is a force in organizing musical experience, for it brings search attitudes into play: ". . . a true search attitude does much more than establish the communication between trace and process, it determines new processes not only through such communication but also by prescribing what the result of the communication is to be: the new process is to be organized in terms of the trace."[17]

The Principles of Pattern Perception

In the statement of the law of Prägnanz to the effect that "psychological organization will always be as 'good' as the prevailing conditions allow" (see p. 86 f.), the term "good" was left undefined. It is to the conditions making for satisfactory and, equally important, unsatisfactory psychological organization that we now turn. These conditions, which are at bottom but corollaries of the axiomatic law of Prägnanz, are expressed in a set of laws and principles formulated by Gestalt psychologists on the basis of empirical evidence.

Although the psychological organization is always as good as possible, this does not stipulate that the organization is always as good as the mind would wish. It is this dissatisfaction with the psychological organization which gives rise to expectation and perception of deviation. "Good continuation and good shape [are] powerful organizing factors, and both [are] in the true sense 'understandable': a line carries its own law within itself, and so does a shaped area or volume. Violations of this law due to external forces are felt as violations; they conflict with our feelings of the fit, hurt our sense of beauty."[18]

Actually they "hurt our sense of beauty" only when their function and significance cannot be understood. A jagged line understood merely as line may be unpleasant; for if it cannot be related to other aspects of experience, its irregularity will seem pointless. Consequently the tensions aroused in perceiving it as pattern will seem meaningless and unpleasant. But the same line placed in an aesthetic context, where its perception is understood as part of a total experience and where belief tends to create a disposition to respond, will seem exciting and significant. Similarly a dissonance or an ambiguous progression which might be unpleasant when heard in isolation may be beautiful within a piece of music where its relationship to past events and impending resolutions is understandable.[19]

The laws and principles that follow are closely interrelated, and their functions often overlap. A violation of the law of completion, for example, almost always involves disturbances in the factor of good continuation, though the reverse of this is not necessarily true. Because of the interaction that takes place, the laws and principles discussed below must be treated as convenient distinctions between various facets of mental organization rather than as clearly separable mental functions. For this reason no rigid and systematic compartmentalization of the discussion has been attempted.

THE LAW OF GOOD CONTINUATION

A shape or pattern will, other things being equal, tend to be continued in its initial mode of operation. Thus "to the factor of good continuation in purely spatial organization there corresponds the factor of the smooth curve of motion and continuous velocity in spatio-temporal organization."[20] Among other things this law helps to account for our being able to hear separate, discrete stimuli as continuous motions and shapes.

Actually, of course, a line or motion does not perpetuate itself. It is only a series of lifeless stimuli. What happens is that the perception of a line or motion initiates a mental process, and it is this mental process which, following the mental line of least resistance, tends to be perpetuated and continued. This is important, not only because we shall, for convenience' sake, often speak of a process as continuing itself, but also because it emphasizes that a line or motion is actually a process of the mind rather than a thing. Since the complexity of a motion often makes it difficult to decide what constitutes continuation and whether it has been disturbed or not, it is the process as determining the motion (both from the standpoint of the perceiver's mind and from that of the composer's technique) which we must examine.

Process continuation is the norm of musical progression, and disturbances in continuation are points of deviation. These disturbances in the process of continuation may be of two kinds: (*a*) gaps in the process in which a process is temporarily halted and then continued again, and (*b*) changes in process, in which there is usually, though not necessarily, a break in line and one manner of progression takes the place of another. Both kinds of disturbances may occur together, as when a process change takes place after a halt in the progress of the music.

The motion by which one process changes to another will be referred to as "process reversal" or simply as "reversal." Since processes may be more and less similar, it follows that reversals may be more and less drastic. For example, during a modulation several types of sequences may be used, one replacing the other. Each change will constitute a slight reversal and will be a point of tension. However, the point at which the modulation process is replaced, say, by a steady statement on the dominant, will constitute a major change in process.

Continuation must be carefully distinguished from repetition. Continuation always implies change within a continuous process, not mere repetition. And while continuation appears to be a normal mode of operation, repetition is so only up to the point at which saturation sets in (see pp. 135 f.). However, even our expectations as to continuation are to some extent subject to our expectations as to change and logic; that is, we expect continuation only so long as it appears significant and meaningful in the sense that it can be understood as motion toward a goal. If meaning becomes obscured, then change will be expected.

MELODIC CONTINUITY

Chopin's Prelude, Op. 28, No. 2 presents a clear example of the establishment of a process, its continuation, a disturbance, and.

finally, the re-establishment of a variation of the original process. The
melodic phrase (Example 5) consists of two similar motives joined

EXAMPLE 5

by the fact that the same tone begins the second fragment as ended
the first. The first and second phrases are similarly linked by a common tone, though the second phrase is displaced by an octave (Example 6). This process of conjunction by common tone establishes a

EXAMPLE 6

strong force toward continuation. We expect the next phrase, even if
it involves new melodic materials, to begin with such a tone conjunction. But this does not take place. The continuity is broken in
measure 14 by the entrance of the A where F-sharp would have
been the expected tone (Example 7).

EXAMPLE 7

The force of this break is not completely apparent until the motive
is completed on the F-natural, since the A to E progression might
simply be taken to be a repetition of the end of the second phrase.
The F-natural enforces the effect of the break because, following
the E, it introduces the first half step in the melody. After this break
in continuity, the original process of progression by tone conjunction is re-established and, with some modifications as to motivic
order, continues until the final cadential formula is reached.

The melodic break which occurs in measures 14 through 16 is paralleled by a break and change in harmonic process, but with this difference: the harmonic change is conclusive, in the sense that the old process is not re-established as was the case with the melody. Without presenting a detailed harmonic analysis of the Prelude, it is clear that the harmonic motion of the first sixteen measures might be symbolized as in Example 8.

EXAMPLE 8

Although the opening phrase is originally heard in E minor, for the sake of simplicity it has been symbolized in terms of G, to which it moves. The second phrase, which seems to be exactly parallel to the first, leads us to expect a D major chord at its conclusion. But this harmony never materializes. Instead there is an irregular resolution to an altered chord, whose root must be considered as being D altered to D-sharp. Here the process changes and the change is, so to speak, suspended during the progressive alteration of this chord until the augmented sixth chord in the last half of measure 14 is reached. The irregular and indecisive character of the harmonic motion gives rise to feelings of ambiguity and uncertainty, which are resolved by the relatively clear and regular cadence from measure 14 to 15, in which the augmented sixth chord (still an alteration of the harmony which should have been D major) moves to the tonic 6/4 in A minor.

One of the most striking things about this progression is that had the sequence continued in the regular manner, with an alteration to minor at the end of the phrase, the same harmonic spot might have been reached with only minimal deviation; that is, beginning with the second phrase, we would have had the following progression:

$$\text{D: } (\text{IV}) - \text{VI} - \text{I}_4^6 - \text{V} - \text{I}$$
$$\text{A: } (\text{IV}) - \text{VI} - \text{I}_4^6 - \text{V} - \text{I} \quad (\text{a minor})$$

It seems perfectly clear that any technical explanations of measures 12 to 16 purely in terms of harmonic goals and modulations must be inadequate, since the same goal could have been reached in a much more regular way. The explanation lies in the importance of doubt and uncertainty in the shaping of aesthetic affective experience.

It is important to realize that certainty and doubt are relative terms. The beginning phrases of this Prelude are only relatively certain, particularly if we consider the stylistic context in which it should be heard and its relation to the preludes which precede and follow it. The constant use of non-harmonic tones and added sixths, etc., in the accompaniment figure together with the over-all subdominant progression (G to D to A) produce a feeling of indefinite tension, a kind of relative uncertainty, from the very beginning. The relative uncertainty moves to much more striking and forceful uncertainty in measure 10, where it is, in turn, resolved to a relative certainty in the arrival of the A minor 6/4 harmony. Complete certainty, toward which the piece progresses from the beginning, is achieved only with the final cadence, the propriety of which is apparent from this analysis.

Intensity is maintained to the end by the delay in the resolution of the 6/4 chord on A minor. Notice that while, from one point of view, the harmonic process is discontinued, from another point of view, the whole motion from measure 12 to the end is at least similar to the original process, though much prolonged:

$$a: \text{IV}_{4\sharp}^{6} - \text{IV}_{3\sharp}^{6\sharp} - (\text{VI, omitted}) - \text{I}_4^6 (\text{prolonged}) - \text{V} - \text{V of V} - \text{V} - \text{I}$$

This example is interesting from several points of view. First, it does not have a beginning in the sense that there is no statement but only a motion and a conclusion. In this respect it is reminiscent of Wertheimer's description of the thinking processes in which we have "......S_1......S_2......"; that is, the opening phrase (S_1) is already part of a process, though in this case the final cadence does represent a final solution. Beginning during a process also contributes to the general aura of vagueness that pervades the whole Prelude. Second, this piece illustrates the difference between discontinuity through a change of process (in the harmonic motion) and discontinuity through a delay and break in a process (in the melodic motion) which is subsequently resumed. Finally, the example is noteworthy because the reversal of process and the break in melodic continuity which constitute the climax do not occur as the result of the typically rising progression but take place, so to speak, in the course of a gradually descending progression.[21]

Some aspects of a process may exhibit continuity while others do not. The sequential opening phrase of the "Liebestod" of Wagner's *Tristan und Isolde* (Example 9) establishes a process which leads us to expect a definite continuation. Up to measure 5 the clarinet and voice present essentially the same line. But at measure 5 the sequential process is broken in the vocal part while the instruments continue the sequence.

EXAMPLE 9

For the sake of clarity, let us turn our attention first to the vocal part, then to the instrumental line, and, finally, to the relation between the two.

Although the sequential process is broken in the vocal line at measure 5, since we expect the line to begin on A and move to D as the horn part does, the over-all line (Example 10), which began with the A-flat in the first measure and moved upward through the

B-flat to C-flat and then C-sharp, is not broken. The tones which we expected are presented, but not in the order expected on the basis of the established sequential process. On the other hand, while the break in process represents no basic break in the line, it does herald a delay in the over-all line, which does not continue its upward surge until the final measure, when the motion to the upper A-flat, a natural point of completion, is reached.

EXAMPLE 10

Notice that this break in the melodic sequence is accompanied by discontinuity of rhythm, which is all the more striking because of the continuousness of the instrumental line. Actually the vocal part in measures 5 and 6 is syncopated against the instrumental line and, as we shall see presently (pp. 113 f.), involves important rhythmic changes. These changes and deviations from the instrumental rhythm should not be confused with the slightly delayed entrances in measures 2 and 3. For though the latter have an expressive effect by delaying and disturbing the process, they work within that process, while the rhythmic changes in measures 5 and 6 are both more striking and more important.

EXAMPLE 11

The instrumental line presents a strong contrast to the vocal line. While the vocal line involves a break in process and rhythm at measure 5, the instrumental line persists with single-mindedness (Example 11) on its sequential way as the whole motion is accelerated. The second measure of the motive is now omitted so that the motion of an ascending fourth followed by descending half steps is heard in each successive measure. The interesting thing about the process is that, though part of the melody is omitted, the intervallic progression upward is not altered, for the new motive always begins on the same tone as the second half of the motive does (Example 12). As a consequence of this modification the process continues basically as before but at a more rapid rate.

EXAMPLE 12

The acceleration is again increased in measure 7, where the entrances of the motive occur at the half measure. However, this increased rate of progression also marks the end of the sequence. For the interval A-flat to D-flat in measure 7 does not continue the sequence but instead serves to reunite the vocal and instrumental lines. Both the point at which the break takes place (the A-flat) and the melodic motion of the union (measure 7) are foreshadowed in the previous measures. The important breaking point, the A-flat, is implied by the motion from D (in measure 5) through the C and B-flat (in measure 6). The melodic motion is implicit in the vocal line of measure 6. That is, if the vocal line of measure 6 had moved upward in fourths, it would have had the same melodic contour as both the instrumental and vocal line have in measure 7. The unification of the instrumental and vocal lines is emphasized and articulated by a more decisive harmonic motion. And both melodic and instrumental lines move upward to the high A-flat, toward which they have been tending from the beginning.

Here, then, we have the simultaneous occurrence of (1) a break in process (in the vocal line) from the point of view of sequential progression but only a delay from the point of view of over-all motion; (2) a continuous process (in the instrumental line) whose mode of progression is altered in detail but not in basic motion; and, finally, (3) the stabilization of both processes through their reunification and through their motion to a point of relative repose. The relationship between the progress of the vocal line and the

instrumental line is particularly interesting. For the feeling of delay
in the vocal line is intensified by the accelerated motion of the instrumental sequence and vice versa.

The melody under consideration presents an interesting example
of alternative possibilities of melodic continuation (see p. 51). The
opening of the two-measure motive creates a structural gap by
skipping from E-flat to A-flat. The ensuing descending motion
(A-flat, G, G-flat, F) begins to fill this gap, establishing a continuity
process which leads the listener to expect a return to the opening
E-flat (see Example 13). But the introduction of a rising progression (G-flat, A-flat, B-flat) during the course of the descent gives
rise to alternative expectations. The tendencies inherent in this new
process are supported by the rising melodic line from measure to
measure (see Example 10). Not only is the arrival of the low E-flat
delayed in favor of this rising progression, but from measure 5 to
measure 8 the ascending motion is itself delayed. And the arrival
of both low and high E-flats (measures 7 and 8), thus make a significant contribution to the feeling of resolution which prevails at
the end of the whole period.

EXAMPLE 13

Notice that just as the point of process disjunction and the beginning of delay in the large melodic shape were marked by an
unexpected tonal sequence and bolder temporal gaps, so in the
smaller motive delay is accompanied by a less regular sequence
of tones and a slight rhythmic disturbance. The parallelism between the motivic construction and the over-all phrase organization
is another instance of the architectonic nature of musical processes.

Since the affective quality of the whole is conditioned by that of
its parts, the smaller delays in continuity must also be examined.
These take the form of those devices that are generally discussed
under the subject of ornamentation. In the example under consideration, the appoggiaturas act to delay the normal continuation of

the quarter-note motion (Example 14). That is, we expect the motion initiated by the skip of a fourth—for instance, from E-flat to A-flat in the first presentation of the motive—to continue on the next beat. Various alternatives are possible within the style system. The motion from the fourth might, for example, move as part of a triad on up to the C; it might move stepwise after the fourth, as in the melody which begins the slow movement of Beethoven's Symphony No. 2; or it might begin to close the structural gap by descending at once, as in the "Faith" motive from Wagner's *Parsifal* (see Prelude, measures 44 f.). However, what does happen is that the tendency toward further motion is delayed by the repetition of the A-flat, and the effect of this delay is heightened because the repeated tone is a dissonance.

EXAMPLE 14

The affective character of the appoggiatura and other ornaments as well as the affective character of chromaticism, which also plays an important role in the effect of this passage, will be discussed more fully in chapters v and vi. At this point we must be content to remark that the expressive affective nature both of ornaments and chromaticism is clearly indicated by evidence from Western, non-Western, and primitive sources.

Continuity always operates within a particular cultural stylistic context, which not only conditions expectations about such obviously cultural factors as harmony but often plays an important part in determining our expectations of melodic continuation. A common example of this is the melodic progression upward through the triad, as in Example 15. This typical pattern forms the basis of such diverse melodies as the main theme of the first movement of Schumann's Piano Concerto, the theme of the slow movement of Haydn's Symphony No. 97 in C Major, and the tune "Three Blind Mice."

EXAMPLE 15

RHYTHMIC CONTINUATION

Thus far continuity has been discussed largely in terms of spatiomelodic and harmonic processes. The vital and ever present factor of temporal organization has received little attention. In view of the numerous and well-known difficulties involved and the incomplete state of our knowledge of the subject, it would indeed be pleasant to ignore the factor of temporal organization altogether. It is, however, so vital in achieving and disturbing continuity that we must at least make some tentative observations on this aspect of the musical process.

Distinctions must first of all be made between pulse, meter, and rhythm.

1. The perception of pulse involves an objective or subjective division of time into regularly recurring, equally accented beats. The ticks of a metronome or a watch are pulses or beats. Such equal pulses will not give rise to an impression of either rhythm or meter unless, of course, the mind of the listener imposes some sort of differentiation upon the separate beats.

Though a feeling of pulse is necessary if an impression of meter is to arise and is generally present in the perception of rhythm, pulse can and does exist alone without creating either meter or rhythm. In order for this to occur, there must be no differentiation of the beats with respect to accentuation. They must be equal. In fact, what are later to be termed "incomplete rhythms" are actually a series of pulses (see pp. 144 f.).

2. The perception of meter involves an awareness of the regular recurrence of accented and unaccented beats. The necessary condition for metric organization is the differentiation of pulses into

accented and unaccented. There must be a feeling of the basic beat if the feeling of meter is to arise. But this pulse of beat need not be actually heard. It may be carried in the mind of the listener (see pp. 118–19, 242). Because the impression of rhythm depends not only upon the existence of accented and non-accented beats but also upon the grouping of those beats, meter can, in a sense, exist alone without any impression of rhythm. For where the listener is unable to group the unaccented pulses in a definitive way—where rhythm is ambiguous—the impression may merely be one of strong beats and weak beats following one another with a given frequency. An instance of this type of organization is discussed in chapter v (see pp. 147 f.).

3. The perception of rhythm involves a mental grouping of one or more unaccented beats in relation to an accented beat. These groupings may, of course, be more and less clear; and within any given meter they may vary indefinitely. They may in this sense be more and less regular. Furthermore, the accents of the rhythmic group, though generally supporting the metric organization, may at times conflict with that organization.

In referring to the patterns which result from such groupings, we shall use the terminology traditionally associated with prosody: iamb ($\smile$ —), anapest ($\smile \smile$ —), trochee (— $\smile$), dactyl (— $\smile \smile$), and amphibrach ($\smile$ — $\smile$). Finally it should be noted that rhythm can exist alone without pulse or meter as it does in plain chant, the rhapsodic fantasias of many different cultures, or recitativo secco.

The basic difference between pulse, on the one hand, and meter and rhythm, on the other, lies in the fact that the latter modes of mental organization involve the differentiation of beats into accented and unaccented, while the former does not. This makes some sort of definition of accent desirable.

Basically anything is accented when it is marked for consciousness in some way. Such mental marking may be the result of differences in intensity, duration, melodic structure, harmonic progression, instrumentation, or any other mode of articulation which can differentiate one stimulus or group of stimuli from others. Even silence, a rest, may be accented, as is the case in the second measure of the fifth movement of Beethoven's String Quartet in C-sharp

Minor (see p. 149). In other instances a tone or group of tones may appear to be accented, not because of any particular distinction which it possesses per se, but because a previously established grouping tends to perpetuate itself, making this type of organization the simplest one.

Accent should not be confused with stress. As observed earlier, silence may be accented; the literature of music is replete with examples of pianissimo accents. Stress is the dynamic emphasis of either an accented or an unaccented tone. Where an accented tone is stressed, the stress may change the rhythmic grouping or may help to clarify an otherwise ambiguous rhythmic organization, but it does not create the accent. Nor does stress placed upon an unaccented beat alter the rhythmic grouping. Such a beat is still perceived as unaccented, not only because of the tendency of a given grouping to perpetuate itself, but also because, as we shall see, the placement in the temporal organization of an unaccented beat, whether stressed or not, is physically different from what it would be were it really an accent. Thus as a rule an offbeat sforzando or forte should be classed as a stress rather than as an accent. A familiar instance of such an offbeat stress is the fortissimo "surprise" in the second movement of Haydn's "Surprise" Symphony. It is clear in this case that the strong stress does not affect the basic rhythmic structure, though it obviously modifies the character of the theme. Indeed, the effect of the fortissimo stress is partly the product of our knowing that it is not the real accent. While it is important to distinguish between accent and stress, it should be noted that there are instances where such an offbeat sforzando or forte should be treated as an accent altering the rhythmic grouping. The performer must be aware of this possibility, for his decision as to the significance of such tones will literally determine his placement of the beats, his performance of the passage.

Rhythm and meter, though obviously intimately interrelated, are nevertheless independent variables. This will be evident as soon as one considers that several different rhythmic groupings can arise within the same metric organization, as the Examples 16–20 show.

a) *Iambic grouping.—*

EXAMPLE 16

BEETHOVEN, FIRST SYMPHONY, MINUETTO

b) *Anapestic grouping.—*

EXAMPLE 17

BIZET, "CARMEN," ACT III, ENTR'ACTE

c) *Trochaic grouping.—*

EXAMPLE 18

MOZART, STRING QUARTET IN A MAJOR (K.464), MINUETTO

d) *Dactylic grouping.—*

EXAMPLE 19

BEETHOVEN, NINTH SYMPHONY, SCHERZO

e) *Amphibrach grouping.—*

EXAMPLE 20

HAYDN, "SURPRISE" SYMPHONY, MINUETTO

In like manner the same rhythmic grouping may arise out of different metric organizations. For instance, an iambic grouping can exist in duple as well as in triple meter, as is the case in the opening theme of the first movement of Brahms' Fourth Symphony; likewise an anapest grouping can arise in duple meter, as it does in the "Gavotte en Rondeau" from Bach's Partita No. 3 for unaccompanied violin; a trochaic pattern can also arise in duple meter, as it does in the tune "Au Clair de la Lune"; and an amphibrach rhythm can exist in duple meter, as is the case in the opening theme of Mendelssohn's Violin Concerto.

However, some rhythmic groupings tend to be incompatible with particular metric schemes. Duple meters, for instance, do not easily give rise to dactylic patterns, while trochaic patterns are difficult to achieve in triple meters. To understand this incompatibility of rhythmic groupings with metric structure, it is necessary to discuss some of the ways in which the mind organizes accented and unaccented beats into cohesive groups.

A series of stimuli of equal intensity and equal duration create no impression of rhythm unless the mind imposes its own differentiation on them. Some of the stimuli must be perceived as accented relative to others.[22] When the mind imposes its grouping upon such a series not only is the vividness of the beats subjectively conditioned by the mind but so also is their position in the series.

If a series of equidistant sounds like the ticks of a metronome are heard the observer may phrase them into iambs, trochees, or dactyls, as he chooses. To the ear, the choice seems to affect merely the vividness of the beats. But if the observer taps a key at each beat of the metronome, it will be found that in the case of the iamb he always misplaces the beats; often the same thing happens in the case of the trochee and the dactyl. Because of the influence of the rhythmic process, the observer does not hear the beats where they actually occur. In the case of the iamb he always hears the beat which he makes subordinate nearer the accented beat than it actually is in the objective clicking of the metronome.[23]

These conclusions were confirmed by the studies of Woodrow,[24] who found that when time intervals are equal and every second sound is accented, the rhythm will appear to be trochaic. If intervals are equal and every third sound is accented, the rhythm will appear as a dactyl. Thus the trochee and dactyl may be grouped together in the sense that both are primarily products of intensity differences rather than durational differences.

Just the opposite is the case with iambic and anapestic rhythms. They are basically products of duration differences. If we start with a trochaic rhythm and gradually increase the interval after the louder sound, we arrive at an iambic rhythm. Similarly if we begin with a dactylic rhythm and gradually lengthen the interval after the louder sound, the rhythm tends to become an anapest. Thus the greater the relative duration of one tone or beat of a group, the greater the tendency for it to complete the group; while the greater the relative intensity of a beat, the greater the tendency for it to begin the rhythmic group. In other words, durational differences tend to result in "end-accented rhythms," and intensity differences tend to result in "beginning-accented rhythms."

This analysis explains why trochaic rhythms do not easily arise in triple meter. For the two-unit trochaic rhythm ($-\smile$) can arise in a three-beat meter only if one of the rhythmic units is two beats long ♩ ♩. And the difficulty with this pattern lies in the fact that such temporally differentiated groups tend to become end-accented. The only way in which such a normally end-accented pattern can become trochaic (beginning accented) is to place a strong stress upon the accent so that intensity differences outweigh, as it were, durational ones. This is precisely what takes place in Example 18. Without the forte-piano on the first beat of measures 1 and 3, the rhythmic grouping would have been amphibrach ♩♩ | ♩♩♩ . But the stress on the first note binds the C-sharp to the A, and the rhythm is thought of and played as a trochee ♩♩ | ♩♩♩ . It is important to emphasize that the performer's conception of the rhythm literally influences his placement of the beats. That is, in interpreting this pattern as trochaic, he actually places the C-sharp nearer to the A than he would had the group been considered to be iambic.

A similar situation prevails in the case of dactylic groupings in duple meter. In order for a dactylic rhythm to exist in a duple meter, one of the two metric pulses must be divided to form the third impulse necessary in the dactyl group: $-\smile\smile$. Thus the pattern

♩♩♩♩ must become ♩♫♩♫; and, again, the temporal differentiation will tend to result in an end-accented rather than beginning-accented rhythm. However, in this case a powerful stress on the accent will also tend to change the normal organization and make it beginning accented. This is what in fact takes place in the opening of Brahms's Rhapsody, Op. 119, No. 4 (Example 21). Were it not for the stress on the first beat of each measure this pattern would tend to appear end accented. Here, too, the performer's conception of the rhythm modifies his rendition of the music. That is, because he thinks of the grouping as dactylic, he literally moves the unaccented beats nearer to the accented one.

EXAMPLE 21

In both the Mozart and Brahms examples the striking effect of the themes is, in large measure, the result of the fact that a beginning-accented group has been forced into a normally end-accented temporal organization.

Whether the rhythm of the Brahms should actually be considered dactylic is open to question. The mind tries to perceive patterns in the simplest possible way, and because of this it tends, particularly in this style of music, to subsume all motion under a single pulse rate. For this reason the two eighth notes of the motive might well be regarded as being a divided weak beat, as the alternative analysis (*b*) shows; in such a case the group would be trochaic rather than dactylic. Probably both types of organization are present in the mind. This possibility of dual analysis seems to indicate that one of the most important things about a given rhythmic organization is not the number of unaccented beats but their placement with relation to the accented one; that is, whether a group is beginning, middle, or end accented.

This examination of the ways in which the mind organizes accented and unaccented beats into cohesive groups also throws light upon the tendency of performers to place unusual stress on the accented beat in amphibrach rhythms (see Example 20). For though a clear temporal differentiation may leave no doubt about there being an anacrusis to the group, the accent must be heavily stressed so that the afterbeat does not become grouped with the anacrusis, that is, so that the amphibrach organization 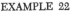 does not become an anapest one ⌣⌣⌣⌣⌣ .

These observations as to the modes of mental grouping are not, however, absolute laws. Their operation is conditioned and modified by the organization of the other elements of the musical structure— melody, harmony, instrumentation, and the like. This is simply illustrated by an analysis of Example 22. In the theme of the first movement of Mozart's Piano Sonata in A Major the second half of each of the first two measures (*a*) is clearly trochaic, despite the normally end-accented (iambic) durational differentiation. This grouping is the result both of the absence of any prior anacrustic organization and of the disjunct motion between measures; that is, the skip from E to B tends to make the motives discrete, isolating the rhythmic groups.

EXAMPLE 22

The relationship between melodic and rhythmic organization can easily be seen if the second measure is changed in such a way that the melodic motion between measures is conjunct, as is the case in part *b* of Example 22. Now the final eighth note of the first measure is clearly heard as an upbeat to the second measure, making the rhythm iambic across the bar.

But even without these major alterations, the grouping can be changed if an upbeat, an eighth note E, is placed before the C-sharp in the first measure of the theme. If the reader sings the theme with such an upbeat, he will find that the last eighth note of the first measure now tends to seem anacrustic. In short, earlier rhythmic groupings influence later ones; or, to put it in another way, an established rhythmic process tends to perpetuate itself. Equally important is the fact that future organization also influences group-ing. Thus the performer will play the first measures of the Mozart theme in such a way that its trochaic pattern is clear because he knows what the organization of the two-measure group is.

It is, then, the total disposition of all the musical materials that determines what the rhythmic grouping will be. This is another way of saying that the entire musical pattern will tend to be perceived in the simplest and most satisfactory terms. For this reason rhythmic organization is not merely a matter of duration and accent but a matter of these elements in relation to all other aspects of the pattern organization. However, while the mental organization of the musical stimuli will be as "good" as possible under the given circumstances, it will not necessarily be as satisfactory as the listener might wish. Often the rhythmic organization is discontinuous, in-complete, or ambiguous.[25]

HIGHER LEVELS OF RHYTHMIC ORGANIZATION

In Example 23 an important rhythmic change takes place in measure 3, even though the quarter-note motion continues as before. The altered grouping is based upon the change in melodic process, a more active harmonic bass line, and the altered phrasing. The second beat of the measure is no longer grouped with the first beat as part of an amphibrach but becomes part of the anacrusis to the

EXAMPLE 23

next measure. This reversal of the rhythm is particularly striking because the new group enters before the old one has had a chance to complete itself. It is so accented for consciousness that one is tempted to analyze the tones D and C as a trochaic subgroup of the larger iamb which ends on the A rather than as an anapest. What is crucial here both for the performer and the critic is that, though we base our interpretation of what the rhythm should be upon the available information supplied by the score, the interpretation itself changes depending on where we place the beats. In this instance, for example, the G in measures 1 or 2 will actually be closer to the B which precedes it than the D in measure 3 will be to the F-sharp which precedes it.

Although the reversal of the rhythmic process is undoubtedly a disturbance in the continuity, from another point of view it is apparent that this very reversal welds the final six beats (counting the rest) of the phrase into a single group, as opposed to the first six beats which form two clearly defined patterns. This unity arises partly because the final group involves no repetition of similar parts and partly because, in a sense, the tone D serves as a pivot belonging both to the preceding amphibrach and to the ensuing anapest. Its anacrustic function is not immediately apparent, though the rhythmic displacement which the performers' interpretation will force upon the temporal relationships will be sensed, and the total group will, in the end, appear as constituting the upbeat to the final A.

It is this creation of a larger rhythmic unit that gives the total phrase its over-all rhythmic form. For just as a series of beats which are equal both in accent and duration will not give rise to an impression of rhythm (except in so far as the mind imposes its own arbitrary differentiation upon the stimuli) so, too, the smaller rhythmic groups will not give rise to larger patterns unless differentiation of accent or duration is present. Thus in this example the grouping might be symbolized as A—A—B or, in terms of duration, as 3—3—6. In rhythmic terms this is nothing but an anapest grouping.

The function of the pivot tone in joining two separable groups together is even clearer in Example 16, where the repeated E in the third measure can be interpreted both as a sort of afterbeat in the iambic rhythm and as part of an anapest foot forming the upbeat to the final G. Here again the construction of a differentiated final group gives rise to an anapest phrase rhythm. This pattern of construction can also be seen in Example 17.

The construction of the Mozart example is quite different (see Example 24). There each two-measure group exhibits a rhythm of its own, but the whole consists of a series of such rhythms rather than a more compact over-all grouping. The rhythm of the first two-measure phases is not absolutely certain but the dynamics would lead one to feel that they exhibit a trochaic grouping. The second group of four measures is quite clearly iambic. If this analysis is correct, then there is a mild rhythmic reversal beginning with the fifth measure. It is mild because the nature of the reversal is not apparent until it is practically over—until we arrive at measure 6—

EXAMPLE 24

and because the opening phrase is not emphatically trochaic. The regularity of the motivic construction and the lack of any strong rhythmic break contribute much to the gracefulness of the total period. Perhaps the most unusual and affective aspect of the whole example is the opening rhythm, whose piquant character is largely a product of the fact that a trochaic rhythm is, as we have seen, forced upon a naturally iambic temporal relationship.

How far one can go in discussing form in terms of rhythm is an open question. It is partly a matter of definition. If, for example, one adopts a motor theory of rhythm, then it seems obvious that one can seldom include as a rhythmic group anything larger than the phrase and sometimes not that. It is also partly a matter of the temporal limits of the psychological response to larger groupings. Certainly Sachs's argument against the concept of form as a type of rhythm, on the grounds that most formal plans do not consist of units that are multiples of two, is no argument at all.[26] For, as we have seen, it is just because not all motives and phrases are of equal duration and accent that we can speak of the rhythm of phrases or larger units at all. Nor should any discussion of form in rhythmic terms be taken to exclude other viewpoints.

Our conception of rhythmic process results not only from the immediate organization of melody, harmony, dynamics, texture, and so forth but also from their past organization within the particular piece being heard. The passage from *Tristan* already considered (pp. 97 ff.) furnishes an interesting illustration of the influence of prior melodic organization upon rhythmic processes. The melodic reversal discussed earlier is accompanied by a striking rhythmic reversal, which we can now examine in more detail (see Example 25). Each of the opening measures establishes a clear iambic rhythm with trochaic subgroups. This organization is supported by the phrasing in the clarinets, the harmonic motion, and by the rhythm of the text itself. Notice that the main rhythmic accent always

EXAMPLE 25

occurs on the top note of the ascending melodic line, after or before a skip of a fourth. When this top tone appears, even though out of its expected order, it is given an important accent partly because of its kinship with earlier accented tones (see Example 26, measure 5). Since it is the first tone of a group, it becomes the accented portion of a trochaic group; and this change from an iambic rhythm to a trochaic one constitutes a rhythmic reversal which in conjunction with the melodic changes is a powerful affective force.

EXAMPLE 26

The analysis would be incomplete, however, if we failed to recognize that this change of process is not confined to the rhythmic organization. The placement of the main accent of the group on the second beat of the measure creates a syncopation in which the metric organization is also disturbed (see Example 27). While the instruments continue the original metric scheme, if anything enforcing it through the accelerated rate of sequential progress, the

EXAMPLE 27

voice part places its primary accent on the second beat of the bar and its secondary accent on the fourth beat of the bar so that, in effect, the whole voice part is syncopated against the instrumental parts.

This cross rhythm is resolved in measure 7, but rhythmic stability is not achieved until measure 8. And here again we see the influence of prior rhythmic-melodic groupings; for the upward skip of a fourth maintains its original anacrustic effect, and the series of fourths in the seventh and eighth measures are without a strong downbeat (Example 28). Even in the instrumental parts where

EXAMPLE 28

downbeats do appear, they are obscured by the over-all series of anacruses, which reach a real downbeat only at the final A-flat.[27] That the accented placement of the A-flat is no accident can be seen if the melodic motion of measure 8 is compared with that of measure 2. The comparison makes it clear that measure 7 is a variant of the first measure of the two-measure motive used at the beginning, but it is so arranged that it achieves no decisive downbeat within the bar. In other words, we again find an example of the welding together of parts which were formerly divided so that ⌣ — ⌣ — becomes ⌣ ⌣ ⌣ —.

This unification of the final two measures has consequences in organizing the structure of the whole period of eight measures. Notice that the reversal in measure 5 not only changes the rhythm within the measure but also that between measures; i.e., that the accented measure in the opening phrase is the second of the group, while in bars 5 and 6 the first measure of the group is accented (Example 29). As a result of this the second phrase does not easily

EXAMPLE 29

split itself into segments, for our attention is carried, so to speak, from the downbeat in measure 5 to the final downbeat in measure 8. In short, the total period might be schematized something like this:

measures measures   measures
1 and 2 3 and 4   5 and 6 7 and 8

iamb   iamb   trochee anapest

METRIC CONTINUATION

Meter is a product of the division of a given time span into parts of equal duration but unequal accentuation. The metric group is measured and numbered in terms of the equal beats from one accent to the next. Thus if the beat is symbolized by the composer as being a quarter note and, counting the accent which begins the group, there are four beats before the next accent, then the meter is said to be 4/4, meaning that there are four quarter notes to a metric unit.

As we have seen, the metric group does not determine what the rhythm is to be. The same metric unit may be the basis for various different rhythms. In other words, although the relationship of unaccented to accented beat is not fixed, there must be accent and release if there is to be meter at all. What is fixed about metric organization is the number of beats, not their disposition.

On the other hand, this does not mean that rhythm and meter are completely independent of one another. A change which alters the position of an accent in relation to other accents will obviously affect both rhythm and meter.

Since the beats which measure the meter may themselves be divided into equal parts, some of which will be accented, it follows that most compositions present a hierarchy of meters. For example, the beats of a 4/4 grouping might be divided as in Example 30.

EXAMPLE 30

Needless to say, other permutations and combinations are possible on all metric levels.

We are inclined to think of there being only one meter—the one designated in the time signature. For purposes of discussion let us call this metric level the primary or fundamental meter. Metric levels which are included within the primary meter will be called inferior metric levels and designated as secondary, tertiary, and so forth, in order of decreasing length. Those metric levels in which the primary rhythm is itself included will be referred to as superior metric levels and will be designated as secondary, tertiary, and so forth, in order of increasing metric length.

Of course, some time signatures do specify the organization of the inferior metric levels and others imply what the organization is to be. Thus a time signature of 3/4 specifies that the primary metric level is to be in threes and implies, but only implies, that the secondary metric level is going to be a division into two. On the other hand, a signature of 9/8 specifies that both the primary and secondary metric levels are to be divided into three. However, composers have been more and more inclined to treat the organization of the secondary and tertiary inferior metric levels with great freedom. A change from this type of metric organization $\frac{3}{4}$ ♫ ♫ ♫ to this one $\frac{3}{4}$ ♫♫♫ is a common occurrence in music of the past two hundred years and is made without any change of time signature.[28] Even less seldom does the composer make any stipulation as to the organization of the superior metric levels. One example that comes to mind occurs in the Scherzo of Beethoven's Ninth Symphony (measures 160–260).

This somewhat casual treatment of changes on the inferior metric levels is a result of the peculiar predominance given to the primary metric level in the style of the past two hundred years. This has not always been the case. During the later Middle Ages and the Renaissance there was (except in dance music or music influenced by dance rhythms) no all-embracing, predominant metric beat. In the polyphonic music of the time each voice tended to have its own metric organization and the relationship of the several metric levels within each voice, both to each other and to the metric structure of the other voices and the whole, was an important facet of the style (see Example 99, p. 244). The importance of the organization of the inferior metrical levels is shown by the fact that they were specified in detail by the time signatures of the period. In this music there is no basic, over-all meter. Each metric line and metric level proceeds, so to speak, on its own on equal terms with other aspects of the metrical organization; that is, the several metrical organizations are not generally speaking subsumed under any single superior beat. For this reason it would seem that attempts to respond to this music in a motor way are misplaced, for motor behavior depends upon and requires a single basic beat to which all others are referred and under which they are subsumed.[29]

The rise of tonal harmony, necessitating a coincidence in the vertical organization of texture, the emergence of the homophonic style, and the increasing importance of dance style music with its emphasis on motor patterns, all made for the predominance of what we have called the primary metric level. During the seventeenth, eighteenth, and nineteenth centuries the primary metric level became the almost exclusive focus of metrical attention. Changes on other metric levels, because they could be and were referred to the regularity of the primary level, went more or less unnoticed, becoming relatively unimportant in the organization and articulation of the rhythmic process. In short, metric continuation became identified almost exclusively with the primary metric level.

Continuation within the style under consideration involves not only the persistence of the motion of the meter but also its unity through dominance. Because of this, disturbance in metric continuation may take three forms: (1) it may involve an over-all change in meter; (2) it may take the form of misplacement in one part of the meter so that although the number of beats is not disturbed their placement is; in other words, there may be syncopation; and (3) it may involve the opposition of simultaneous meters.

An excellent example of a temporary metric change, the hemiola rhythm, which is common in the baroque style, is to be found in the final movement of Handel's Concerto Grosso No. 4. In order to understand the function and effect of the metric disturbance in measures 97 and 98, it is necessary to note that there is some doubt as to how the preceding measures (85–96) will continue. The doubt arises because the sequence that recurs here previously led to several different consequents (measures 5–8, 23–27, and 27–30) and the listener is uncertain about the outcome in this case. From measure 90 on the listener begins to expect a strong cadential progression. This expectation is intensified and colored by the doubts which arise as a result of the continued repetition of the short motive and the essentially static harmonic structure of these measures.

In measure 96 the situation becomes clear and certain, and the listener eagerly awaits the cadence which he now knows will be in the tonic, A minor. But instead of giving us a regular rhythmic structure as well as the expected harmonic progression (see Example 31), Handel heightens our now definitive expectations by delaying and prolonging the cadence and by disturbing the meter, thus intensifying the motion from tension to rest.

EXAMPLE 31

In these measures we have a clear metric grouping in twos. But the feeling for the basic triple meter is not lost. It continues as part of our mental set and our motor response so that the new metric group, conflicting with the old, intensifies the drive toward resolution and unification. The resolution is inevitable, in the sense that any conflict of meters, barring further changes, must finally reach agreement on a superior metric level. That is, groups of threes against groups of twos must eventually meet—have coinciding downbeats every sixth beat—as they do here.

The disturbance of the metric organization not only acts as an intensification it also acts to recondition the metric scheme present throughout the movement. It makes the meter seem fresh and new when it once again moves with its usual regularity. This process of reconditioning is particularly common where triple meter is used because, since triple meter does not generally admit of secondary accents, it tends to become more tiresome and singsongy than meters which are or can be easily compounded.

One of the particularly striking things about passages such as this one is that the disturbance of the meter is so much more forceful—more so than in many seemingly more irregular metric schemes—than in many works of the twentieth century. There are several reasons for this. In the first place, it is obvious that in the music of the eighteenth and nineteenth centuries regularity is more or less the norm, especially in the formation of the chief melodies. In much contemporary music the main melodies are irregular in metric structure. Second, and this is related to the first point, in music of today metric disturbance is part of the general ongoing musical process, while in earlier music metrical irregularity is something special, a deviation functioning in conjunction with other deviant processes. Finally, I should like to suggest that contemporary music sometimes looks much more irregular than it actually sounds.

As an example of this let us examine a passage from the Soldier's March in Stravinsky's *Histoire du Soldat* (see Example 32).[30] The

EXAMPLE 32 *

meter appears to be very irregular, alternating between 2/4, 3/8, and 3/4. Yet if we look more closely we see that the bass part and the violin, which coincides with the bass part in the score, are very regular. Their meter is clearly 2/4. Looking more closely at the upper line we can see that the first measures could have been written as in Example 33. Stravinsky writes the meter as he does be-

* By permission of the copyright owners: J. & W. Chester, Ltd., London.

cause he wishes to enforce and guarantee the syncopation of the tones B and C-sharp in the second measure. In other words, the meter is not irregular, but the meters of the accompaniment and melody do not coincide; the melody is syncopated against the accompaniment.

EXAMPLE 33

With this clue to Stravinsky's mode of working, the metric scheme of the whole passage is seen as a syncopation with minor irregularities rather than as a series of irregular meters. This is clear if the passage is rewritten as in Example 34. Notice that there are two degrees of syncopation. The first occurs in the third bar. Here the syncopation is at the half bar, i.e., the primary accent in the melody

EXAMPLE 34

coincides with the secondary accent of the accompaniment. The second syncopation begins at the spot marked (y). Here the main beat of the melody fails to coincide with either accent in the accompaniment. The syncopation of the upper voice is resolved at (z) through the prolongation of the end of the melodic fragment in the previous measure.

The points of metric disturbance occur not at the seeming points of disjuncture, i.e., where they appear in notation, but at the beginning of each of the syncopations. In other words, the melody enters earlier than expected at (x) and later than expected at (y) and (z).

The effect of syncopation in this passage is somewhat problematical. On the one hand, it seems clear that within the context of this particular work and style, syncopation does not per se represent a deviation nor, as such, is it normative. Rather deviation and intensification are accomplished through changes in the placement of the syncopation relative to the basic beat. On the other hand, the effect of syncopation is there as part of the basic primary beat. The desire of the listener for simplicity and unity of beat gives this passage its special feeling of urgency—of striving for the point of metric coincidence, which is reached at No. 9.

The question ultimately is a matter of process continuation. Syncopation becomes an affective force, as distinguished from a force toward characterization, when it creates a disturbance in an ongoing process. When the syncopation is itself the process, then *qua* syncopation no longer functions as a powerful affective *modus operandi*.

The same thing is true of polymeters. In the second movement of the Ravel String Quartet (Example 35), for instance, a polymetric structure within the bar is present from the outset, and its normative nature is shown by the fact that it characterizes all of

EXAMPLE 35 °

the main melodic ideas—the stable musical formations. From a rhythmic point of view, tension is produced largely through the weakening of the rhythmic pattern, as at No. 17 in the Durand miniature score, by creating gaps in the temporal continuum, as is

° Reprint permission granted by Durand et Cie, Paris, France, copyright owners; Elkan-Vogel Co., Inc., Philadelphia, Pa., agent.

the case just before No. 15; or, less decisively, by increasing the rhythmic complications somewhat, as before No. 17.

In order for a polymetric structure to be felt as such, each part of the structure must be precisely and definitely articulated. If one part of the structure is so uniform in its rhythm as to present only a vaguely articulated meter, then it will probably be perceived as a ground to a single line. This is what occurs after measure 70 in Debussy's *Nocturne*, "Fêtes" (Example 36). That is, the tendency to hear a relatively uniform part of a texture as being as uniform as possible so that other figures will appear more clearly shaped (see pp. 186 f.) weakens our feeling for the meter of the string accompaniment in this section almost to vanishing point. Thus what we hear is a figure in the flutes, oboes, and clarinets against a general background of strings, horns, and lower woodwinds.

EXAMPLE 36 *

However, where the introduction of polyrhythm interrupts the rhythmic process, it may play a vital role in articulating the musical form and, consequently, in shaping the emotional response to the music. This does not mean to imply that the metric structure of a theme, such as that of the Ravel Quartet, plays no part in creating musical responses. It does play such a part, but, in so far as the process proceeds in a regular manner, the part is that of establishing the basic metric process to which other later processes will be referred. It also creates what, for want of a better term, we shall call "character" or "spirit." With the former we are directly concerned in this study; with the latter we are concerned only in so far as spirit or character may effect expectation (see p. 30).

* Reprint permission granted by Jean Jobert, Paris, France, copyright owner; Elkan-Vogel Co., Inc., Philadelphia, Pa., agent.

Real polymeters are not as common in music of the classical period as are other forms of metric disturbance. But when they are used, they serve a very clear purpose—they act as deviants. The next example is taken from the first movement of Mozart's Piano Sonata in F Major (K. 332). It includes almost the entire "bridge" section between the first and second themes in the exposition (see Example 37). The rhythm in the left hand is consistently in triple

EXAMPLE 37

meter, while the meter of the melody in the right hand at first seems to waver between twos and threes. The measures numbered 1 and 2 and 5 and 6 seem to be made of three times two. At the very least, the metric structure is ambiguous. Measures 3 and 4 and 7 and 8 are apparently in triple meter. From measure 9 through measure 14 the meter of the right hand is clearly duple, while the left hand continues in threes. Notice that this specification of the polyrhythmic structure is paralleled by a more decisive harmonic motion: both begin a new process that delays the arrival of a "solid" G in the soprano, which the motion from the B-flat (measures 3 and 4) through the A to A-flat (measures 7 and 8) leads us to expect. The importance of this delay is demonstrated by the emphasis the G receives when it finally does arrive. Notice, too, that the definition of the polymeter coincides with the definition of the harmonic process and that both are, so to speak, resolved together in measure 15.

Any discussion of the superior metric levels is faced with numerous difficulties and problems. The difficulties are those of space, the fact that the larger metric structures cover a large portion of a composition. The problems can only be touched upon. The crucial one is, as mentioned earlier (p. 112), that of the span of attention and, concurrently, the relation of metric perception to motor habits. If the response to the metrical scheme can extend beyond the phrase, how far can it extend and with what sort of accuracy? How are sections which are dovetailed or overlapped to be interpreted metrically, etc.?

In view of these problems we shall merely point out that we probably do feel phrases partly in metrical terms and that larger metrical schemes will usually demonstrate regularity and irregularity just as the metrical scheme of the basic beat does. If we turn again to Example 37, we can see this plainly. If we count each bar as a quarter note, then the metric organization of the passage (including the final three measures which are not given) might be schematized as in Example 38. There seems to be little doubt but that measures 9–14, coming as they do after the regular succession of four-measure phrases in the first-theme group and the two four-measure phrases which begin this section, create an appreciable disturbance on the superior metric level.

♩= 1 measure

| ♩ ♩♩ | ♩ ♩♩♩ | ♩♩♩ ♩♩♩ ♩♩♩ | ♩♩♩ |

(2+1+1)+(2+1+1)+(2 + 2 + 2)+(1+1+2)

mm: 1 — 4,   5 — 8,   9 ——— 14 , 15—18.

EXAMPLE 38

FURTHER CONSIDERATIONS

Before closing this section, there are several further aspects of continuity processes that need consideration. In the examples thus far examined, disturbances in continuity have, on the whole, resulted from either a reversal of an established musical process, a delay in the process, or both. But continuity can also be disturbed

by anticipation. Syncopation is, in a sense, simply a rhythmic anticipation in which an accent in one of the parts enters too soon. This
is the case in the example cited earlier from Stravinsky's *Histoire
du Soldat,* where the repetition of the motive begins one beat too
soon and continues in this way (see pp. 120 f.).

The second movement of Beethoven's Third Symphony (Example
39) furnishes an excellent example of the disturbance of continuity
by anticipation. Here the B-flat in measure 20 disturbs the established sequence by entering one beat earlier than expected. This

EXAMPLE 39

anticipation is important, not only because of the immediate affective aesthetic consequences which it has, but also because it alters
the rhythmic and melodic structure of the last two measures. The
rhythm groups of the opening four measures are amphibrachs. But
the displacement of the B-flat together with the occurrence of a rest
where that tone should have been breaks the motive in two so that
the detached B-flat is no longer felt as the downbeat of an amphibrach rhythm. As a consequence the rhythm of measures 21 and 22
is reversed, and these measures are perceived as being anacrucial
to the final G in measure 23. Furthermore, the displacement of the
B-flat enables that part of the motive which was formerly the begin-
ing to come at the end, that is, the tone C, which is a continuation
of the over-all motion from A-flat to B-flat, has a new melodic-
rhythmic function within the motivic structure.

Although continuity and its disturbance have been treated
largely in terms of melodic and rhythmic processes, it is obvious
that the law of good continuation is relevant and applicable to other
musical processes as well—e.g., harmony, instrumentation, texture,
form, and so forth. Any aspect of the musical progress governed by
probability relationships, whether these relationships are products
of learning or the result of relationships created within the context
of the particular work, establishes preferred modes of continuation.

A detailed treatment of all these aspects of the musical materials is beyond the scope of this study. Some have already been described in the discussions of melodic and rhythmic continuation. Others will be examined when we deal with further aspects of the perceptual process. And it is hoped that the reader will, on the basis of the general viewpoint adopted in this chapter together with his own musical experience, be able to elaborate upon and systematize the observations made here.

These various aspects of process continuation are not, of course, compartmentalized and separated from one another in the mind of either the composer or the listener. As a rule melody, rhythm, harmony, and so forth are perceived together as a single unitary process. Thus in the Chopin Prelude already discussed (pp. 93–97) melodic, harmonic, and rhythmic processes were found to be congruent: they all acted together in creating and disturbing continuity.

Though this is generally the case, it is not always so. Sometimes one aspect of the musical organization will continue an established process while other aspects of the organization which were at first congruent with that process become changed in important ways. We saw this to be the case in our examination of the "Liebestod" where, it will be recalled, the total process established by the voice and instruments together is continued by the instruments but is broken in the vocal part.

In the first movement of Beethoven's String Quartet in B-flat, Op. 130, such a bifurcation of process continuation takes place at the beginning of the recapitulation. It is particularly interesting because of its effect upon the form of the whole movement.

All that need concern us about the exposition section is the fact that there is a general congruence of harmonic and other processes and that from a tonal point of view there is a motion from B-flat to G-flat. An enharmonic change at the beginning of the development section (measure 97) establishes the key of D major. At measure 104 a new process is established, which is regular and very well organized from the point of view of figuration. The harmonic motion of this process consists in a regular progression through the circle of fifths, from D to G to C minor and so forth. Because this is a time-honored norm of harmonic progression in the classical style, it establishes a specially powerful tendency toward continuation.

The other processes established continue along with the harmonic movement until the tonality of B-flat major (the tonic) is reached. At this point the bifurcation occurs. For the melodic, rhythmic, textural, and other processes begin to recapitulate the materials of the exposition section while the harmonic motion continues on through the cycle of fifths, from B-flat to E-flat, skirting A-flat, to D-flat.[31] This is schematized in Example 40. In other words, while thematically the recapitulation begins when the earlier B-flat (in

EXAMPLE 40

measure 132) is reached, harmonically or tonally it is not securely established until the second group is presented in the tonic at measure 174. The thematic recapitulation is unsteady, not only tonally, but also melodically, because the order of the parts is constantly being shifted around. Although there is a kind of recapitulation of the first group, the basic reversal, the change from an ongoing, developing process to a relatively stable one, does not take place, as is usually the case, at the point where the first group is repeated but rather at the point where the second group is heard in the tonic.

IV

Principles of Pattern Perception:
Completion and Closure

General Considerations

To assert that incompleteness gives rise to expectations of completeness is tantamount to tautology. For things seem to be incomplete only because we entertain definite feelings, latent expectations, as to what constitutes completeness in a given stimulus situation.

Our opinion or feeling as to the completeness of a given stimulus is a product of the natural modes of mental organization. These function both within the framework of what is given in the style and within the sound terms established in the particular work. In other words, the mind, governed by the law of Prägnanz, is continually striving for completeness, stability, and rest. But what represents completeness will vary from style to style and from piece to piece.

For instance, to the listener practiced only in the music of the eighteenth and nineteenth centuries, the cadential formula which closes and completes many pieces written during the Renaissance will seem to be a semicadence. It will be felt to be incomplete, to lack finality. However, to a listener who understands the Renaissance style, the same cadence will seem to be a final, satisfactory conclusion. Similarly the practiced listener will not feel a sense of real completeness and conclusion after only the minuet part of a minuet movement of a classical symphony has been heard, though the same series of sound terms will appear as final when they are repeated later. He expects the trio and minuetto repetition to follow, partly, because of a desire for repetition and, partly, and this is important, because he knows, though perhaps only unconsciously, what constitutes completeness for this kind of movement in this particular style.

Our sense of completeness or incompleteness is also a product of those patterns or sound terms which become established as more or less fixed, given parts of a particular work. That is, once a sound term has been established as a coherent, though not necessarily as a complete or closed unit, then part of the series taken by itself will, generally speaking, seem to be incomplete, particularly if the fragment occurs in the earlier parts of the total work. Thus repetitions of the beginning of a well-shaped theme already heard several times will arouse expectations that the theme will be completed as it has been in the past.

Even this seemingly plausible statement is subject to important qualifications. Particularly in the later stages of a work, part of a sound term or an abstraction of its essential motion or its motives may come to stand for and represent the whole sound term. In such a case, the repetition of a fragment of a larger part may not be felt to constitute incompleteness but, on the contrary, be taken as a sign of closure, making the whole work seem complete and stable.

This observation illustrates the difficulties involved in setting up any accurate distinctions between the various laws of perception. For our feeling of expectation where a normal stylistic process is broken off or where an established theme is only partially presented is as much a result of the desire for good continuation as it is a result of our desire for completion and closure. Indeed, it would appear reasonable to consider the law of completion as a corollary of the law of continuation, since all incompleteness is, in some sense, a lack of good continuation and since that which is complete must have been well continued.

Completeness and closure are possible only because the motions presented in music are processes involving relationships between antecedents and consequents. Completion is possible only where there is shape and pattern. Repetition in itself does not make for completeness and closure, nor does change in itself. For completion is not simply cessation—silence. It involves conclusion—almost in the syllogistic sense that the conclusion or completion is implicit in the premises, in the earlier phases of the musical motion. It is for this reason that, granted a sensitivity to the style in question, it is not difficult to know when a sound term is incomplete, partially complete, or finally closed.

Furthermore, completeness and closure exhibit the same architectonic order as the music itself. That is, what is felt to be a completed process on one level may appear to be incomplete on a higher architectonic level. This is important because the mind of the listener is able to take certain patterns as units, to close them out, so to speak, and take them as given.

This analysis makes it clear that neither continuity nor completeness create shape or pattern. Rather they are products of shape and pattern. The problem of what makes a shape or pattern is an extremely intricate and difficult subject, which can be investigated only superficially in this study (see chap. v).

Two types of incompleteness can be distinguished: (1) those which arise in the course of the pattern because something was left out or skipped over; and (2) those in which the figure, though complete so far as it goes, simply is not felt to have reached a satisfactory conclusion, is not finished. The first type of incompleteness may be said to be a product of a "structural gap," the second type, a product of a delay in the need and desire for "closure."

STRUCTURAL GAPS

A structural gap occurs where something is felt to be left out. The hiatus created by such a gap need not disturb the process of continuity. In fact, it might be better to consider such a break as a disturbance in continuity rather than as a structural gap. For instance, the hiatus created by the rests in measures 45 and 46 of the Minuetto from Haydn's Symphony No. 104 in D Major (Example 41) can be considered as a structural gap only in a Pickwickian sense. For the term "gap" implies the possibility of subsequent completion.

EXAMPLE 41

And though a temporal process can be broken off and then continued again, the subsequent continuation does not in any real sense fill the gap thus created. Such a break in process may arouse the keenest expectation, as indeed it does in this instance; but expectation is satisfied after the rests, not because something which was missing is introduced, but because that which was interrupted is begun again.

It should be noted that though this is not properly speaking an instance of a structural gap, it is an example of lack of closure. For the break in process is effective because, when it occurs, the figure is patently incomplete, not closed. Had the hiatus occurred two measures later, after the progression to D major, it would have been a weak, insipid anticlimax.

The tendency for structural gaps to be completed is most clearly seen in the case of melodic structure. It is to this aspect of the musical organization that we shall devote most of the ensuing discussion.

In the music of a culture the tonal materials given in the style system establish a norm of melodic completeness. That is, in any tonal system there is a normal repertory of tones which mark off the distance between tones of equivalence or duplication, usually the octave. The total complement of such tones constitutes completeness for the system. When the practiced or cultivated listener becomes aware that one of these steps has been passed over (left out) he expects, albeit unconsciously, that the missing tone will be forthcoming later in the series. He expects, in short, that the structural gaps created by such a skip will eventually be filled in.

This tendency for structural gaps to be completed and filled in is evident in the music of many different countries. "But a large number of these 'crooked' forms of Hindu *Rags* consisted in creating gaps in ascent to be filled up in descent, or vice versa. This not only avoids anticlimax, but includes climax. To pass over a note immediately creates a desire for it, and it then becomes a fit note to bear the climax." [1] Studying the intervallic motions of extremely diverse types of music, Watt found that the larger the interval (the larger the skip), the more likely that it will be followed by contrary motion (motion which will fill in the tones passed over). He also notes that the studies of Turkish music made by Hornbostel and Abraham and the study of Swedish folk tunes made by Fox Strangways reveal similar tendencies.[2] In their article on "Muhammedan Music" in *Grove's Dictionary*, Lachmann and Strangways note that "after a third, return is usually made to one of the notes which have been leapt over."[3] In our own culture the rule of counterpoint which states that after a skip the melody should move by stepwise motion in the opposite direction is simply an application of the law of completion to a particular practice.[4]

Of course, different cultures as a rule have different style systems, different ways of organizing musical space. In one system the normal repertory of tones may be five, in another seven, and in still another only three; and the distances between the tones comprised in the system may be equal or unequal. For this reason, an intervallic distance which would constitute a skip or gap in one system might not be one in another system. In a style system in which the musical space between identical tones, the octave, is divided into seven steps, a skip of a third will probably be perceived as a structural gap. But in a tonal system in which the octave is divided into only five steps and in which one of the normal distances is a third, such an interval will probably not be considered as being a structural gap.

The preceding statements were intentionally conditional. The cultural criterion of completeness is by no means absolute. We are able to evaluate completeness aside from purely cultural facts. For if, as is the case in most tonal systems, the distances between tones are not equal, the mind will assume the smaller distance as a standard and accordingly judge the larger distances as having gaps which require completion. In short, a series which is differentiated into larger and smaller distances will, so to speak, have structural gaps built into it.

According to the present analysis, there would be a tendency for such a series of unequally spaced steps to become filled in. This is, in fact, what has happened to most unequally spaced scales. There is a strong tendency for tonal systems to become more complete. Most scales (the abstracted linearization of tonal materials) have developed in the direction of closure, toward the elimination of gaps in their structure.

The Chinese, for instance, have introduced *pièn* tones into their essentially pentatonic tonal system, thus filling in the open thirds of the pentatonic scale. Other folk cultures and primitive cultures have done likewise.

> It has no doubt been noted . . . that the Quechua musician often fills up one of the minor triads of his pentatonic scale with an extra tone which he uses in an ornamental capacity—usually as a passing tone between two more important melodic notes. . . . Often a kena-player will take a well known pure pentatonic melody and ornament it *ad libitum* with these extra tones.[5]

In his book, *A Theory of Evolving Tonality*,[6] Joseph Yasser traces the growth and development of tonal systems, attempting to show that this development follows certain characteristic mathematical patterns, but he does not attempt to account for this process. The present analysis would seem to present an explanation for the gradual increase in the tonal materials comprising the octave. For the new tones, introduced at first for the sake of both completion and, as we shall see later, expression, eventually become fixed parts of the tonal repertory—norms of the tonal system. If this new repertory of tones also exhibits inequalities of distance, then new "filler tones" will be required, since the system will still be felt to have structural gaps.

But there is another possible course which the development of a tonal system may follow, and this raises questions as to the necessity for the mathematical evolution prescribed by Yasser. This is the possibility of equal temperament. The Javanese, for instance, eliminate structural gaps from their music, not by adding new filler tones, but by making all tones equally distant.

> It is surely worthy of note once again to see this tendency to equidistance at work in Malay music; the same tendency which once before, i.e. in Further India, had already turned the same basic scale into an equidistant sequence of tones. In the latter case, however, this was not done by inserting two new tones, but by dividing up the octave into seven equal intervals of approximately 171C, each.
>
> A third instance of this tendency to equidistance may be observed . . . in a number of slendro scales.[7]

A seven-tone tempered scale can, according to Tracey, also be found in Portuguese East Africa.[8] This inclination toward temperament also appears to have been felt in the Near East.[9]

Thus the tendency toward equal temperament and the propensity to add new tones to a scale with unequal distances both seem, from this point of view, to be products of a more general psychological need for structural completeness—for the elimination of structural gaps not only in the melodic line of the individual piece but also in the tonal system itself. This, to borrow a term from Kunst, is the "tendency toward equidistance."

If a general tendency toward equidistance does in fact exist, and there seem to be reasonable grounds for believing that it does, and if the continued development of tonal systems, the gradual accretion of new tones which fill structural gaps, is a manifestation of this tendency, then Yasser's supposition of a kind of inevitable growth (up to the limits of the physio-psychological ability of the human ear and mind) would be open to question. For the process of accretion would logically cease once the need for completion was fulfilled in equal temperament. An important proviso must, however, be made: Should all the tempered tones of a system become structural points (norms), then new tones, tendency tones, would have to be introduced into the system so that meaningful relationships would exist within the tonal system.

A structural gap, then, creates a tendency toward "filling in." And if this tendency is delayed, if the completion of the pattern is blocked, affect or the objectification of meaning will probably follow.

If, for instance, we compare the opening theme of Bach's Branden-

EXAMPLE 42

burg Concerto No. 5 with a part of the aria "Che faro senza Euridice!" from Gluck's *Orfeo ed Euridice* we find that the opening notes

EXAMPLE 43

of both themes create the same structural gaps. In the Bach theme, however, the filling in of these structural gaps begins immediately;

and, partly for this reason, this theme, though definite and forceful in both mood and character, is not itself affective. The affective experience of this movement is rather a product of the progression of the larger parts. But the fragment from *Orfeo* is, Hanslick's derision notwithstanding, notably affective.[10] The poignancy of this passage is due in part to the tensions which arise, the tendencies which are inhibited, because there is a delay in the filling in of the structural gaps created by the opening motive. And it is only after all the skipped tones have been presented that these tensions subside and the melody concludes.

Notice that disturbances in process continuation also play an important part in creating the affective quality of this passage. For the repetition of the C after the triadic motive creates a break in both melodic and rhythmic processes. That is, we expect the triadic motion of the opening motive to continue. The powerful effect of the high E is partly a result of the fact that it was unconsciously expected at the beginning of the first complete measure. The eighth-note motion is also expected to continue, and for this reason the quarter note C becomes a particularly effective appoggiatura.

SATURATION

The principle of saturation is related, on the one hand, to the laws of good continuation and completion and, on the other, to the beliefs which the listener entertains as to the nature of aesthetic experience. Since the meaning of any sound term is a function of its relationships to other consequent terms which it indicates, our normal expectation is of progressive change and growth. A figure which is repeated over and over again arouses a strong expectation of change both because continuation is inhibited and because the figure is not allowed to reach completion. Our expectation of change and our concomitant willingness to go along with the composer in this apparently meaningless repetition are also products of our beliefs in the purposefulness of art and the serious intentions, the integrity, of the composer. We believe that he will bring about a change.

A particularly clear example of the arousal of expectation through saturation is to be found in the first movement (measures 16–26) of Beethoven's Symphony No. 6, where the same motive is repeated ten times with only minimal dynamic and orchestral changes (see Example 44; also see the development section of this Symphony and that of Beethoven's Symphony No. 8). The use of saturation is common particularly in the slow introductions and development sections of eighteenth- and nineteenth-century works where there is expectation of a return to a theme already heard. For at such places the fragment need only be repeated one or two times in order to achieve the desired effect.

EXAMPLE 44

Koffka observes that there is an intimate relationship between saturation and emotion: "Saturation is emotional behavior. Its analysis revealed an interplay of forces leading to increasing tension within the Ego system. . . ." [11] Although it was found that, generally speaking, these tensions could be relieved by varying the tasks being performed, it would seem that in the case of musical perception tensions may arise even though variation is present. That is, even with variation in harmony or range or dynamics a very marked figure may, in the proper context, give rise to saturation if it is repeated with great enough insistence.

It is necessary once again to emphasize the importance of context upon these processes. A repeated pattern at the end of a work need not give rise to saturation, since at this point the listener understands, or thinks he understands, the significance of the repetition: that is, because this is the end of the piece, lack of forward motion, a composed fermata, is expected and desirable. Thus the law of saturation is conditional: In a situation where repetition is not normal and understandable, the longer a pattern or process persists, the stronger the expectation of change. [12]

In the last analysis everything depends upon our ability to comprehend the significance of the repetition. If it is understandable, then there will be no saturation. For instance, a repeated pattern or figure may, because of its position in the work and its relationship to other patterns, be understood as an ostinato. If it is to be heard

in this manner, the composer must so articulate the texture that the
listener grasps the significance of the figure as an ostinato, He
must as a rule make evident the fact that the repeated pattern is a
ground, e.g., it must be more homogeneous than the other patterns
and will, as a general rule, surround the other figures temporally,
begin before they do. An ostinato must also have a less palpable,
well-figured shape than the other figures of the work so that it is
clear that it is not the chief pattern. In other words, it must not
develop tendencies of its own, as did the figure in Example 44. This
relative weakness of figure is what distinguishes an ostinato, such
as the one employed by Debussy in his Piano Prelude "Des Pas sur
la Neige," from a ground bass. For a ground bass develops tendencies of its own; it has shape, and it is a shaping and controlling

EXAMPLE 45 °

force in the articulation of the musical progress and growth. That
is, the ground bass changes its meaning as it forms new and changing relationships with the other parts of the texture. It is not simply
a given static entity.

It should, however, be observed that an ostinato-like pattern may
at times seem ambiguous, though it need never do so. The listener
understands that the function of the pattern is to establish a continuous and repeated ground against which other more clearly
articulated figures are to be projected. If no other more substantial
figures are forthcoming, then the listener may begin to entertain
doubts as to whether the motive in question really is an ostinato.
Then as the repeated figure becomes the center of attention, the
listener will begin to expect changes to take place. And if the figure
remains stable or is subjected to only minor variations, saturation

may set in. This would seem to be what takes place in the opening section, "Prélude à la nuit," of Ravel's *Rapsodie Espagnole,* where the ostinato figure is dominant even during the brief appearances of the theme.

MELODIC COMPLETENESS AND CLOSURE

One of the most powerful and persuasive forces conditioning and controlling the sense of completeness which a melodic pattern gives is the tonal organization or scale of the culture. It "establishes a system of order, a system of expectancies, a system of tonality. . . ." [13] Since the importance and functioning of tonality has been discussed in chapter ii and will be the subject of further discussion in chapter vi, its overwhelming significance need only be recalled at this point: Tonality is probably the most important single facet of style, the *sine qua non* of even the most primitive musical organization.

It is important also to recall that the norms of style, of tonality, important as they are, can be altered through training and knowledge. For the individual musical work also establishes norms which condition our feelings and opinions as to completeness and closure, and these norms of the individual work may be unusual within the style. A composer may, for instance, by dint of repetition within a work, establish as final, as representing closure, a melodic pattern which might not normally seem finished or final. The listener's sense of closure and finality can, as Farnsworth has shown, be altered through training.[14] W. V. Bingham [15] has shown that opinions as to the finality of a series of tones can be influenced by information stipulating the number of tones to be heard in the series. If, for instance, listeners were told that the fifth tone of the series was to be the last, it appeared to possess a finality which it did not as a rule have otherwise. This furnishes experimental evidence, if any was needed, for the statement that what we know, either because we have been told or have learned through practice and experience, influences our judgment of what we perceive and hence our feeling of completeness and our expectation based upon that feeling.

Our sense of completeness is directly related to our ability to understand the meaning of a particular pattern. A stimulus series which develops no process, awakens no tendencies, will, if it becomes the focus of attention, always appear to be incomplete. A sustained tone, for instance, will give rise to expectations of change, unless, of course, it is not the main object of attention or can be understood more easily in another way, e.g., as a pedal point.

Moreover, the direction in which the tone may be expected to move is also related to our sense of completeness. "The direction of expectation, whether to a tone below the first tone of a melody or above it, depends largely on the absolute pitch of the latter. In general, the lower this is the less will the melody be expected to descend on the next following tone; while correspondingly the higher it is the less will the melody be expected to rise on the next tone." [16] Actually the situation is somewhat more complicated than this. For our expectations depend upon our awareness of potential range as well. That is, a tone which would be "high" for one voice or instrument, and would consequently be expected to descend, might be low for another voice or instrument and would consequently be expected to rise.

Although not directly related to the Gestalt principles of pattern perception, our sense of closure is in part a product of the general configuration of relaxation and quiescence. Melodically speaking, relaxation is associated with the decline in tension which is effected when pitches are lower—when a progression descends at its close.[17]

Curiously enough, however, the lowering of the dynamic level, which is also a normal concomitant of relaxation, does not necessarily accompany closure. The reason for this would appear to lie in the fact that the dynamic level is intimately associated with those aspects of the musical materials which tend to designate the character of the piece. More particularly, the dynamic level would seem to be linked to tempo and general range. These elements are themselves interassociated so that fast tempi, loud dynamics, and high ranges (but not necessarily ascending melodic lines) are usual together, while slow tempi, soft dynamics, and low ranges are also usual together. Of course, there are pieces that get softer at the end as well as ones that become slower; and both of these changes play a part in making closure more emphatic. But, on the whole, the slowing down which brings a piece of music to its close is not a slowing down in the physical tempo but a slowing down of the rate of musical process. That is, though the tones may fly by with great rapidity, the melodic, harmonic, and rhythmic changes which create a sense of tendency are brought to a standstill. The music no longer progresses; it marks time; it is static.

In any particular musical work certain melodic patterns because of their palpable and cohesive shapes become established in the mind of the listener as given, axiomatic sound terms. They set the mode of continuation, completion, and closure which are the norms of the particular work. And if part of such a pattern is introduced, it will arouse definite expectations as to the manner of continuation and completion.

The following melody is established as such an axiomatic sound term in the first movement of Hindemith's Symphony, *Mathis der Maler* (Example 46). This is not the place to make an exhaustive

EXAMPLE 46 °

analysis of this melody, particularly since Hindemith himself deals with it in some detail.[18] However, one point with which Hindemith fails to deal in his own analysis must be discussed, for it plays an important part in the organization of the melody and, therefore, in conditioning subsequent expectations and feelings of completion. This is the fact that the over-all motion of the melody is triadic, moving (as indicated in analysis A of Example 46) from the initial

° Copyright 1934 by B. Schott's Soehne, Mainz; used by permission of Associated Music Publishers, Inc., New York.

G, through B and D, up to F-sharp. The first motion is up to the D; but this tone is, so to speak, left dangling in mid-air. It does not really move to anything when it is first heard. Rather the B which precedes it moves downward to the C in measure 48 (see analysis *B*). This is of special interest in the present discussion since this effect creates a definite sense of incompleteness. We feel and expect that we must return to the D and move in a coherent manner from it.

Before the higher D is picked up in measure 50, the intervallic and rhythmic motion which first led to it is re-established in a lower range (measures 47–48). The whole motion from measures 48–49 is, in a sense, nothing but a composed upbeat to the higher D. Notice in this connection that the important tones in this sequence, the B, D and A-sharp (enharmonically, B-flat), are also the vital tones in the figure in which the D first occurs (measure 43). The return to the high D leads to a stepwise motion to the F-sharp and then down through the D to B.

In making a further abstraction of the essential melodic motion of this melody, it would seem that the G in measure 49 plays a much more important role than it would appear to have at first. It serves to tie together the first and second phrases and by doing so to provide a long delayed resolution of the motion from B to A in measures 41–42. From this point of view, and it is certainly not the only one possible, the over-all scheme of the melody might look something like Example 47.

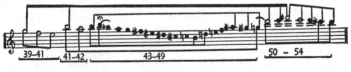

EXAMPLE 47

In this analysis the hiatus created with the break in measure 42 involves both incompletion of the motion down to the G, which arrives only in measure 49, and a halt in the upward motion begun in the first four measures. What really happens is that the significance of the D remains to be established. This is accomplished by its upward motion to the F-sharp, which marks the reversal of process in the melody as a whole. That is, it not only literally marks the first major descent in the over-all line but it is also preceded and marked by a significant harmonic clarification, a fact which Hindemith notes in his own analysis.

In terms both of its motive and its over-all triadic motion, this melody provides one of the normative sound terms in the first movement of *Mathis der Maler*. Its analysis furnishes a basis for understanding how subsequent deviations arouse expectation.

In the passage that follows the melody given above, the first part of the theme is presented in an incomplete form. It therefore arouses

EXAMPLE 48

our expectations both because we have a standard of completeness, we know how it should continue, and because the structural gaps remain unfilled until the whole melody is heard beginning at measure 63. But we do have a very strong sense of direction and continuity once the first two fragments have been heard. We expect the rising motion to continue because it is incomplete and because it has been established as a mode of continuation in the melody itself. Notice, incidentally, the fact that the motion from G to D to F-sharp, which was somewhat veiled in the original melody, is here made very clear and forceful.

The arrival of the F-sharp in measure 60 has a decisive effect upon our expectations for two reasons. First, it crystallizes and fixes the basis of the ascending progression, making clear the fact that the sequence is rising through the major triad, and second, it marks the onset of saturation.

Up to measure 60 we expect that the progression will rise, but we do not know precisely what form the ascending progression will follow. Once the F-sharp is reached, this is made clear. And it is this knowledge which enables the composer to repeat the motive on the F-sharp. For had it been repeated sooner, it would not have appeared as so strong a delay in the line, and it is partly this feeling of delay that contributes to the effect of saturation.

Actually the effect of saturation is cumulative. Even though the motive is at first stated on different degrees of the scale, it is felt as repeated. And the powerful effect of the exact repetition on the F-sharp is, in part, a product of the earlier statements of the motive. The effect of saturation is also dependent upon the fact of incompleteness. Hindemith emphasizes this by making these later versions of the motive even shorter than the earlier ones. This also has the important effect of increasing the psychological tempo. For our sense of timing is guided by the time span between the entrances of the motive, which at first are ten beats apart, and later become only six beats apart, and, finally, only five beats apart. This hurrying plus the repetition of the F-sharp motive (which heightens our expectation both because it represents a delay in the process of continuation and because it becomes a sign that the main event, which we have been awaiting, is about to take place) build up tension, which is climactically released at the arrival of the high A and a complete, though somewhat varied, statement of the whole melody.

RHYTHMIC COMPLETENESS AND CLOSURE

The difference between meter and rhythm was discussed in chapter iii. The distinction is important in connection with an examination of rhythmic completeness. For rhythm may be incomplete though meter remains intact; and, conversely, rhythm may be complete without there being any meter.

The completeness of a rhythm depends upon the apprehension of a relationship between accented and unaccented parts of a cohesive group. The sequence of rhythmic feet may vary considerably so long as the relationships within the various feet are clear. That is, trochees may follow iambs, iambs may follow anapests, and so forth without creating incompleteness, though continuity will, of course, be disturbed in such a sequence. The accented or unaccented parts of a rhythmic grouping may be implied, imagined by the listener, rather than stated, but not both. However, whether the relationship is explicit or implied, it must exist if there is to be any sense of rhythm. A series of unaccented beats will seem incomplete and give rise to expectations of completeness, expectations of an accent. Conversely a series of accents will appear incomplete and give rise to expectations of a return to an understandable relationship between accent and release. One might well contend that there is no difference between a series of accents and a series of beats which are unaccented, since we can know either one only in terms of the other. Both are, in a sense, only pulses. Finally, it should be noted that, since rhythms form an architectonic hierarchy, a passage which is rhythmically incomplete on a higher architectonic level may be complete on a lower one. However, the reverse of this is not true; for if the lower level is incomplete, fails to differentiate beats into accented and unaccented, then the higher level is deprived of the basis for its organization.

The apprehension of meter depends upon the establishment of a regularly recurring accented beat. The disposition and number of unaccented beats in such a metric group is a matter of indifference. The temporal recurrence of the main beat is all important. Hence a meter is incomplete when the main beat of the group is missing. Since the listener expects an objective stimulus to correspond to his "inner beat," metric completion cannot be subjective.

It should be noted that, although metric incompleteness of necessity involves metric discontinuity—for the absence of a beat where one is expected creates awareness of a break—metric discontinuity need not involve incompleteness. For discontinuity may arise because the beat, though arriving at the proper time, is no longer felt to be accented, as, for instance, in the bridge passage (measures 23–25) from the second movement of Mozart's Jupiter Symphony (K. 551), where there are obvious metrical disturbances but no metric incompleteness.

One other aspect of the problem must be considered. Though the perception of meter does not depend upon the existence of a fixed relationship between accented and unaccented beats it does depend upon there being a difference between the several beats within a metric group. That is, some beats must be accented, others not. For this reason a series of equally accented pulses will no more give rise to an impression of meter than it will give an impression of rhythm. Such a series will be ambiguous; and its significance will lie in the very fact of ambiguity: the fact that the series indicates and points to, leads the listener to expect, clarification and normality.

Since these matters can best be discussed in the light of a specific example, let us turn to an examination of a portion of the fifth movement of Beethoven's String Quartet in C-Sharp Minor, Op. 131.

The main theme of this movement is regular and symmetrical. Each of its two four-measure phrases is composed of two complementary motives (see Example 49). The first is labeled *a*, the second, *b*. Three levels of rhythmic organization can be distinguished in each of the phrases. Level 1, the rhythm within the bar, is trochaic. This is true for every measure of the theme. Level 2, the level of the half phrase, is iambic. An iambic rhythm continues on this level throughout the period. Level 3, comprehending the whole phrase, is also iambic; that is, the second two measures are accented relative to the first two because of the change of harmony and the more decisive motion both within and between the several voices. The pattern of the consequent phrase is the same as that of the antecedent phrase.

EXAMPLE 49

After this basic rhythmic structure has been well established in the mind of the listener by repetition both within the phrase and the total period, Beethoven detaches motive *a* from the phrase and bases a six-measure sequence upon it (measures 19–24, Example 50). This change makes the rhythm on level 3 incomplete. For motive *a* now has no accented motive to move to. Considered on this rhythmic level, the sequence (measures 19–24) is a series of anacruses. It is incomplete, and this incompleteness, creating tendency and expectation, gives rise to affect and aesthetic signification.

EXAMPLE 50

Since it is the relationship between motives within the phrase which is changed in the construction of this sequence and not the relationships within the motive, the completeness of the rhythm of the first two levels remains intact. This accounts for the fact that, though there is evident incompleteness, there is no discontinuity, no break in the basic motion.

At measure 25 a somewhat varied version of the second half of the motive is separated out, and, if we include the slight variations to which this fragment is subjected, it becomes the basis for the organization of the following twelve measures (measures 25–36, Example 51). Rhythmic level 2, which depended for its existence upon the differentiation between, and a juxtaposition of, an unstressed first measure and a stressed second measure, is destroyed by the repetition of this fragment. That is, since we are presented with a series of precisely equivalent measures, it is impossible to differentiate them into accent and release; and, consequently, on level 2 the rhythm is now felt to be incomplete. This is, of course, precisely what took place in measures 19–24 on rhythmic level 3.

EXAMPLE 51

The variation in the half note fragment is a necessity if rhythmic suspense is to be maintained. For had measure 25 begun on the beat with a half note F-sharp, this would have created a powerful accent on both the second and third rhythmic levels, and a new rhythmic process would have begun.

This omission of the first beat of the measure creates metric incompleteness as well as rhythmic incompleteness. For since the listener's sense of the metric pulse, once it has been established, tends to persist, the suppression of the downbeat is felt as a gap or incompleteness. Notice that Beethoven has been careful to make sure that no displacement and reconstitution of the metric beat takes place. For instance, had the figure been written as a syncopation with half notes beginning on the second and fourth beat, the listener might eventually have heard the meter as complete, though it would be displaced relative to its original position. As it is, the listener's sense of the original metric organization is supported by the fact that the unaccented portion of the meter comes where it formerly did, and this helps to emphasize that the accented portion of the metric group is missing.

In spite of the patent incompleteness of the meter and rhythm on the second and third levels, some feeling of rhythmic organization remains. For on the first level a differentiation between accent and release still exists. However, the omission of the first quarter note of the measure has brought about a change in the rhythm. That is, the fragment which was formerly trochaic (as in measure 20) is now iambic. This reversal creates a certain amount of indecision in the feeling for the rhythmic organization. This feeling is subjected to further strain when the tempo changes at measure 33. In fact, our feeling for the relationship between the metric organization built up and maintained within the listener and the objective metric organization is all but destroyed at this point. And our feeling for the rhythm suffers the same fate with the change in tempo in measure 36.

The progressive incompleteness of the rhythmic and metric organization from measure 25 through measure 36 not only creates a desire for a return to the well-defined structures of the theme itself but it also makes the listener feel that further disintegration is impossible. Consequently the return to a regular, uninterrupted series of pulses and the use of new material, based on the first measure of the motive, are at first understood to constitute this expected return. But this understanding soon proves to be illusory. For though there is continuity of pulsation and a clear rhythm should emerge, there is no differentiation into stressed beats and unstressed ones. Since the successive but overlapping entrances of the motive on the same pitch level provide no basis for a distinction between accented and unaccented beats, these measures (38–41, Example 52) are perceived as a series of equal pulsations. In spite of the regular pulsation, there is no meter, for there is no differentiation. If there is any differentiation at all, it exists on the subprimary level as a trochaic rhythm of quarter notes. But it is doubtful, in view of the rapid tempo, whether this succession of quarter notes is perceived as a rhythmic grouping at all.

EXAMPLE 52

Even the return in measure 41 to the general range used in the beginning of the movement, though it certainly whets our expectations, does not clarify the situation completely, since overlapping still takes place. In fact, since it appears that the rebuilding of the rhythm is supposed to be gradual, it seems important that no special accent be given to the first beat of this group. The D-sharp in the first violin (measure 41) should probably be underplayed rather than the other way around. More precisely: it is clear that regularity is definitely established only after the fermata between measures 44 and 45. If tension is to be maintained, then the whole rhythm of the phrase should, as it were, be held back. This can be achieved by making the rhythm in measure 41 indecisive and ambiguous. If this is the case, then the rhythm of level 1 becomes established in measure 42, and the rhythm of level 2 becomes established in measures 43 and 44. However, since the rhythm of measure 41 was ambiguous and unformed, measures 41 and 42 fail to set up a rhythm on level 2; and, consequently, these four measures are unable to give rise to a feeling of rhythm on level 3. In short, the significance and efficacy of this period (measures 37–44) lie in the fact that while it re-establishes the original rhythmic organization, it does not do so completely. The listener remains in a state of suspense until the theme is presented as a total unit.

This analysis also increases our understanding of the over-all rhythm of the first section of this movement (measure 66) and enables us to understand better its psychological effect and intellectual significance. For it is clear that the incompleteness of rhythm in measures 19–44 creates suspense. The measures are an anticipatory upbeat, an anacrusis, to the complete thematic statement which begins at measure 45 and extends through measure 66. Seen in this light, the significance and importance of the two introductory measures also become clear. For they not only provide a brief but effective anacrusis to the whole first statement of the main idea (measures 3–18), but they also establish the basic iambic rhythm which is continued throughout the section. For even though the second measure is a rest, it is accented—strongly marked for consciousness by the mind of the listener. The over-all rhythm of this section might be schematized as follows:

measures: <u>1–2</u> <u>3–18</u> <u>19–44</u> <u>45–66</u>.

HARMONIC COMPLETENESS AND CLOSURE

Rhythmic organization does not operate as an isolated independent variable without reference to other aspects of the total musical organization. The formulation and operation of the rhythmic organization are conditioned and modified by the melodic structure, the disposition of the texture, and, in Western music at least, by the harmonic organization. In the fifth movement of the C-Sharp

Minor Quartet the relationship between harmonic completeness and rhythmic completeness is very clear. For this reason it might be well to discuss the question of harmonic completeness with reference to this example.

A feeling of harmonic completeness arises when the music returns to the harmonic base from which it began or moves to one which was in some way implicit in the opening materials. In this movement (see Example 49) both the opening period and its repetition, though rhythmically complete, are harmonically incomplete because they end not on the tonic but on the dominant of the submediant, the chord built on the sixth degree of the scale.

This harmonic incompleteness leads the listener to expect that this main theme will eventually close on the tonic. In measures 10–24 the harmonic progression from VI to IV to V in E major, a typical cadential formula, together with the incompleteness of the rhythm activate strong expectations of a close. But these are disappointed. For in measures 25–28 the dominant harmony is not resolved to the tonic but rather is weakened by the omission of the all-important leading tone and continues only by implication. In measure 29 this dominant feeling is not so much resolved as simply replaced by another incomplete triad whose significance is ambiguous. The subsequent harmonic changes in this passage are likewise vague and indeterminate. This lack of decisiveness is important because it enables the incompleteness of the rhythmic and metric organizations to make themselves felt. And the converse of this is also true: the rhythmic incompleteness makes the harmonic motion seem particularly vapid and ambiguous.

One might say that, though harmonic motion continues, harmonic progression is suspended. From measure 25 through measure 41 the harmony changes, but it does not appear to have direction. This permits the rhythmic structure to be progressively weakened without destroying the listener's sense of tonality. The listener knows what key he is in. This is proved by the fact that, although various preparations are made for a cadence in G-sharp minor (measures 42–44), the listener never really expects them to materialize; and, consequently, the motion to E major in measure 45 comes as no surprise.[19]

The effect of this whole section is clearly dependent upon the intimate co-operation of rhythmic and harmonic organization. The harmonic incompleteness establishes the forces toward completion, and the tendencies thus established give force and urgency to the rhythmic delay. Because this delay takes place at the beginning of the movement, Beethoven does not wish to destroy or weaken the tonal orientation of the listener. Indeed, had the feeling of E major been destroyed, the whole *raison d'être* of the passage would have been lost, for its purpose is precisely to delay the cadence in the tonic E major. For this reason Beethoven avoided extensive chromaticism and the use of very irregular chord progressions, turning rather to rhythm to create the feeling of suspense which he wanted. Here, again, we see the complementary relationship between harmony and rhythm. For the rhythmic incompleteness necessary to create delay and suspense was possible only because the harmonic motion was weak and indecisive.

THE PRINCIPLE OF RETURN

The different tonal systems upon which the music of various cultures has been built, whether they are primarily melodic or both melodic and harmonic, are all basically special, though vitally important, instances of "what has been called the *law of return,* the law that, other things being equal, it is better to return to any starting point whatsoever than not to return." [20] This law apparently influences the structure of primitive melodies built upon only two or three tones as well as the organization of the complex musical structures of art music. [21] Of course, once a tonal style has been established, has become part of the habit responses of the cultural group, the term "return" need not be taken literally; that is, the opening materials may indicate what the final tone of a piece is to be without explicitly presenting it in the opening moments.

The law of return depends for its operation upon "recurrence," a form of repetition which must be distinguished from "reiteration." Recurrence is repetition which takes place after there has been a departure from whatever has been established as given in the particular piece. There can be a return to a pattern only after there has been something different which was understood as a departure from

the pattern. Because there is departure and return, recurrence always involves a delay of expectation and subsequent fulfilment.

Reiteration, whether exact or varied, is the successive repetition
of a given sound term which, even if it is very extensive, is nevertheless perceived as a unit. Reiteration does not necessarily give rise
to expectations of further repetition. On the contrary, if repetition
is fairly exact and persistent, change rather than further repetition is
expected, i.e., saturation sets in.

Reiteration is the basis of what may be called the principle of
successive comparison. A given pattern establishes an intra-opus
norm, a base for expectation within the particular piece. Subsequent deviations from the pattern, occurring in repetitions, give
rise to affective or aesthetic responses because they function to
arrest or inhibit the tendency toward precise repetition. There are
no long-range delays that give rise to suspense. Expectation is
latent, and affect tends to be ephemeral. The composer plays, as
it were, with the listener's latent expectations of precision and
regularity.[22]

The operation of the law of return may be contrasted with that of
the principle of successive comparison by noting that in the latter
case tension arises out of deviations involved in the repetition of
the sound term, out of the fact of repetition, while in the former case
tensions arise because repetition is expected but is not as yet forthcoming. The recurrence itself represents, not tension, but the relaxation phase of the total motion. It creates closure and a feeling of
completeness. Notice, too, that while the principle of successive
comparison tends to emphasize the differences between the pattern
and its repetition, the law of return tends to emphasize the similarity between the pattern and its recurrence. This does not mean, of
course, that differences will not be noticed. Whenever there is
repetition there is bound to be successive comparison; and, though
differences will tend to be minimized in the case of return, they will
nevertheless be aesthetically effective.[23]

In spite of these significant differences, it is not always possible to
designate a passage as involving only return or only reiteration. In
the first place, some aspects of a given sound term may return while
others do not. For more than a melodic or harmonic norm is estab-

lished as given in any particular piece. Norms of tempo, dynamics, texture, instrumentation, and good shape are also established; and the recurrence of these, either singly or in combination, may give rise to feelings of partial return. In the development of Mozart's String Quartet in D Major (K. 575), for instance, a new theme is introduced. This theme creates a feeling of partial return, not because its melody is similar to that of the opening theme or because it is in the same key as the opening theme, but because its texture is like that of the opening. Furthermore, since it is preceded by less palpable patterns, it appears to be well shaped, like the opening theme. To take another example, the first fugue of the *Well-tempered Clavier* clearly involves melodic reiteration, but its harmonic articulation is a result of the operation of the law of return. Thus there are degrees of return both because recurrences may be only partially similar and because some aspects of the sound term may recur while others do not.

The law of return appears to operate most effectively where the given sound term is left incomplete. Since the sound term is a Gestalt which sets up forces toward a particular kind of closure, the only way it can be closed is by repeating it with a new and more final ending. A corollary of this would seem to be the fact that a varied recurrence of a well-shaped but incomplete term which has developed strong tendencies toward completion will seem more like a return than will a somewhat more exact recurrence of a closed sound term. In the former case the changes are understood as arising out of the necessity for closure. Conversely the more closed a sound term is, the more its recurrence is likely to be exact or almost exact.

The listener's opinion of the significance of any given repetition, and hence his impression of completeness, is partly a result of the experience of that aspect of style which is called form. Repetition has one meaning in a movement which is believed to be a fugue, another in one which is believed to be a theme and variations, and still another in one believed to be a sonata form. Moreover, the same general scheme of repetition may have different significations in different contexts. For instance, in a piece known to be a fugue, the imitative entrances of the fugal exposition arouse expectations of continuity and continuation. The repetitions do not give rise to saturation. However, a similar series of imitative entrances gives rise to different expectations if it forms part of the development section of a sonata-form movement, as, for instance, in the first movement of Beethoven's Piano Sonata, Op. 111. Here repetition and the texture to which it gives rise are not the norm; continuity of process is not expected, at least for any period of time; and repetition may well give rise to saturation if it continues for any length of time. In both cases not only are different expectations aroused but different standards of completeness are brought into play.

Fortunately the modes of repetition and the law of return are among the best understood principles in music. Therefore rather than expatiate in general upon these principles, let us return to the examination of a particular piece of music. Since the opening section of the fifth movement of Beethoven's String Quartet, Op. 131, furnishes an excellent example of the operation of the law of return, we once again turn to this music rather than to another example whose explication would involve a fairly lengthy preliminary analysis.

After the two introductory measures already discussed, the section opens with an eight-measure theme. The theme is patently incomplete both melodically and harmonically. But the listener's attitude at the end of it is neutral; that is, though he knows that the music will continue, he does not know whether the theme will be completed by a consequent phrase or will simply be repeated. Observe that had the consequent or concluding phrase been presented immediately after the antecedent, as indeed it easily could have been, no feeling of return would have been engendered. In other words, had Beethoven written the following (see Example 53), the second period would have constituted a varied and concluding reiteration of the first phrase. There would have been no feeling of strong tension toward closure, no suspense, and it would have received little attention. It would have been a pert theme with a rather witty conclusion, a sort of O'Henry ending. There would clearly have been no feeling of return.

What Beethoven actually does, however, is to repeat the opening phrase in a higher register. Once this has taken place, further reiteration is impossible. Another repetition of this phrase, even in its concluding form (measures 45–54), would have resulted either in anticlimax or in saturation. In order to create a forceful desire for return, it is necessary both to depart from the regularity and conciseness of the theme and, at the same time, to create unambiguous expectations. Beethoven at one and the same time begins to create rhythmic incompleteness and moves toward a harmonic position whose incompleteness will be more patent, i.e., the dominant (measures 19–24, Example 50). In the following measure the harmonic incompleteness is, as we have seen, heightened by increasing rhythmic incompleteness (Example 51). In fact, both grow together.

EXAMPLE 53

Notice that every feature of the music is changed in order to heighten our desire for return: rhythm and harmony are incomplete and, in the end, quite ambiguous, whereas earlier they were very clear and well formed; melodic motion, which in the opening phrase was strong and well patterned, is also destroyed; the tempo too is changed; and, finally, in measures 37–41 (Example 52) the distinction between figure and ground is almost completely annihilated.

But at the very moment when rhythm, harmony, texture, and even melody in the sense of pattern seem all but destroyed, the little figure which opens the movement and the first phrase raises our hopes and redirects our expectations of completion and return. Now we are certain as to what is coming. Expectation is definite and powerful, a fact which makes the delay created by the ritard

and fermata all the more forceful. Then in measure 45 there is a
return to the opening theme, which is now completed; and the completion is emphasized by the measures which follow. The satisfaction created by this return is not merely a function of the incompleteness of the opening measures but also a product of the creation
of further incompleteness in the middle part (measures 19–44).

What we experience at measure 45 is not simply the reiteration of
a theme heard earlier. We have returned to a melody which almost
had been destroyed, to a texture which is familiar, to a harmonic
motion which is certain and regular, to a tempo which had been
altered, and to a palpable unified Gestalt which had been dis-
rupted. Indeed, the feeling of return, the pleasure of resolution, is
so strong that the rather piquant flavor of the additional closing
measures (51–54) goes almost unnoticed unless it is called to our
attention. At all events, the effect of these measures would have
been much more noticeable had this version of the theme immediately followed the opening phrase, as in the construction given in
Example 53.

V

Principles of Pattern Perception:
The Weakening of Shape

Throughout the two preceding chapters we have been concerned either directly and explicitly or indirectly and by implication with the problem of shape and its articulation. Generally speaking the discussion has involved an examination of the way in which expectations are aroused and tendencies inhibited when well-articulated figures or processes are disturbed or delayed in some manner. Indeed, such delays and irregularities are most effective precisely when patterns and shapes are distinct and tangible; for it is then that expectations of continuation and closure are most clear and unambiguous.

The Nature of Shape

The apprehension of a series of physically discrete stimuli as constituting a pattern or shape results from the ability of the human mind to relate the constituent parts of the stimulus or stimulus series to one another in an intelligible and meaningful way. For an impression of shape to arise an order must be perceived in which the individual stimuli become parts of a larger structure and perform distinguishable functions within that structure. A shape or pattern, then, is a sound term, as defined in chapter ii, and it is meaningful and significant because its consequents can be envisaged with some degree of probability.[1]

One of the absolute and necessary conditions for the apprehension of shape, for the perception of any relationships at all, no matter what the style, is the existence of both similarities and differences among the several stimuli which constitute the series under consideration.

If the stimuli comprising the series cannot be perceived as being similar in any respect whatsoever, then they will fail to cohere, to form a group or unit, and will be perceived as separate, isolated, and discrete sounds, "signifying nothing." Since contrast and comparison can exist only where there is similarity or equality of some sort, the mental impression created by such a series will be one of dispersion, not disparity; of diffusion, not divergence; of novelty, not variety.

Complete similarity, proximity, and equality of stimulation, on the other hand, will create an undifferentiated homogeneity out of which no relationships can arise because there are no separable, individual identities to be contrasted, compared, or otherwise related. There will be coexistence and constancy, but not connection; uniformity and union, but not unity. In short, both total segregation and total uniformity will produce sensation, but neither will be apprehended as pattern or shape.

Because from both a temporal and a musico-spatial point of view the factors which in large measure are responsible for segregation and uniformity—factors such as similarity, proximity, and equality of stimulation—admit of varying degrees or gradations, the appraisal of shape is a relative one, depending upon the general level of differentiation and homogeneity prevalent in a particular musical style. That is, in a style in which the members of the stimulus series are not differentiated or segregated from one another in a particularly emphatic or marked manner, modest differences (though necessarily appreciable ones) will give rise to well defined, palpable shapes. While in a style marked by radical segregation and extreme differentiation, these same modest differences will produce only uniformity. To take the reverse case: a stimulus series which appears to be well articulated and clearly organized in a piece where differences are very marked might well seem chaotic and incoherent in a piece in which the level of uniformity was higher.

These observations call attention to another necessary condition for the apprehension of shape and pattern. Namely, it is not enough that differentiation and unification simply exist. The articulation must be sufficiently marked and salient relative to the context in which it appears to be noticed. The gradual accretion of relatively slight differences, which in the given stylistic context are subliminal, will not give rise to an impression of shape. For instance, inequality of stimulation will tend to produce segregation only "provided that the inequality entails abrupt change."[2] Thus a mode of differentiation which would have been incisive in a context of moderate similarity, proximity, and equality, might be subliminal in a style where these factors were more extreme. These remarks are also applicable to the perception of unification: if the factors making for unification are subliminal within the context, then no impression of shape will arise.

The fact that the apprehension of shape is a function of the norms of articulation established within a given style does not mean that any stimulation can create an impression of shape. As we have seen, neither total segregation nor total uniformity—no matter what the style—will create an impression of shape. But even between these extremes, shape does not seem to be completely relative. Some series of stimuli do, in fact, seem better shaped than others, irrespective of style. Indeed, were this not the case, all styles would seem aesthetically and psychologically equivalent—which they do not.

The basis for this seemingly absolute standard of articulation and differentiation is to be found in the fact that our comprehensive, over-all stylistic experience, our experience of Bach as well as of Bartók, of Mozart as well as of Monteverdi, gives rise to an all-embracing norm of pattern and shape, just as our total stylistic experience becomes the foundation for comprehensive norms of consonance and dissonance and for an over-all norm of texture. And the peremptory presence of this general standard enables us, even compels us, to compare (albeit unconsciously) the quality of Schubert's patterns with those of Schoenberg and those of Debussy with those of Dufay.

However, within the context of a particular work in a specific style the evaluation and appraisal of shape is relative. This relativity is a product of the psychological demand for distinct, substantial, good shape: it is a result of the operation of the law of Prägnanz.

If there is any articulation of the stimulus group into similarity and difference, proximity and remoteness, equality and disparity of stimulation, then the mind will probably find some basis (no matter how feeble or farfetched it may appear to be) for relating the stimuli to one another in an orderly and meaningful way—for apprehending the stimulus group as a shape or pattern. Indeed, even where no objective differentiation exists, the mind will, if at all possible, impose such differentiation. But neither the differentiation of the stimulus series nor the existence of unification between its several parts are sufficient conditions for the impression of shape. For the parts of the series must be related to one another in a consistent and orderly manner. They are so related and ordered by the social phenomenon we call style. And if we do not understand a given style, if we lack the proper habit responses, we will either fail to apprehend shape or, if we apprehend it in terms of another style, we will fail to comprehend it. That is, the impression of shape may arise because two style systems have sound stimuli in common, but such an impression will be incorrectly interpreted and, in point of fact, not really comprehended at all.

The Weakening of Shape

The fact that the appraisal of shape varies from style to style, and even from work to work within a single style, does not mean that all patterns or shapes in a particular work will be perceived as equally good. Some shapes will at times appear to be significantly stronger, more clearly articulated, than others.

The words "good" or "strong," "poor" or "weak" as used in the discussion of shape are not to be construed as implying value judgments. On the contrary, weak, ambiguous shapes may, as has been mentioned from time to time throughout this study, perform a valuable and vital function in creating and molding the affective aesthetic musical experience. For the lack of distinct, tangible shapes and of well-articulated modes of progression is capable of arousing powerful desires for, and expectations of, clarification and improvement.

This aspect of musical structure and expression is one which has unfortunately received but scant attention from music theorists, aestheticians, and critics, who, enticed and befuddled by the honorific garlands so plausibly bestowed upon regularity, symmetry, and pristine clarity, have continually construed "inevitability" to mean unequivocal progression. These scholars, in their intricate and ingenious attempts to derive all the melodic materials of a musical work from a single motivic "germ" or to subsume all harmonic changes under the structure of a single cadence, have with Talmudic tenacity confused both unification and uniformity with unity. Yet the fact of the matter is that some of the greatest music is great precisely because the composer has not feared to let his music tremble on the brink of chaos, thus inspiring the listener's awe, apprehension, and anxiety and, at the same time, exciting his emotions and his intellect.

A stimulus series, then, is well shaped when its progress, its articulation into phases of activity and phases of rest, its modes of continuation, its manner of completion and closure, and even its temporary disturbances and irregularities are intelligible to the practiced listener and enable him to envisage with some degree of specificity and accuracy what the later stages of the particular musical process will be. Because good shape is intelligible in this sense, it creates a psychological atmosphere of certainty, security, and patent purpose, in which the listener feels a sense of control and power as well as a sense of specific tendency and definite direction.

Because, as has already been observed, the apprehension of shape is in part dependent upon the existence of a balanced relationship between uniformity and differentiation, the impression of shape can be weakened by the exaggeration or intensification of either force within the context of a given musical work. Shape may, from this point of view, be regarded as a kind of stylistic "mean" lying between the extremes of chaotic overdifferentiation and primordial homogeneity. Thus while a balanced relationship, as established within the style, produces an impression of well-organized patterns, exaggerated differentiation gives rise to *dis*organized ones, and intensified uniformity results in *un*organized ones.

It is extremely difficult, if not impossible, to weaken the impression of shape through exaggerating differences without destroying shape completely—without producing meaningless chaos. The causes of this difficulty lie in the characteristics of the musical stimuli themselves, in the capabilities of the human ear, and in the nature of the human mind.

Because musical stimuli are necessarily similar to each other in many respects, it is almost impossible to isolate tones through dissimilarity. The very fact that musical materials are as a rule tonal means that they have such physical characteristics as frequency, amplitude, and timbre in common. It is likewise difficult to achieve an impression of tonal segregation (non-proximity). For the mind can with the aid of the overtone series relate pitches in widely separated registers.

Furthermore, differences in pitch, volume, and duration are limited by the physiological abilities of the human ear. For only certain pitches can be used in music, are audible to human ears, and those must be of a certain volume and duration if they are to be perceived. Thus the number of stimuli and their quality is limited.

Most important of all is the fact that if segregation or differentiation, whether spatial or temporal, is not so extreme as to preclude all possibility of pattern apprehension, then some sort of shapes will probably arise. For the human mind, operating under the aegis of the law of Prägnanz, will go to almost any lengths to avoid the doubts and anxieties which are created by ambiguity. That is, the mind will tend to apprehend a group of stimuli as a pattern or shape if there is any possible way of relating the stimuli to one another.

Indeed, if weak shapes have resulted largely from exaggerated segregation of stimuli (e.g., extreme distance between pitches, excessive temporal disjunction, or both), then the mind will prefer to regard the stimulus series as being incomplete (see pp. 130 f.); and since further developments will be expected to complete what was incomplete or to effect some other sort of clarification, the feeling of mental control will not be lost. Or uncertainty and doubt may be avoided if the series can be or is understood as having a special designative meaning. For example, if segregation (non-proximity), disparity (non-similarity), and inequality of stimulation can be understood as a humorous or grotesque distortion of some normative type of pattern construction, then the doubt and anxiety which might otherwise have arisen can be rationalized and removed.

Though exaggerated differentiation would theoretically provide a method of weakening shape, it is extremely difficult to achieve and hence extremely rare. Indeed, this author has been able to discover no clear-cut example which is not programatic in character.

Uniformity

Uniformity arises where the several elements of musical organization—pitch progression, rhythm, harmony, and timbre—combine to create equality, similarity, and equiproximity of stimulation on the same architectonic level.

In terms of pitch progression, uniformity is produced when a series of tones, whether conjunct or disjunct, are equidistant from one another and are differentiated in no other way; e.g., rhythmically or harmonically. For it is only by virtue of the existence of difference of distance that the mind is able to establish ordered relationships between successive tones. If all the members of a series are equally distant, none will be marked for consciousness, and hence there will be no focal points in the series with reference to which organization can take place and shape can arise.

Psychologically speaking, what happens here, and this applies with equal force to rhythmic and harmonic uniformity, is that the uniform series, lacking internal articulation, establishes no points of activity and rest. Consequently the listener is unable to envisage the ultimate goal, the logical stopping place of the series. He is able to apprehend the mode of continuation but is unable to comprehend the basis for completion and closure. The series is, so to speak, frictionless and out of control. Doubt and uncertainty arise not because the listener does not know what the next stimulus is going to be—he knows, for instance, if the series is a chromatic scale that the next tone will probably be a half step away from the one being heard at the moment—but because he is unable to envisage where the series will end, to control its destiny mentally.

Of course, if equal stimulation is only momentary, if the ambiguity is resolved almost immediately, then doubt, uncertainty, and anxiety will be transient and evanescent. But when uniformity persists for a relatively long time, the series will have a cumulative effect, arousing strong desires for a return to more intelligible and controllable shape and a more certain and secure psychological atmosphere.

Because chromatic and whole-tone scales and augmented and diminished triads all involve intervallic equidistance, they create uniformity and produce ambiguity. And it is no accident that such weakly shaped, ambiguous series have tended to become identified with affectivity and have so often been used to express intense emotion, apprehension, and anxiety (see pp. 218 f.).

The following fragment from Liszt's Piano Sonata is a particularly interesting example of uniformity of pitch succession because it is doubly chromatic; that is, chromaticism exists both within the groups of sixteenth notes and between them (Example 54). Theo-

EXAMPLE 54

retically this series could have ended anywhere and closed in any key at all. For instance, had motive *x*, which breaks the series, occurred after the first group in the second measure, the final key would have been either B major or G-sharp minor. Or had the series continued until the end of the measure, the final key would have been F minor or A-flat major. This duality is possible because the cadential motive (*x*) is itself somewhat ambiguous. For the final tone A might have been the tonic of A major as well as the third of F-sharp minor. This, incidentally, is entirely appropriate since the passage quoted comes at the conclusion of a section which consistently employs, both melodically and harmonically, a diminished seventh chord that might have been in either A major or F-sharp minor.

Uniformity of pitch succession must be supported by uniformity of rhythm if an impression of homogeneity and weakened shape is to arise. Conversely rhythmic uniformity, produced by equality of accent and duration, must be complemented by uniformity in other aspects of the series—such as pitch succession, harmonic progression, and timbre—if the over-all impression is to be one of homogeneity. Thus a major scale or a cadential chord progression, though realized in tones of equal duration, will not seem weakly formed or ambiguous because their articulation literally creates accentuation, even where no change in physical intensity is made.

Uniformity like articulation may be architectonic in nature. It may be established on all levels, as in the example from the Liszt Sonata, or it may exist on some levels but not on others. In the latter case it is generally one of the higher levels, though not the highest, which is uniform. Furthermore, on some levels all aspects of the stimulus series may be uniform, while on other levels some aspects may exhibit uniformity and others may not; for instance, rhythm may be uniform though pitch succession is not.

In Example 55 from the first movement of Bruckner's Seventh Symphony, the stimulus series is well articulated on the lowest level but is weakly shaped on the higher architectonic level. On the lowest level the articulation of the rhythm into an anapest foot is clear and unambiguous. But since the series consists only of anapests, the rhythm of the next higher level is uniform. It is a series of beats

EXAMPLE 55

of equal duration and apparently equal accentuation.[3] The same is true of pitch succession. On the primary architectonic level a well-shaped motive consisting of a fourth, followed by a half step, followed by a minor third arises. But on the second level pitch progression is uniform—merely a succession of minor thirds (see analysis *a*). Or the series might be analyzed as a series of augmented fourths a minor third apart.

Notice, however, that the primary groups are not all precisely equivalent in pitch succession. For the third group in each measure is slightly different in organization from the other two (see analysis *b*). However, because of the general uniformity of pitch succession and temporal duration as well as because of its inconspicuous placement in the series, this slight differentiation between groups, though important in facilitating the changes which bring the series to its conclusion, does not upset or weaken the prevailing feeling of homogeneity. In short, the differences are subliminal. The listener becomes consciously aware of the differentiation, if at all, only in retrospect, only after the passage is over and the existence of the difference has been pointed up by the part it plays in moving the line smoothly to its conclusion.

Harmonic uniformity may arise: (1) as a result of equality of interval within the vertical harmonic organization itself; (2) because, though the vertical organization is differentiated, all the harmonies in the series are precisely alike; (3) where, though differentiation between successive harmonies occurs and a process is developed, the progressions making up the series are all equal; and (4) where any or all of these modes of achieving uniformity are combined.

As was the case with pitch succession, if the vertical organization is undifferentiated as to intervallic distance, then there can be no focal point around which organization can take place—out of which shape can arise. Thus, for instance, a diminished seventh chord, an augmented triad, or a harmonic structure built upon equal fourths will have no root and no shape and hence no tendency. In many contexts the root is implied or the series is "controlled" in some other way. This is the case with the following series of diminished seventh chords occurring near the end of the last movement of Brahms' Second Piano Sonata (Example 56). The ambiguity of

EXAMPLE 56

this series, resulting not only from the uniformity of the constituent chords but also from the uniformity of their succession by equal half steps, is somewhat mitigated by the presence of the G in the bass, which acts as a focal point in relation to which the upper part can be organized. The G creates a sense of tonal stability and control which makes the feeling of ambiguity and uncertainty less forceful than it might otherwise have been.

The ambiguity resulting from uniformity of chord construction can also be considerably meliorated by good melodic or rhythmic articulation. Thus in the following example from the conclusion of Schumann's *Humoreske*, Op. 20 (Example 57), though the chords

EXAMPLE 57

are all diminished sevenths and hence potentially ambiguous, the over-all rhythmic and harmonic sequence keeps the listener oriented and assures him that the last chord is the dominant of C.

As noted above, uniformity may arise because all of the chords are constructed in precisely the same way, though the several chords comprising the series are in themselves differentiated. This is the case in the following succession from Debussy's *Nocturne*, "Nuages" (Example 58). Here uniformity of chord succession is somewhat

EXAMPLE 58 *

* Reprint permission granted by Jean Jobert, Paris, France, copyright owner; Elkan-Vogel Co., Inc., Philadelphia, Pa., agent.

intensified by the manner of chord construction; that is, the outer voices are very consonant and tend to make the internal differences seem minimal. On the other hand, there is some melodic articulation in the series, though this is too minimized by the fact that the two halves of the series are in this respect equivalent.

Finally, it should be noted that in the Debussy example and to some extent in the Brahms example as well ambiguity is also a product of rhythmic uniformity. To put it somewhat differently, the equality of rhythmic stimulation allows the uniformity of the other elements to take their full effect.

On the higher architectonic levels harmonic melodic uniformity may result, not from the fact that the chords themselves are constructed of equal intervals or from the fact that all the chords of the series are of the same construction, but because the successive groups, whether primarily melodic or both melodic and harmonic, are equivalent. Uniformity here is a matter of continuous and equivalent process. What is commonly called a "sequence" is a type of uniformity.

One of the most common types of melodic-harmonic sequences is one that moves harmonically through the cycle of fifths, either descending (as in A1 in Example 59) or ascending (as in A3).

EXAMPLE 59

Uniformity results, not only from the fact that every other chord is the dominant of the chord which follows it, but also from the fact that one of the voices follows a chromatic line while the other voice moves in minor thirds and half steps. Other versions of such a sequence of dominants are possible; as, for instance, in *A2*, where the series follows not the cycle of fifths but a chromatically descending pattern, or in *B1*, where the implied root progression moves by minor thirds and fifths and the guiding or conjunct line moves by whole tones.[4]

Any series in which a continuous process is developed will tend to be ambiguous because the point at which the process will be broken or the series concluded is in doubt. This is the case in the following continuous schemes (Example 60). In the first of these

EXAMPLE 60

(*C1*), tonal harmony is employed and, though the steps of the conjunct line are not all equal, the groups are equal: the conjunct line moves by half step, whole step, half step, etc. Because of this equality of groups, the series could continue indefinitely in a frictionless way; and there is no way of knowing at what point the series will be articulated and reach its conclusion. Many other such series might be constructed. For instance, in *C4*, *C5*, and *C6* there are no functional, classical harmonic relationships, but the sequences are, nevertheless, uniform in their mode of progression.

Such equal though harmonically non-functional passages are not uncommon in contemporary music. The following excerpt from the Finale of Bartók's Fifth String Quartet is given as an example (Example 61). In this instance we find not only uniformity in the succession of two-measure groups which descend in whole-tones but also uniformity within the groups. For a glance at the pitch succession of the lower voices makes it clear that the lower voices are moving through the augmented triad (see analysis of reduction given in Example 61). In addition to this uniformity of pitch succession, there is also uniformity of rhythm and motive between measures in both upper and lower voices.

EXAMPLE 61 *

Many different forms of continuous uniformity are possible. For instance, the suspension technique used in fourth-species counterpoint or a variant of it, a series of prepared appoggiaturas, may give rise to continuous processes, particularly where the controlling line is tonally ambiguous. Although in the example given here the interval "pulling" the upper tone down, causing the series to move, is either a major or minor seventh, this need not be the case. Theoretically such a series could be constructed at any interval. As a matter of fact, some of the sequences given in Example 59 (*A2* and *B2*) are also forms of fourth species (suspension) counterpoint.

EXAMPLE 62

Continuous sequential processes need not, of course, seem ambiguous. If the series is tonal (or differentiated in some other way) and well articulated as to rhythm and melody, both the successive steps of the sequence and the ultimate point of its completion may seem to be predictable. But where other aspects of the series tend toward uniformity such a series may give rise to uncertainty and doubt, even though it is not completely uniform. For once such a continuous sequential process is established, it develops an inner momentum and drive which enable it to veer very easily in the direction of uniformity or away from the envisaged point of completion. For this reason irregularities in such processes will not, as a rule, be apprehended as articulating the process but will appear as disturbances and deviations from the process which add to the insecurity and uncertainty inherent in the fact of continuous process itself. Where the process is regular and uniform, the listener knows or believes that he knows what the next stimulus will be but is in doubt as to where the process will be broken. Where such seemingly continuous processes are irregular, the listener is able to envisage neither where the process will break nor what the next step in the process will be.

The statement that the listener does not know or is doubtful as to where such continuous processes will end or break must be understood in a conditional sense. What the listener really doubts is the manner in which a sometimes only dimly envisaged goal will be reached. He has a general feeling as to what the final goal of the series is, but he is uncertain as to how the present process will get him there and what detours and obstacles will be encountered en route. And it is only at the point of "reversal," the point at which the process is broken and another mode of continuation takes its place, that the listener finally is able to envisage his goal with any degree of security. It is thus the point of reversal of process which constitutes the climax and turning point of the passage, the point at which doubt and anxiety are replaced by more certain anticipation.

These facts of process continuation are well understood by the practiced listener. Because of this, sequential process will generally tend to raise doubts in the listener's mind, will seem more or less ambiguous. The controlling factor for the listener is context. If the sequence occurs in a generally controlled context, for instance, as part of or in connection with an important and well-articulated theme, then it would probably give rise to minimal tension and uncertainty. But if the continuous process occurs in connection with other types of uniformity—in a passage which is clearly developmental—it might well create powerful doubts and anxieties, even though it apparently is quite tonal and well articulated; for in this case the listener is aware that such passages are unpredictable, that the series may veer with great ease from its present course.

Finally, it is important to make clear that it is the hypothetical meaning of the several successive stimuli which is ambiguous, not necessarily their evident meaning. A series is ambiguous because the listener is unable to envisage with any reliable or decisive degree of probability what the future terms will be. Indeed, because of the listener's attitude toward such passages, almost all sound terms tend to seem equivocal. However, once the consequent term arrives, the listener may well be able to understand its relationships to the terms which have preceded it. Yet even this understanding is conditional. For the determinate meaning of any given sound term can only be known when the whole passage has been completed and a clear point of stability and orientation has been reached.

The development section (measures 72–86) of the Finale of Haydn's Piano Sonata in A-Flat Major furnishes an excellent example of uniformity of rhythm and pitch succession coupled with continuous sequential processes (Example 63).

EXAMPLE 63

In the first place, a glance at the example shows that there is general rhythmic uniformity. At the beginning the rhythmic structure within the measure is somewhat problematical. Because the passage begins with an anacrusis, the first rhythmic group is perceived as an amphibrach, and this feeling of amphibrach rhythm tends to perpetuate itself. In order for this to take place, the second beat of each measure must function both as the end of one group and the beginning of the next (see Example 64). This impression of the dovetailing of groups is strengthened by the fact that the final tone of each measure is a preparation for the first beat of the following measure and also a resolution of the first beat of the measure in which it appears. The rhythmic articulation within measures could be clarified were the performer to make the final eighth note of each measure an anacrusis to the first beat of the next measure

EXAMPLE 64

by playing it slightly nearer to the downbeat and accenting it somewhat, as in Example 65. However, since such a performance would tend to weaken the effect of the passage, this would seem a questionable interpretation. Indeed, any "interpretive" accentuation on the part of the performer is unnecessary and uncalled for. The passage should be played quite uniformly. Incidentally this is an example of meter without rhythm. The beats are clearly differentiated into accented and unaccented but grouping is inappropriate and undesirable.

EXAMPLE 65

After measure 7 (as numbered in Example 63) this overlapping of rhythmic groups ends and a fairly clear trochaic rhythm, implicit in the lower voice from measure 3, emerges within each measure. But there is still uniformity between measures; hence no impression of rhythm arises on the higher architectonic level. Incidentally it is just at this point, where the rhythm within the bar becomes clarified, that the melodic and harmonic structure of the series becomes most uniform, counteracting the clarification of rhythmic shape.

The line of pitch succession, though not completely uniform, could hardly be termed well articulated or distinctly shaped, since it lacks those changes in pitch direction and those differences in accent and duration which create well-defined substantial shapes.

Nor is the scale described by the outer voices unambiguous. At first it might be interpreted as the scale of F minor, later as C minor, or, even, as an altered scale in B-flat. And just as it seems fairly clear that the scale is that of E-flat major, which it really is, the uncertainty of chromatic uniformity is introduced.

The absence of a well-shaped melodic pattern is important. For were rhythm and melody distinctly shaped, the attention of the listener would be directed to these and the feeling of security and control found in such clearly articulated shapes would considerably diminish the suspense and uncertainty engendered by the uniformity of the other aspects of the musical process. This occurs at times in music of the nineteenth century, where ambiguous harmonic progressions bear such distinct and palpable themes that the uncertainty of the harmonic continuum is more or less nullified because the listener focuses his attention upon the expressive and well-shaped tunes.

The listener's doubts and anxieties are partly a product of his own stylistic experience, his awareness that this is part of a development section and that passages in such sections tend to be unpredictable, deceptive, and irregular. And the general uniformity coupled with the presence of obviously sequential processes confirms the listener's attitudes and accentuates his feeling of tension.

At the outset of this passage a combination of suspension technique and harmonic sequence create a momentum of process in which what articulation there is, is more than counterbalanced by the ever present possibility of equiprobable alternative consequents. A schematization of these measures (measures 1–6) is given in Example 66 together with some of the alternative consequents which might have been forthcoming. For instance, the sequences might have continued unvaried (as in *a*), moving through E-flat major and D-flat major to a cadence in F minor, the key in which the passage begins. Such "false" modulations are not uncommon. The process might (as in *b*) have been broken by using an augmented sixth chord, which would have moved to the dominant of C minor, and after this new *modus operandi* the harmony might have progressed through B-flat to the tonic A-flat major. Or the suspension technique might have continued for another measure (as in *c*), reaching the dominant E-flat earlier than is actually the case. Finally, had the original *modus operandi* been perpetuated still further (as in *d*), the same point would have been reached that is actually achieved through the introduction of chromaticism.

EXAMPLE 66

This last observation points up the fact that neither the introduction of chromaticism in measure 7 nor the passage taken as a whole can be understood and accounted for solely on the basis of the necessities of modulation and the desire to return to the tonic. Had Haydn's purpose in writing this passage been merely to return to A-flat major, then it would seem that he went to a lot of unnecessary trouble. For as every student of elementary harmony knows, there is no trick to modulating from F minor to A-flat major. It can be done with a couple of diatonic chords.

The introduction of chromaticism in the upper voice serves several different though complementary purposes. First, it creates enough variety within the continuous process of harmonic sequence to preclude tedium. Second, it allows the sequence to become more uniform, avoiding the more apparent articulation such as takes place in measure 5. And third, it allows the basic process to continue without creating a stylistically unacceptable whole-tone scale in the upper voice, which would have been the case had the suspension technique been continued (see Example 67).

EXAMPLE 67

But these ends could have been achieved with other means. It is to meaning and content that we must turn if the reasons for this change are to be fully comprehended. By emphasizing the uniformity of pitch progression in the upper voice and of harmonic sequence progression throughout, chromaticism and regularity intensify the inner impulsion and drive of the series, weakening the listener's sense of control, his ability to envisage the point at which the series will break and articulation will take place. While in process the chromaticism and potential uniformity of chord progression make the passage seem almost formless and, in terms of more remote tendencies, incomprehensible.

Yet the passage is really not as uniform as has been implied in the foregoing discussion. Though the outer voices are uniform and regular, the inner voice moves in a somewhat deceptive manner. The irregularity of this voice not only produces a certain amount of variety, though this is minimized by the more patent uniformity of the outer voices, but, by effecting changes and deceptive progressions in the harmonic progression, it also intensifies the listener's sense of doubt and insecurity. For the listener is now able to envisage neither the terminal point of the series nor even the next term of the series. This is illustrated in Example 68, in which the sequence, together with its presumed line of harmonic root progression, is schematized as it would have been had it been completely regular.

In this version of the sequence the roots of the chords, beginning in measure 6, are all a fifth apart. From measure 7 through measure 9 each chord is the dominant of the one which follows it, so that the progression is, in a sense, completely uniform even between chords; that is, as A is to B, so B is to C, and so forth. Between measures there is precise equivalence of process. Here each successive chord

Implied root progressions

EXAMPLE 68

of the sequence is predictable, but the terminal point of the series is not.

In Haydn's variant of this regular, uniform progression, measures 8 and 9 contain irregular, deceptive resolutions (Example 69). Because of its place in the sequence, the diminished triad in the beginning of measure 8 sounds as though it were the dominant of A-flat; but this chord moves deceptively to F minor. Since the ambiguous diminished triad has already been resolved in two different ways, the listener is almost completely undecided when it appears again in measure 9 whether it will move to G-flat major (in the manner of measure 7), to E-flat minor (in the manner of measure 8), or, perhaps, even to C minor. In short, he is now in doubt not only as to the terminal point of the series but also as to the following term of the series.

EXAMPLE 69

The insistence in the foregoing discussion upon the importance of uniformity and ambiguity in arousing uncertainty and anxiety does not imply that this passage is chaotic or unstructured. If the main outlines (Example 70) of the series are abstracted from the vitally important ornaments which tend to obscure them, it be-

EXAMPLE 70

comes apparent that the series follows a definite over-all plan, in which the outer voices, moving in parallel tenths, delineate a descending scale in the key of E-flat (major and minor). But this structure becomes clear and is understood only after it has been completed and the series has been terminated. Only when the sequence is timeless in memory can the relationship of its parts to one another and to the total series be comprehended.

The terminal part of this series, its return to more decisive, clear-cut shape takes place in measure 10, where the upper voice changes the direction of its motion from descending to ascending, and the lower voice moves by skips of a fourth from F to B-flat to E-flat, creating an incisive accent and motion in the bass.

When measure 11 is reached (Example 71), the listener is, so to speak, "out of the woods"; he knows where he is going and envisages

EXAMPLE 71

the goal with clarity and certainty. He expects a return to the tonic, which is necessary for a feeling of completeness, and to more distinct and palpable shapes, in particular to the first theme of the movement. Though expectation is now very specific, it is not to be fulfilled straightaway. There is a waiting period, a delay on dominant harmony, in which the mind is able to orient itself, evaluating what has taken place and adjusting itself to what is now impinging.

Minimal Differences

Uniformity is a mental fact, not a physical one. Not all differentiation necessarily creates an impression of good shape. The differentiation must be decisive enough and salient enough, relative to the particular context in which it appears, to play an appreciable role in articulating shape. Some instances of subliminal differentiation have already been cited, e.g., in connection with the Bruckner and Debussy examples. The present discussion will, for the most part, be concerned with certain aspects of harmonic differentiation, with the uniformity that arises through the accretion of small differences.

Harmonic uniformity may arise because the difference between harmonic terms is not great enough to create a sense of progression. That is, a change may appear to be a variation of an already presented term rather than a motion to a new term. There may be alteration, but not succession.

Although the criteria determining what constitutes harmonic progression—unambiguous chord succession—become established as part of the listener's stylistic responses, the stylistic norms of well-articulated succession are themselves, in part at least, products of the need for sufficiently marked differentiation between harmonic terms. It is partly because of the necessity for appreciable differences between successive harmonic terms that the harmonic progressions that are least ambiguous are those which involve changes of at least two tones between chords. This is made amply clear by an examination, for instance, of Piston's "Table of Usual Root Progressions" (see p. 54). The most decisive progression of all in the delineation of tonality, the one from the subdominant to the dominant to the tonic, is so devised that the first two triads have no tones in common and that each of these triads has only one tone in common with the tonic to which they resolve.[5] Other progressions might be devised involving complete tonal change, but all of them would of necessity employ one chord having two tones in common with the tonic, thus weakening the total effect of progression. Further evidence of the importance of marked and appreciable pitch changes between harmonic structures is furnished by the fact that when chords have their root and third in common, they tend to serve as substitutes for one another in terms of function. The submediant (VI) may serve as a substitute for the tonic (I), the supertonic (II) may serve as a substitute for the subdominant (IV), and the mediant (III) may serve as a substitute for the dominant (V).

Harmonic articulation is not merely a matter of pitch differences between successive chords. The degree of articulation also depends upon the manner in which the chords are constructed (whether there is general uniformity of construction or not), the way in which the voices (pitches) move from chord to chord (whether by conjunct or disjunct motion), and the rhythmic articulation of the harmonic changes in question. For instance, a progression from the tonic chord to that built on the sixth degree of the scale can be accomplished by moving only one tone (as in I*a* in Example 72), in which case the feeling of progression is minimal; or it can be achieved using disjunct motion in the outer voices (as in I*b*), in which case the sense of harmonic progression is substantially

EXAMPLE 72

strengthened. Likewise, variety of chord construction may create a sense of well-defined motion, as is the case in II*b* as contrasted with II*a*. It is clear, from this point of view, that the apprehension of harmonic progression is partly a function of melodic articulation. Hence the continued prohibition of parallel fifths and octaves, even after linear independence was no longer a prime concern of musical style.

Decisive, clearly articulated harmonic progression is not, of course, necessarily a desideratum. Vague and ambiguous progressions, created by minimal differentiation, may play an important role in creating tensions, uncertainties, and expectation.

This is the case in the introductory measures of the second movement of Berlioz's *Symphonie Fantastique* (Example 73). Before discussing the nature and effect of minimal differentiation in this passage, it should be noted that these are able to take their full effect because the passage (measures 1–29) is quite uniform as to pitch succession, texture, and instrumentation and quite indecisive and ambiguous as to rhythm. The opening measures of the movement establish the general pattern, which continues through the first twenty-nine measures:

EXAMPLE 73

The triadic figure in the cellos and basses in the third and fourth measures and the arpeggio in the fifth measure in the harp could hardly be called well shaped since they involve no real melodic progression. The continuous tremolo in the strings tends to accentuate the general uniformity of instrumental color and texture. What rhythmic articulation there is, is a product of harmonic change; and, since, as we shall see, this is minimal, so is the feeling of rhythmic accentuation. Only toward the end of the passage where the triadic figure recurs at two measure intervals and the harmonic changes, though still ambiguous, are more marked does there seem to be an intensification of rhythm, creating a feeling of increased excitement, quickening tempo, and the approach of a resolution to clarity and certainty.

The harmonic ambiguity of this passage is the product of minimal differentiation between successive vertical structures. This is made very clear by the abstract of the harmonic motion of the first thirty-three measures of the introduction (Example 74). Observe, for in-

EXAMPLE 74

stance, (1) that up to measure 13 only one tone is changed in each successive harmony; (2) that the slight disjunct motion in the lower voice (the skips from A to F to A and so forth), though they do articulate the motion somewhat, are minimized by the static quality of the basic bass line, which moves only from A to A-sharp; and (3) that stylistically the harmonic relationships established by this particular series give rise to no clear-cut probability relationships, provide no basis for envisaging the nature of the next term in the series. Even the motion from measure 12 to measure 13, the first stylistically unambiguous progression, involves as little motion and change as possible. Only after measure 19 does the degree of harmonic change increase, i.e., two tones are changed in each succeeding chord and once (from measures 21 to 22) three. But these progressions, though they are more marked and create a sense of increased motion, are no less ambiguous. For not only does this series fail to establish stylistically unambiguous harmonic relationships but just at this point other aspects of the musical structure become increasingly uniform (see brackets in Example 74). That is, the chords in general move in parallel motion; the outer voices move chromatically in octaves, tending to obscure what inner articulation there is; and the measures are motivically and rhythmically precisely equivalent to one another.

Though the listener is not able to envisage the next term in the series with any greater specificity than before, the increased harmonic motion in these measures (measures 20–26) does perform an important function. It creates a feeling of intensified activity, a sense of the approach to, and impending arrival of, a decisive point of structural articulation. This feeling is heightened in several ways. First of all, more marked and noticeable harmonic changes together with more regular motivic repetition bring about an increased sense of accentuation from measure 19 on. Both because of the general uniformity of the passage and because of the listener's awareness that this is not the real substance of the movement, this repetition of the motive in the bass gives rise to those expectations of change which we have called "saturation." The gradually growing crescendo also intensifies the sense that important musical events, the arrival at regular progressions and well-shaped themes, are in the offing. These expectations receive final confirmation just at the end of these measures, where the entrance of the woodwinds (measure 28) acts as a sign of the coming change. But it is only when the six-four chord (so striking because of its brilliantly major sound, its open spacing, and its full orchestral setting) arrives that the listener is really sure of his orientation and certain that his expectations will not be disappointed.

Before concluding this discussion of minimal differences, it should be pointed out that the distinction between uniformity and differentiation is not always as marked and obvious as it has been in most of the examples cited above. Uncertainty may arise because the listener is unable to decide whether the stimulus series is thematic or not. For instance a sound term that is neither markedly uniform nor clearly articulated may make the listener uncertain as to how to interpret the series as a whole. He may not be sure whether he is hearing the real theme or an introduction involving thematic anticipation.

The opening measures of the second movement of Schubert's Seventh Symphony in C Major (Example 75) provide an instance of this equivocal type of articulation. Here the upper voices are, generally speaking, quite uniform and homogeneous. There is little melodic motion and what there is not only moves by semitones but

Andante con moto.

EXAMPLE 75

is confined to the inner voices where its effect is minimized. Although stylistically the harmonic progressions are unambiguous, there is only a limited feeling of harmonic progression because of the minimal linear changes and because the changes consist only of an alteration of tonic and dominant harmony. What rhythmic articulation there is in the upper voices is produced by the harmonic fluctuations, and these could hardly be said to produce a strongly articulated rhythmic structure.

Taken by themselves these aspects of the stimulus series would probably lead the listener to conclude that this was definitely an introduction, an accompaniment figure over which a melody was still to appear. But the presence of a rather well-shaped melody in the bass precludes such a definite, unequivocal interpretation. Rhythmically this lower voice is very distinctly articulated. And even though the pitch successions seem somewhat static because the melody continually moves through the tonic triad, the passage as a whole might seem thematic, were it not for the listener's awareness that in music of this style the melody is usually, though not invariably, in one of the upper voices.

The equivocal balance between the forces of uniformity and

those of differentiation, together with the listener's stylistic experience, create uncertainty as to whether the series is to be understood
as an introductory "prestate" of the theme or whether it is the theme
itself. The expectations of clarification to which this ambiguity gives
rise are satisfied in measure 8, where the entrance of what is obviously the real theme enables the listener to understand, in retrospect, the significance of the opening measures. He now knows that
the passage was an introduction in which some features of the main
melody were anticipated. Thus while the hypothetical meaning of
the passage is ambiguous, its evident meaning is clear and unequivocal.

The equivocal character of such passages is perhaps best demonstrated by showing that other equally ambivalent series may in other
cases be the real thematic substance of a piece. The opening measures of Mozart's Piano Concerto in D Minor (K. 466), for instance,
are just as doubtful in character as those in the second movement
of Schubert's Seventh Symphony. Rhythmically and melodically
they are more uniform, more like an introduction or even like an
accompaniment over which a melody or theme might be expected
to appear (Example 76). Yet, as the passage gradually evolves and
the series becomes progressively more differentiated, the listener
realizes that this is the main material of the opening section of the

EXAMPLE 76

movement. In short, though the hypothetical meaning of the opening of the Mozart Concerto is in a very general way similar to that
of the Schubert movement, the evident meaning is very different.

The mental demand for good shape is, of course, conditioned and
modified by the stylistic experience of the listener and his awareness
of the kind of music to which he is listening. For instance, while
listening to the development section of the Haydn Sonata discussed
above or the introduction to the second movement of the Berlioz

Symphony, the practiced listener is aware that these passages are not as well shaped as they should be relative to the stylistic norm—that they are not, in a sense, the "main event."

But in other musical stylistic situations his attitude toward weakly defined shape may be quite different, and this difference in attitude will modify his responses. For example, the free, rhapsodic, toccata-like pieces of the baroque period, though perhaps exhibiting intelligible shape when viewed as a whole (after the piece has been concluded), often appear to be diffuse and amorphous when viewed in terms of their parts and their succession. Though this lack of well-defined, articulate patterns does arouse the desire for, and expectation of, more distinct and substantial shapes, the practiced listener who understands the nature of such free and effusive pieces tempers his psychological desire for better shape with the knowledge that such "preludes" will eventually lead either to more defined shapes within the piece or to another piece with a more palpable pattern. Such a listener, following musical progress as best he can, awaits the outcome, if not with perfect equanimity, at least without the intense impatience and anxiety that similar passages might arouse in other stylistic contexts.

Texture

Texture has to do with the ways in which the mind groups concurrent musical stimuli into simultaneous figures, a figure and accompaniment (ground), and so forth. Like other musical processes textural organization, or the lack of it, may give rise to expectation.

According to Koffka, "if conditions are such as to produce segregation of larger and smaller units, the smaller will, *ceteris paribus*, become figure; the larger ground." [6] Does this mean that in a polyphonic piece smaller fragments will necessarily be perceived as figures and the longer parts as ground? For instance, will a well-articulated theme presented in augmentation become a ground on which shorter though equally well-articulated motives will appear? The answer is that such a distribution of texture is not necessarily apprehended in terms of a figure-ground distribution but can quite readily be perceived as the co-existence of several independent, well-articulated figures.

Koffka tends to emphasize the necessity of a figure-ground distribution because he is primarily concerned with visual experience. Figures seen in visual space always appear to be projected against or framed by a ground of some sort just as these words are seen on a ground, the white paper on which they are printed. It is difficult, if not impossible, even to imagine a visual figure without also imagining the more continuous, homogeneous ground against which it appears. But in "aural space," in music, there is no given ground; there is no necessary, continuous stimulation, against which all figures must be perceived. The only thing that is continuous in aural experience is unorganized, timeless silence—the absence of any stimulation whatsoever.[7]

Due to the absence of a necessary, given ground in aural experience, the mind of the listener is able to organize the data presented to it by the senses in several different ways. The musical field can be perceived as containing: (1) a single figure without any ground at all, as, for instance, in a piece for solo flute; (2) several figures without any ground, as in a polyphonic composition in which the several parts are clearly segregated and are equally, or almost equally, well shaped; (3) one or sometimes more than one figure accompanied by a ground, as in a typical homophonic texture of the eighteenth or nineteenth centuries; (4) a ground alone, as in the introduction to a musical work—a song, for instance—where the melody or figure is obviously still to come; or (5) a superimposition of small motives which are similar but not exactly alike and which have little real independence of motion, as in so-called heterophonic textures.

Which of these various organizations or combinations of them the mind imposes upon the sensory materials presented to it depends upon the psychological demand for good shape (upon the operation of the law of Prägnanz) and upon the attitude and expectations of the experienced and practiced listener.

The psychological demand for good shape not only impels the mind to articulate the stimuli presented to it into well-shaped figures and patterns but also makes the total set of relationships resulting from such articulation as simple and distinct as possible. For instance, if the over-all articulation is simpler when a piece for a single instrument is understood as implying several "lines" or voices, then this mode of organization is the one that will probably appear; while if the final result of articulation is more distinct and the patterns perceived of better shape when the stimuli are apprehended in terms of a figure-ground distribution, then this mode of organization will probably emerge.

Furthermore, whichever textural organization emerges, it will be made to appear as simple and distinct as possible. The mind will tend to improve the over-all articulation even if this means weakening some of the individual shapes. For example, if the "field" is most easily perceived in terms of a figure-ground distribution in which one part is well shaped and the other tends toward uniformity, then the unified part of the field will seem as uniform and as homogeneous as prevailing conditions allow. If, however, it is easiest to apprehend the stimulus field in terms of a single shape or in terms of several more or less equal shapes, then the mind will tend to improve both the individual shapes and the relationships between shapes as much as possible.

The mind of the listener which produces such organization is not a kind of neutral, disinterested *tabula rasa.* The stimulus field is organized, partly at least, on the basis of past experience—the learned habits of discrimination and perception of the listener. Such learning, by directing the listener's attention to certain parts of the total field, conditions what is looked for and expected and hence modifies what is perceived; "where the center of our interest lies there, *ceteris paribus,* a figure is likely to arise." [8] Learning also tends to influence the quality of the figures which arise, because "attention, adding energy to the particular field part, will increase its articulation, if it is not articulated as well as it might be." [9] In other words, the practiced listener has learned to direct his attention in particular ways, depending upon the stylistic circumstances; hence he not only tends to improve articulation in general but tends to favor certain types of organizations over others in a given set of stylistic circumstances.[10] Thus, in perceiving music which he supposes to be polyphonic, the practiced listener will tend to emphasize the equality of more or less equally well-articulated figures; while in attending to music which is presumed to be homophonic, the listener will favor one strand of the texture over the others, and these latter aspects of the texture will appear more uniform than might otherwise be the case.

Whether a given textural organization is felt to be satisfactory depends upon the specific disposition of the various parts within the total perceptual field, the norms established within the particular work, and the listener's stylistic habits of perception.

There are textures in which the organization of the field into co-existing figures, into figure and ground, or into some other type of relationship is clear, complete, and normative within the style and in which changes in texture are immediately understandable. Such textures will not in themselves become the basis for expectation.

There are also textural situations in which the nature and organization of the texture, though clear and immediately understandable, is nevertheless felt to be incomplete. By way of illustration, three different "incomplete" textural situations may be distinguished.

First, texture plays a part in determining the listener's sense of formal completeness. For, since the law of return (see p. 151) applies to the organization of the total musical structure and, at times, even to the recurrence of separate aspects of that organization (such as melody, tonality, or texture), a change from one type of textural organization to another or changes within one genus (homophonic, polyphonic, etc.) will activate expectations of return to previously established modes of organization. Even this general statement is subject to qualification. For the expectation of return depends upon the listener's understanding of the passage in question. For instance, in an opera or oratorio the introduction of new characters in a scene may bring about changes in texture—what was a homophonic aria may become a polyphonic quartet; but because these changes are understood in terms of the stage action, they will probably not arouse expectations of return to the original texture of the number.

Texture does not as a rule act as an independent variable. Changes in texture are usually made in conjunction with changes in other aspects of the musical organization. And it is not only an established texture which will be expected to return but rather the whole complex of the stimulus series, of which texture was but one aspect.

However, melody, tonality, instrumentation, and so forth may vary indefinitely while the basic textural organization remains constant.

Because of the desire to organize the textural field as it was organized when an established melodic harmonic rhythmic pattern first appeared, expectation will be particularly active and intense in cases in which the salient shaping forces of a work remain constant while texture changes, e.g., where a theme or melody already established as a norm in one textural organization is repeated or recurs in different textural setting. Moreover, such deviant textures often tend to create uncertainty and tension in the mind of the listener. This is particularly evident in cases where a theme which originally appeared as part of a homophonic texture is subsequently used in conjunction either with other equally well-articulated shapes or in imitative counterpoint with itself. Here there is often a conflict, though only a minor one, between the subjective organization which the listener attempts to impose and the objective facts of the textural distribution. In such cases the introduction of additional figures which are well shaped appears as an intrusion, as a disturbance of what was supposed to be a homophonic texture.

Second, a sense of incompleteness of texture may arise as the result of abnormally wide distances between the parts of the textural field. That is, whether the field is organized into equally well-articulated figures or into a figure-ground distribution, the several parts of the texture may be so widely separated in musical space that they are expected to come together or to be "filled in" by other stimuli.[11] Such abnormally wide spacings may be considered as a special case of structural gaps. In Berg's *Lyric Suite* (Example 77) the very wide spacing between the first violin and the cello is first gradually filled in by the other instruments, and then all the parts move toward a common meeting point in the middle range. Notice, incidentally, that the tendency of the outer voices to move is not a result of dissonance—at least, not at first. The feeling of tension toward a middle range is almost entirely textural. The entire fifth movement of the *Lyric Suite* may be taken as an illustration of the fact that though generally speaking texture does not act as an independent variable, it does at times become a very important factor in creating motion and in shaping musical experience.

EXAMPLE 77 *

Finally, a series of stimuli may seem incomplete because they
are so uniform that they are understood as constituting a ground
or accompaniment for a theme or melody which is still to come—
which is expected. This is the case in the introduction to the fourth
movement of Mendelssohn's "Italian" Symphony (Example 78).
Not all instances are, of course, as clear as this one; for at times it
may be doubtful whether the stimulus series is really an accompaniment or not.[12]

EXAMPLE 78

The psychological effect of textural change depends not only upon
the particular manner in which the changes take place (whether
they are gradual or abrupt and whether they are accompanied by
marked changes in melody, tonality, etc.) but also upon the stylistic
experience of the listener, his judgment as to the nature and genre
of the piece in question. The practiced listener knows that in certain
types of music, texture tends to be constant, while in other types of
music marked changes of texture, though not necessarily expected,
are at least not unusual or unexpected. The difference is important
because in the former case the psychological effect of change is that
of disturbance and interruption, while in the latter case the change

is understood as simply constituting a change of materials, the beginning of a new section.

In a fugue, for example, a single type of texture generally persists throughout the entire piece, though there will be variations within this general genre. Because continuity of texture is expected in a fugue, the significance of a decisive textural change may not be immediately apparent. If the meaning of such a change is not clear, doubts may arise in the listener's mind about the composer's intentions and about the relevance of his own expectations, which were brought into play partly on the basis of his belief as to the nature of the work being heard. In other words, the change creates a feeling of uncertainty because it weakens the listener's ability to envisage the future course of the music.

The last movement of Handel's Concerto Grosso No. 2 furnishes an excellent example of such an interruption of a texture which is expected to be continuous.[13] The movement begins like a normal fugue (Example 79), and the listener expects the texture to con-

Allegro, ma non troppo

EXAMPLE 79

tinue with the customary modifications and variations until the conclusion is reached. However, at measure 27 (Example 80) a

EXAMPLE 80

radical change of texture takes place. The organization becomes as homophonic as possible. Because these changes constitute a dramatic deviation from stylistic norms, they raise doubts and anxieties both as to the significance of the textural discontinuity and as to the relationship between the parts of the movement. Only gradually as the accompaniment becomes more active melodically, as though influenced by the fugal sections with which it alternates, does the listener begin to understand that the homophonic texture will eventually become part of the general polyphony of the fugue. The real meaning of the textural disturbance becomes apparent in measures 66 (Example 81), 74, and 82, where the two melodic ideas are combined.

EXAMPLE 81

The powerful effect of this change of texture is particularly interesting since, in a sense, the homophonic texture is simpler than the polyphonic one; that is, it involves less expenditure of mental effort and would probably in other circumstances seem rather relaxed and calm. The crucial factor creating tension in this example is the listener's difficulty in understanding the significance of the textural changes. This is shown by the fact that homophony coming at the conclusion of a fugue, where it is immediately understandable, creates no doubt or uncertainty in the mind of the listener.

The preceding discussion was concerned with textural organizations which were, taken separately and individually, unambiguous. Ambiguity arose, if at all, because the relationship between successive textures (each of which was clear in itself) was not immediately understandable. Only where the change of texture involved no concomitant changes in the other aspects of the stimulus series could the textural organization itself be said to have been ambiguous.

Ambiguity may, however, arise because the organization of the field is itself unclear. This may occur either because the progressive weakening of the figures obscures a previously clear organization or because the number, diversity, and placement of the several parts of the texture obscure the definition and articulation of the individual constituents of the texture.

If the number and diversity of the individual elements in a texture are so great as to obscure one another or if their placement is such that they cannot be perceived as clearly separated entities, then ambiguity may arise. But, in a sense, it is not really the texture which is ambiguous, rather the number of elements and their placement make the individual shapes appear unclear and ambiguous. Such textures are not common. For the most part they occur in program music where the resultant obscurity has a more or less obvious designative meaning and creates little uncertainty or tension. An instance of this type of ambiguity occurs in Strauss' *Also Sprach Zarathustra,* where a fugue written in the lowest register creates a muddy, indecipherable texture, which supposedly depicts academic obscurity and befuddlement.

A uniform texture does not necessarily appear ambiguous. It may simply be understood as constituting a ground for some sort of theme which is still to appear. For this reason uniformity of texture will seem ambiguous only under special conditions: i.e., where it persists for a seemingly intolerable length of time and hence gives rise to saturation or where a previously clear organization becomes progressively weakened either because the figures lose their definition or because the ground becomes more distinctly articulated or both.

The opening measures of Beethoven's Ninth Symphony furnish a striking example in which a progressive weakening of texture, together with both harmonic and motivic incompleteness and ambiguity, create powerful expectations whose inhibition and ultimate resolution into a clearly defined theme produce a powerful affective experience. In the sixteen measures of introduction (Example 82) the structural gaps are not only melodic, they are harmonic as well. For within the cultural context in which this work is heard, the complete triad is the norm, and the open fifths presented throughout the introduction are felt to involve incompleteness. Indeed, this

EXAMPLE 82

incompleteness is signified by the very fact that such fifths are commonly referred to as "empty." Moreover, the harmonic incompleteness creates ambiguity as to mode; the listener is in doubt as to what the completion will be. Thus, the powerful effect of the first theme is, at least in part, due to the fact that it presents a completed triad and in this way removes the previous ambiguity and completes what was clearly incomplete.

But the forceful impression of the first theme is even more the product of the fact that it is a distinct, substantial shape. The whole introduction is built upon a motive which is obviously psychologically unsatisfactory. It is not merely incomplete, it lacks direction and coherence. The listener senses that it must have meaning, but he has no idea of what that meaning is since he can envisage its consequents only in the vaguest terms. Because the motive establishes no progressive motion, either melodically or harmonically, the listener has little feeling for where this passage is leading; he is merely aware that it seems to presage some momentous, fateful event.

In a sense, the only really satisfactory, unambiguous aspect of measures 1–12 is the relationship between the figure and the ground. All the factors making for a clearly articulated relationship are present: not only is the ground much more uniform than the figure, but it begins before the figure is introduced, thus surrounding it in a temporal sense.[14] But this clarity also gives way to ambiguity (Example 83). For as the point of culmination approaches, the figure becomes progressively weaker—more like the ground. First, the rhythmic articulation of the motive is lost in the rising crescendo of volume and the psychological accelerando (measures 13–14, Example 83). Then its intervallic definition becomes obscured in the general octave motion; and, in the end, when the distinction between

EXAMPLE 83

figure and ground is obliterated altogether, the texture becomes completely ambiguous and the listener is uncertain as to what the textural organization is.[15]

The feeling that a momentous event is impending is heightened by the crescendo which begins in measure 11 and by the increased psychological tempo at that point. For the figure instead of being repeated every two beats is now repeated on every beat. And in measure 13 it occurs at a still shorter time interval. It should also be noted that when the motive is stated in sixteenth notes (beginning in measure 13), the metric opposition of twos against threes, implicit in the opening measures, becomes actualized and tends to increase the general ambiguity of the whole texture.

Although the entrance of the low D in the horns and bassoon in measure 15 is not strongly emphasized, not marked for consciousness, it plays an important part in intensifying expectation at the very end of the passage. Since it creates the first harmonic motion in the whole introduction, the listener senses that "this is it," that at last he will know and understand what heretofore had been only a powerful premonition.

The sense of the relentless power of inexorable fate which characterizes the main theme of this first movement is a result not only of the elemental force of the theme itself and of the ambiguities and expectations excited by the introduction but also of the particular manner in which the introduction leads into the theme. Unlike most introductions (see Example 74) this one does not conclude with a dominant preparation, a waiting period, in which the listener is given an opportunity to orient himself to what has passed and prepare for what is to come. Instead the music moves on without pause, without pity, to its stark and awful declaration.

> As flies to wanton boys are we to the gods.
> They kill us for their sport.

These compelling lines call attention to those inexplicable and inescapable events of our existence which the Greeks attributed to "fate," the Renaissance to "fortune," and we ascribe to "chance."

Chance is an uncompromising fact which permeates all the realms of being: the physical, the biological, the social, the personal, and the aesthetic. It is but chance that there is a solar system; but chance that life developed on this planet; but the chance of a series of fortuitous mutations that there is human life as we know it; but chance that any particular human consciousness comes into being; and, once living, both past and present chance events continually condition and modify the course and tenor of our lives.

Thus it is that music, mirroring the essential shape and substance of human experience, from time to time contains sudden, shocking clashes with unpredictable chance. Lesser composers tend to eschew such harsh encounters with the unexpected, avoiding them by employing a single-minded sameness of musical materials or minimizing them by making a fetish of well-oiled, smooth transitions. But the great masters have faced fate boldly, and capricious clashes with chance are present in much of their finest music.

The pedants have piously attempted to explain away the inexplicable in order to make their analyses jibe with their mechanistic misconceptions of what constitutes the basis for musical unity, logic, and inevitability. But chance will not be denied. And while such encounters must of course be possible within the style employed, we must accept the fact that one passage may follow another not because of inescapable inner necessity but merely because chance will have it so.

Nor do such seemingly fortuitous encounters weaken our feeling of musical coherence and credibility. Rather, since such things have been experienced in life as well as in art, these encounters often strengthen our impression of the truth and reality of the aesthetic experience. Initially they must be understood as chance. But as they become part of our experience of the musical work, causing us to revise our opinion of what has passed and conditioning our expectations of what is still to come, their significance emerges and we discern their influence upon the shape and the course of the musical process. This does not, however, mean that the tendencies developed before chance intervened are obliterated and canceled out. They persist; but their course and mode of fulfilment are necessarily conditioned and modified by the unexpected intrusion of chance. It is pointless to attempt with tortuous argument to analyze away such unpredictable encounters. They can be truly understood only by boldly facing the fundamental fact of chance.

VI

The Evidence: Deviation in Performance
and Tonal Organization

The Nature of the Evidence

The present study seeks to establish and explain the general causes
and conditions for the affective aesthetic response to music. It is thus
relevant that the basic hypothesis adopted is applicable to the music
of different cultures and various cultural levels. The evidence presented in support of the hypothesis has been chosen from many
different kinds of music: from folk music, primitive music, jazz,
oriental music, as well as from the music of Western Europe. The
very diversity of the musical style systems that can be used as evidence increases the probability that the hypothesis is sound.

The evidence to be considered consists of: (1) statements of
composers, performers, theoreticians, and competent critics which
relate specific musical practices to affect or to aesthetic pleasure;
(2) statements which relate a specific musical passage to affect or
to aesthetic pleasure; (3) musical processes in Western music which
are by common consent considered to be affective, e.g., chromaticism; (4) musical examples, taken from the familiar style of Western
music, where common habit responses will allow the assumption of
common understanding and interpretation.

All four types of evidence will be used in the case of the familiar
Western music. However, because it is impossible to assume a
common response and because of the danger of reading Western
meanings and expectations into passages where they are not relevant, only the first and second type of evidence will be used in

discussing non-Western music. In dealing with oriental, primitive, folk music, or Western music before the seventeenth century, we will rely upon the stated responses of those familiar with and sensitive to the nuances and tendencies of the particular styles in question.

The statements of composers, performers, theoreticians, and competent critics are not, however, always precise and unequivocal. Often they require interpretation and explication. Before introducing the evidence itself, several problems relating to its meaning and interpretation must be considered.

Both the theoretical and critical literature about music abounds with references to its emotional character. Innumerable works or parts of works are cited as emotionally "moving," "exciting," and so forth. Yet simply labeling a passage, a mode, or a *rāga* as having emotional quality tells us nothing about the basis for such a response. What in the passage or mode is affective? Most references of this sort do not refer to affect as we have been using the term; they refer instead to mood and associative responses. They are based upon a response to those aspects of musical materials, such as range, tempo, dynamic level, which do not change in the course of an excerpt. To be of value as evidence in the present study, statements about affectivity must connect emotion or aesthetic satisfaction with a specific musical process in the passage cited—a process in which the relationship of deviation and norms to affective aesthetic responses can be examined and discussed.

It was argued in chapter i that the same stimulus conditions give rise to both the affective and the aesthetic intellectual response to music. Which one emerges depends not upon the musical organization which brings it into being but upon the disposition and training of the listener. Self-conscious minds tend to rationalize musical processes by bringing their observations to the level of conscious awareness. They tend, that is, to respond on the aesthetic intellectual level. Because most of the evidence presented here comes from persons with a technical interest in music—from persons who tend to rationalize the musical process (see p. 40)—many of their statements connect the musical processes with aesthetic satisfaction and with affect only by implication.

Even the writings of composers and performers are not always as explicit as one might wish. For the composer and performer tend to view the musical process in a special way. For them aesthetic satisfaction comes from the overcoming of difficulties (see p. 69). The difficulties overcome are the norms which fix the regular and expected. Thus when reference is made to the excitement and pleasure engendered by technical difficulties, the process described is usually one of deviation from the normal and regular. This process has, in turn, been viewed as an aspect of play, and the number of references to the play factor in the performance and creation of music is very striking.

Performance and Deviation

The musical relationships embodied in a score or handed down in an oral tradition do not fix with rigid and inflexible precision what the performer's actualization of the score or aural tradition is to be. They are indications, more or less specific, of what the composer intended and what tradition has established. The performer is not a musical automaton or a kind of musico-mechanical medium through which a score or tradition is realized in sound. The performer is a creator who brings to life, through his own sensitivity of feeling and imagination, the relationships presented in the musical score or handed down in the aural tradition which he has learned.

The amount of freedom allowed to the performer in his creative realization of a score or oral tradition varies from culture to culture and within different epochs of the same culture. In some periods of Western music composers have indicated in great detail exactly how they wish their music to be played, and the performer is not supposed to add to or embellish with new patterns the notes that the composer has set down. This "detailing" of the score reached its most extreme stage at the end of the nineteenth century. Yet even here, as we shall see, the performer does play a creative role. In other styles the performer is given much more freedom to add to and embellish the schematic guide given by the composer or handed down by aural tradition. This is the case in almost all non-Western music, in folk music, and in much of the music of the West, e.g., the music of the seventeenth and eighteenth centuries. Thus, in a sense, one might say that qualitatively the performer's role is always the same; he is always an active creator, shaping and moulding the abstract scheme furnished him by the composer or by tradition. Quantitatively his role varies. At times his task is limited to communicating the meaning latent in a relatively fixed set of musical relationships; at other times, in other cultures, the performer adds to, alters, and makes major modifications in the materials which serve him as a point of departure.

Distinctions between deviations in pitch, rhythm, or tempo and deviations which involve ornamental additions to the basic scheme furnished by the composer or by tradition involve differences in degree rather than kind. The present discussion arbitrarily limits deviations in performance to those which involve slight modifications of the substantive pattern furnished by tradition or the composer. Alterations and additions to that pattern will be discussed under the topic of ornamentation. Though such minor deviations in pitch, rhythm, dynamics, and the like exist in non-Western music, they are more easily observed in Western music, where the scheme of relationships is more definitely fixed by traditions of intonation and by the score of the composer.

EXPRESSIVE PERFORMANCE IN THE WEST

Since it is impossible to study bygone modes of musical performance directly, evidence of deviations before the invention of the phonograph must come from the writings of theorists and critics. These tend to deal with deviations in dynamics, tempo, and rhythm explicitly and with deviations in pitch only by implication.

C. P. E. Bach, for instance, maintains that "certain purposeful violations of the beat are often exceptionally beautiful."[1] Leopold Mozart notes that he who accompanies a true virtuoso "must not allow himself to be seduced into hesitating or hurrying by the prolongations and anticipations of the notes that the soloist knows how to bring in so skillfully and touchingly. . . ."[2] Much the same relationship between melody and accompaniment is implied by Chopin, who is reported to have said that "the singing hand may deviate from strict time, but the accompanying hand must keep time."[3]

L. Mozart also prescribes a special mode of performance for chromatic notes, which, as we shall see, are themselves to be regarded as deviants.

The vibrato (also see p. 66) is essentially a deviation in pitch, an oscillation about a basic pitch. At times it is coupled with crescendo and diminuendo effects. That the vibrato was considered particularly expressive may be seen from Geminiani's discussion of it:

When it [the vibrato] is long continued swelling the sound by degrees, drawing the bow nearer to the bridge, and ending very strong it may express majesty, dignity, etc. But making it shorter, lower and softer, it may denote affliction, fear, etc., ... And with regard to musical performances, experience has shown that the imagination of the hearer is in general so much at the disposal of the master, that by the help of variation, movements, intervals and modulation he may stamp what impression on the mind he pleases.

These extraordinary emotions are indeed most easily excited when accompany'd with words; and I would besides advise as well the composer as the performer, who is ambitious to inspire his audience, to be first inspired himself; which he cannot fail to be if he chuses a work of genius, if he makes himself thoroughly acquainted with all its beauties; and if while his imagination is warm and glowing he pours the same exalted spirit into his own performance.[4]

The affective aesthetic value of deviations in the performance of music is perhaps even more clearly illustrated by the criticisms which chide the performer for "merely playing the notes" or playing "mechanically."

Employing more accurate techniques for the study of musical performance, recent research has shown that deviations from exact pitch, tempo and rhythm are present in most musical performances. Carl Seashore and his associates found that in contemporary performance at least, "The conventional musical score—the composer's documentation of the tonal sequences which he feels will express beauty, emotion, and meaning—is for the singer only a schematic reference about which he weaves, through continuous variations in pitch, a nicely integrated melodic unit."[5]

In part such deviations must be regarded as attempts to add emphasis to the tendencies of tones whose motion is strongly directed or to those which already function as deviants within the tonal system employed. Partly, however, deviations in pitch, rhythm, and volume appear to be products of the performer's own expressive intentions.

In music and speech pure tone, true pitch, exact intonation, perfect harmony, rigid rhythm, even touch and precise time play a relatively small role. They are mainly points of orientation for art and nature. The unlimited resources for vocal and instrumental expression lie in artistic deviation from the pure, the true, the exact, the perfect, the rigid, the even, and the precise. This deviation from the exact is, on the whole, the medium for the creation of the beautiful—for the conveying of emotion.

The variation from the exact which is due to incapacity for rendering the exact is, on the whole, ugly. The artist who is to vary effectively from the exact must know the exact and must have mastered its attainment before his emotion can express itself adequately through a sort of flirtation with it.[6]

At first glance Seashore's viewpoint appears to be quite similar to the one adopted in this study. But on closer scrutiny several important differences are evident.

Although Seashore sees emotion and beauty (notice that he ascribes the same cause to both) arising from deviation, yet his basic philosophical position is in many respects diametrically opposed to the one taken here. Seashore views the norms and deviants as absolute and fixed. He believes that aesthetic quality can be quantitatively measured.[7] However, if one considers the great variety of style systems and tonal organization which exist in various cultures —tempered twelve-tone scales, tempered five- or seven-tone scales, and all the many untempered scales and modes—it seems very evident that there are no absolute norms.

Moreover, although we may know that a particular deviation is not accidental (because it tends to be constant within a given style), the criterion of aesthetic deviation is itself culturally and stylistically determined. What is considered an expressive deviation in one style may be considered an abomination in another. The wide pitch deviations in Hawaiian guitar playing, though perhaps expressive to some, are most distasteful to those accustomed to the more modest departures of European art music.

Many problems arise in connection with Seashore's method and the data developed by it. He himself admits that there are deviations which result from causes not relevant to expressive deviation; e.g., the use of Pythagorean or natural-scale intonation, the non-linear relationship of pitch and frequency, and the relation of pitch production to motor behavior.[8] How is one to determine which deviations are expressive and which are not? Only by a careful study and analysis of the general plan of expression, both within the style in general and within the particular piece in question, and by attempting to correlate expressive deviation with the total affective aesthetic musical structure.

Because Seashore advances no theory and attempts no explanation of the relationship between deviation and affective aesthetic experience, his viewpoint lacks substance and plausibility. He demonstrates a correspondence but no causality. Furthermore, in failing to explain or account for the relationship between deviation and "beauty in music," he also fails to see that deviation in performance is only one aspect of what is actually a much more comprehensive and general principle.

EXPRESSIVE DEVIATION IN NON-WESTERN MUSIC

Such expressive deviations are by no means confined to the tradition of Western music. Although some of the variability in the intonation of primitive singers may be attributed to the lack of instrumental accompaniment and some, where instruments are present, to peculiarities of their intonation, not all of the variability need "necessarily be ascribed to lack of training. . . . It has definite limits, and changes in intonation often have an expressive function. . . ."[9]

Primitive singers also employ vibrato as a method of pitch deviation.

One of the characteristics of Chippewa singing observed during this study is that a vibrato, or wavering tone, is especially pleasing to the singers. This is difficult for them to acquire and is considered a sign of musical proficiency. The vibrato may seem to indicate an uncertain sense of tone, but the singer who uses it is ready to approve the song when sung with correct intonation. He declares, however, that this is not "good singing."[10]

Expressive fluctuations in intonation are likewise common in folk singing. "The intonation of a traditional folk singer is not necessarily worse than ours, but it is often more flexible. A tone is often taken somewhat higher or lower than might be expected, for expressive and ornamental purposes." [11] Bartók notes that the deviations of pitch in folk music "since they show a certain system and are subconsciously intentional, must not be considered faulty, off-pitch singing. This is the essential difference between the accidental off-pitch singing of urban amateurs and the self-assured, self-conscious, decided performance of peasant singers." [12]

Deviation also plays an important role in the performance of oriental music, and there also it is considered to be affective and aesthetically pleasing. In his book, *Ten Rules for Playing the Lute,* Wu Ch'ên at the turn of the thirteenth century writes that "if one just plays the music as it is written, one will not be able to express the sentiments of the composer." [13] And in the sixteenth century Yang Piao-cheng stresses the necessity for interpretation, connecting this with an understanding of the tendency of the music (though it is doubtful if he is using the word "tendency" in the same sense as it has been used in this study). "When one knows its meaning, one understands its tendency; when one understands its tendency, one may (truly) understand the music. Though the music be technically well executed, if its tendency is not understood, what benefit shall it give? It is nothing but a big noise, that avails nothing." [14] In a collection of Javanese poetry, the Tjentin, the following comment on the playing of the *rebab* appears: "Every now and then there was a little deviation from the correct pitch so as to enhance the charm of the music." [15]

Ornamentation

In a sense the expressive deviations discussed above are merely unclassified forms of ornamentation. Certainly the distinction between the expressive deviations made by performers of all cultures and the devices which the various cultures systematize as ornaments is very difficult to draw. Deviations in pitch which in Western music would be considered as expressive deviations are, for instance, in the music of India often classified as ornaments. Even within a single culture the same device may at one time be classified as an ornament and at another time may simply be part of the style of the performance or may be incorporated into the body of the composer's score. For example, the vibrato, which was once classed as an ornament, became an aspect of traditional string performance; while the appoggiatura, once an ornament, became part of the composer's basic plan. In the final analysis, whether an expressive device is classified as an ornament, as an expressive deviant, or as a compositional technique depends largely upon the particular theory of music in which it appears and not upon its basic function.

Unfortunately the term "ornament" has taken on pejorative connotations.

It will be found that most of the words (for ornament) which imply for us the notion of something adventitious and luxurious, added to utilities but not essential to their efficacy, originally implied a completion or fulfillment of the artifact or other object in question; that to decorate an object or person originally meant to endow the object or person with its or his necessary accidents with a view to proper operation. . . .[16]

We must revise our attitude toward ornamentation. Ornaments are of the essence of music. Indeed, since music is architectonic, it is possible to consider even the largest sections of a composition as being essentially ornamental, though of course this involves a special use of the term. From this point of view the analytic method developed by Schenker partly consists in exhibiting this process of ornamentation on higher architectonic levels.[17]

Ornaments, then, must be considered as inseparable from the structural tones and basic plan which they ornament and to which they give meaning. They themselves are likewise inseparable from and meaningless without the basic substantive tones, harmonies, and rhythms which they ornament. From this point of view, the basic structural framework of a passage or composition may be considered as a norm, and the ornaments which breathe meaning and feeling into this plan may be regarded as deviants.

"A melody without ornament," says an Indian theoretical treatise, "is like a night without a moon, a river without water, a vine without flowers, or a woman without jewels." [18]

ORNAMENTATION IN THE WEST

Because ornamentation (or embellishment), in the strict sense of the word, became codified and systematized during the baroque period of Western culture and because of the concern of composers and theoreticians of that period with emotional expression, the relationship between ornamentation and affective aesthetic experience is clearer and more explicit in the writings of this period than in those of most other epochs. For instance, though Reese's discussion of ornamentation in music of the Middle Ages makes it clear that the process was of considerable importance,[19] its relation to affective aesthetic experience is not made explicit. Similarly in the Renaissance, though other aspects of the process of deviation can be related to aesthetic experience, embellishment is not generally discussed in detail nor is it, generally speaking, explicitly correlated with aesthetic considerations. After the baroque period as composer and performer began to be specialists, composers detailed their embellishments into the score, and ornamentation as a separable resource of musical expression all but vanished from musical practice.

The typical baroque attitude toward embellishments is concisely and forcefully stated by Blanchet, who writes that they are "greatly befitted to move powerfully the soul; to deprive music of such ornaments would be depriving it of the most beautiful part of its essence." [20] Ornamentation has also been connected with the spirit of play and, by implication, with the pleasure of the creative performer in surmounting difficulties and overcoming resistances. "To this exactness they [the Italians] join all the embellishments an air is capable of; they run a hundred sort of divisions upon it; they in a manner play with it. . . ." [21] Although the elaborate embellishments, coloraturas, and cadenzas invented by performers perhaps involve a certain amount of exhibitionism, only a viewpoint saturated with nineteenth-century prejudice would imply that this is their basic *raison d'être*. Cadenzas and other embellishments have an aesthetic function, delaying an expected resolution, deviating from the normative melodic curve, or otherwise creating psychological tension.

Having thus established the connection between ornamentation and affective expressive experience, it remains to show that ornamentation involves the inhibition of a tendency or habit. Embellishment functions in two ways in creating inhibition or tension.

In the first place, since most embellishments are not structural tones, they delay (inhibit) the arrival of the expected and anticipated structural tone. As C. P. E. Bach puts it: ". . . the small notes rather than the principal tone are struck with the bass and the other parts," [22] and because these ornamental tones are, as a rule, dissonant with the bass their tendency is very clear and the expectation of consonance is active. Bach himself notes that "appoggiaturas retard the chords which are called for by the bass." [23] Discussing ornamentation in the Palestrina style, Jeppesen notes that "the third note of the *cambiata* is followed by the skip of the third upward, followed in turn by a step of the second downward, through which the real note of resolution comes at last and is thus doubly delayed." [24]

In the second place, many ornaments tend to create doubt and uncertainty, however momentary, as to which tone is the structural or substantive one. Trills, turns, or even the very wide vibrato tremolo effect present in some types of primitive music (see p. 203) often obscure the musical pattern temporarily. In other cases momentary uncertainty arises as a result of the manner in which the ornament is performed. This would appear to be true of the embellishment which Couperin calls the *accent*. "Couperin's ornament is derived from lute technique, being originally the stopping of an auxiliary note on the lute without actually plucking it. . . . The effect . . . cannot really be translated into terms of the harpsichord; the player approximates it by playing the auxiliary note, usually a tone above and in dotted rhythm, as faintly and vaguely as possible." [25]

The relationship between embellishment and uncertainty is clearer where an elaborate ornamental mode of performance, usually improvisatory, is sustained for a considerable time. This is well illustrated in the following passage in which François Raguenet compares the French and Italian styles of musical performance at the beginning of the eighteenth century.

The French would think themselves undone if they offended in the least against the rules; they flatter, tickle, and court the ear and are still doubtful of success, though everything be done with an exact regularity. The more hardy Italian changes the tone and the mode without any awe or hesitation; he makes double or treble cadences of seven or eight bars together upon tones we should think incapable of the least division. He'll make a swelling of so prodigious a length that they who are unacquainted with it can't choose but be offended at first to see him so adventurous but before he has done they'll think they can't sufficiently admire him. He'll have passages of such an extent as will perfectly confound his auditors at first, and upon such irregular notes as shall instill a terror as well as surprise into the audience, who will immediately conclude that the whole concert is degenerating into a dreadful dissonance; and betraying 'em by that means into a concern for the music, which seems to be on the brink of ruin, he immediately reconciles 'em by such regular cadences that everyone is surprised to see harmony rising again, in a manner, out of discord itself and owing its greatest beauties to those irregularities which seemed to threaten it with destruction.[26]

Here both the relationship between embellishment and affective aesthetic experience and the relationship between doubt and uncertainty and aesthetic experience are made clear and explicit.

These relationships, which are the very ones asserted by the hypothesis of this study, are implied in descriptions of the response to music of widely different styles. For instance, a similar type of experience is reported by the Renaissance theorist, Heinrich Glarean, who describes the effect of Josquin's "De Profundis" in the following words: "I wish every one to observe closely . . . with how much passion and how much majesty the composer has given us the opening words . . . with astonishing and carefully studied elegance, he has thrown the phrase into violent disorder, usurping now the leap of the Lydian, now that of the Ionian, until at length, by means of these beautiful refinements, he glides . . . from the Dorian to the Phrygian." [27] Spanning both time and style, a very similar experience is described in Stanley Dance's account of a performance by Sidney Bechet, the jazz clarinetist: "His most daring flights of improvisation may momentarily have made the listener a little nervous, a little doubtful of the outcome, but all were accomplished with confident ease." [28]

ORNAMENTATION IN ORIENTAL MUSIC

When we turn from the art music of the West to the art music of the Orient, to folk music, or to the music of primitives, we encounter musical styles which are largely improvisatory. Even where notation is present, only the basic plan of a piece is written down. The realization of that plan is left to the creative ability of the composer-performer. What he adds to the basic plan, which he has learned by ear or studied in score, might all be said to lie in the realm of ornamentation. "The task of the Indonesian singer, in contrast to that of the European executant musician, is a *creative* one. Each time a *lagu* is sung, the song flowers again from the traditional melodic ground work, the unalterable melodic nucleus; often to the delight of those who have learned to esteem the native . . . style of performance." [29] Notice that ornamentation would seem to be particularly affective in such traditional music since expectation is quite precise; that is, the performance of such music involves a kind of double deviation, a deviation both from the general stylistic norms and from the norms which are specific to the particular song being embellished.

In India, too, the distinction between the performer and the creative artist is non-existent. The *rāga* is the melodic structure or ground plan "which the master first of all communicates to the pupil; and to sing is to improvise upon the theme thus defined." [30] However, since successive variations, whether in art music, folk music, or primitive music, made upon a given ground plan will be discussed in chapter vii, we will here discuss ornamentation only in the more limited sense.

The importance of embellishment in the music of the Orient is made apparent by the elaborate classification of various types of ornaments. As Sachs remarks:

So vital in East Asiatic Music is the delicate vacillation that dissolves the rigidity of pentatonic scales that all possible artifices have carefully been classified, named, and, by syllabic symbols of their names, embodied in notation. . . .

Few notes he would leave clear and hard; mostly, the string, after plucking, is given additional tension, so that the tone goes up for a moment or for good; or else, the stopping finger leaves the tone just plucked and rubs along the string with a wiping noise rather than a melodious glissando. Such continual wailing and sobbing, though certainly against our taste, is indispensable when East Asiatic music appeals to the heart.[31]

The relationship between embellishment and affect is clearly implied in this quotation. The relationship is emphasized again and again by oriental musicians and poets. For instance, the Javanese poet of the Tjentin collection writes that "The *wirama* which found its expression in the *wilet* strove after touching the heart. . . . More and more opulently did the *wilet* entwine itself, striving after the awakening of emotion."[32] The *wirama* is the tempo expressed in time intervals; the *wilet* denotes the time intervals filled by a melody sung or played on the *rebab* (a string instrument), and it also means the elaboration of basic tones, i.e., embellishment.[33] Another stanza of the Tjentin poems is interesting because it specifies the presence of expectation in response to this music. "The power of emotion gripped the heart; the *wilet* intoxicated the senses . . . the gripping power of the *gending* [orchestral composition] . . . awakened a feeling of hankering expectation, as of one looking forward, full of longing.'"[34]

In books about Indian music and in the works of the theorists themselves the relationship between ornamentation and affect is made explicit or is implicit in the names given to the various embellishments. "But in India the note and the microtonal graces compose a closer unity, for the grace fulfils just that function of adding light and shade which in harmonized music is attained by varying degrees of assonance. The Indian song without grace would seem to Indian ears as bald as the European art song without the accompaniment it presupposes." [35]

Both the delaying function of embellishment and its expressive effect have been discussed by Strangways in connection with Indian music.

A musical purpose of importance is served by this Predominant and its consonant. One of the most effective resources of melody is appoggiatura, i.e. the delaying of a note, the raising of pleasing expectations. . . . The essential condition of appoggiatura is that the delaying note should be felt to be only transitory and the delayed note to be relatively final or permanent. This is effected in our music by the harmony, expressed or implied. . . . But when there are no chords at all in question the substantive nature of the delayed note has to be established in some other way. In Indian, as no doubt in Greek and probably in the ecclesiastical melodies, this is done by the Predominant (*amśa, mesē,* reciting *note*); notes receive the force of appoggiaturas as they delay this.[36]

As was the case with Western music, some types of embellishment do not so much act to create a delay in the arrival of an expected substantive note as they do to create uncertainty as to which tone is the substantive one; or, to put the matter in another way, some embellishments delay the arrival of the substantive tone as a simple, clear, definite point in the musical structure.[37]

The function of coloratura and embellishment in Byzantine chant has already been touched upon in another connection (see p. 67). The importance of embellishments in Jewish chant of Asia and eastern Europe is made clear in the following:

. . . for the outpouring of the heart in prayer-texts musical embellishments offer added power of interpretation, and the solo-recitative insures freedom for the expression of rising devotion.

The coloratura in the Eastern European *chazzanuth* is like the soul in the body; without it that *chazzanuth* loses its vitality, its charm, its fascination.[38]

Generalizing on the subject of oriental melody, Sachs writes that "'Melody,' in the Orient, has always meant one of those flexible patterns that the Arabs finally classified as *maqamât* and the Hindu as *rāgas,* which imposed upon the singer their specific genera, scales, pitches, accents, tempos, and moods, but granted him full personal freedom for their elaboration." [39]

FOLK MUSIC AND PRIMITIVE MUSIC

The line between folk music and the improvisatory types of art music seems to be drawn on the basis of musical theory rather than musical practice. For the folk singer like the oriental creator-performer or the performer of the baroque period in the Western tradition also performs his creative task by ornamenting and varying a basic plan. The chief difference between the folk singer's art and that of the trained musician lies in the fact that the plan of folk song is handed down in an oral tradition and embellishments are not codified but are traditional or invented by the singer himself.

The primitive musician unhesitatingly alters the traditional material he has inherited from thousands of unknown talents and geniuses before him. . . . He not only remoulds old ditties, but also weaves together fresh combinations of more or less familiar phrases, which he calls 'making new songs'. . . . It would be difficult to exaggerate the extent to which such traditional singers embellish so-called 'simple melodies' with a regular riot of individualistic excrescences and idiosyncrasies of every kind, each detail of which . . . is a precious manifestation of real artistic personality.[40]

Since folk material has no theoretical codification of ornaments and no theoretical literature, we shall have to rely for testimony as to the relation of embellishment to affect in folk music on the experts in the field of folk music. Writing of Yugoslav folk music George Herzog says:

Musical rhythm is treated more briefly, since its patterns in Yugoslav folk music are free, very rich, and even diffuse; the basic structures are overlaid by a free rubato performance and luxuriant ornamentation. . . .

South Slavic music has an especial appeal. This may well be due to the contrast between the essential simplicity of its basic materials and the pulsing quality of life achieved through an abundance of expressive devices, including the ornamentation.[41]

Bartók also discusses certain aspects of the rhythmic style of these songs and relates the rhythmic irregularities to expression. He says that a characteristic feature of the Serbo-Croatian and Bulgarian folk melodies is that "the line–, word–, and syllable–interruptions effected by shorter or longer rests [are] not for articulation's sake, but for decorative—one might almost say for expressive—purposes."[42]

Each folk culture has its own basic plans and its own style. Within the limits of these the singer embellishes, alters, and often distorts, making the impact of his own creative personality felt and reveling in what has been called "the joy of being a cause." He takes pleasure in technique and its mastery, and, in the course of exhibiting it, he will deliberately attempt the difficult. American folk fiddle players, for example, seek "deliberately for certain 'wild notes'."[43] In *The Book of American Negro Spirituals* James Weldon Johnson mentions the "curious turns and twists and quavers and the intentional striking of certain notes just a shade off the key, with which the Negro loves to embellish his songs." [44] And Metfessel relates these embellishments to emotional expression, saying that "the ornaments are excessive, but fit into the general emotional intoxication of the singer." [45]

Real jazz is also a kind of folk music involving the improvisation about and embellishment of a basic plan or structure. In their concerted improvisation the players ". . . worry and cajole the rhythms and phrases of their solos, extemporizing here and there, introducing solo 'breaks' and otherwise ornamenting the printed skeleton that has been provided for their collective guidance." [46] The importance of these improvisations from the aesthetic artistic point of view is stressed by Jelly Roll Morton:

You may have noticed that in playin' jazz the breaks are one of the most essential things that you can ever do in jazz. Without breaks and without clean breaks; without beautiful ideas in breaks, you don't need to even think about doin' anything else. . . . Without a break you have nothin'; even if a toon hav'n' a break in it, it is always necessary to arrange some kind of spot to make a break because as I said before, you haven't got jazz. . . . A riff is a background—a riff is what you would call a foundation (as like what you would walk on), and a break is something that you break. . . ." [47]

The quotation is particularly interesting because it relates the foundation or riff (the norm) to the breaks (the deviation).

Rex Harris stresses the emotional aspect of the jazz performance: "Jazz . . . like all folk music, is emotional in outlook. It is 'playin' from the heart'. . . . Inspiration, spontaneity, exuberance, absence of inhibition, all these qualities are axiomatic in jazz." [48] In short, "a popular song played 'as written' is seldom 'hot'; it is the series of artistic distortions given to the tune that makes it jazz." [49]

Much primitive music is intimately connected with ritualistic observances and magic ceremonies, and it is probably for this reason that it often tends to be less subject to variation and ornamentation. The religious sanctions imposed upon primitive art and the communal nature of the primitive ceremonies prohibit creative deviation on the part of individual performers. [50] When, however, primitive art becomes separated from ritual and magic, we find the same tendency towards ornamentation and embellishment that is usual in folk music and art music.

The tendency toward elaboration of a basic plan, and elaboration exhibiting the creative abilities and tendencies of the performer, is found in almost all primitive musical styles.[51] In African music:

The individual performer has complete freedom for his own individual and inspired variation within these fixed limits. Provided he keeps to the main rules an African performer may introduce as many subtle variations as he pleases—and all conceived on the spur of the moment. It is spontaneous music. You never hear the same song done exactly the same way.[52]

Even where music has an avowedly utilitarian function as in African drum language or in the Jabo language of western Liberia, an aesthetic element often enters. Commenting upon the way in which a horn player calls on another man by sounding his name in music, Herzog writes: "The free variation of tempo and prosody injects a semi-aesthetic play-element. But a definite departure from mere speech representation toward musical ornamentation is achieved in the occasional transposition of the signal from its normal level to the lower one. . . ."[53] Helen H. Roberts also notes and comments upon the aesthetic play element in primitive music and embellishment.[54]

Tonality and Deviation

The term "tonality" refers to the relationships existing between tones or tonal spheres within the context of a particular style system (see pp. 45 ff.). As Strangways has put it: "A tonic is a tendency rather than a fact."[55] That is, some of the tones of the system are active. They tend to move toward the more stable points in the system—the structural or substantive tones.

But activity and rest are relative terms because tonal systems are generally hierarchical: tones which are active tendency tones on one level may be focal substantive tones on another level and vice versa. Thus in the major mode in Western music the tonic tone is the tone of ultimate rest toward which all other tones tend to move. On the next higher level the third and fifth of the scale, though active melodic tones relative to the tonic, join the tonic as structural tones; and all the other tones, whether diatonic or chromatic, tend toward one of these. Going still further in the system, the full complement of diatonic tones are structural focal points relative to the chromatic notes between them. And, finally, as we have seen, any of these twelve chromatic notes may be taken as substantive relative to slight expressive deviations from their normal pitches.[56]

At the other end of the architectonic scale it should be noted that tonality plays a part in the articulation of musical forms larger than those of the phrase or melody. A musical section of considerable length may be in a tonal sphere which, relative to the tonal spheres of other sections, is structurally active, so that the whole section may be said to tend toward another section whose tonal sphere is substantive. However, even within a tonal realm of a section that is, relatively speaking, "at rest" there are tensions and releases which function at the sectional level.

If the architectonic structure of tonal levels is viewed from the smallest deviation to the larger ones, it might well be argued that the whole structure can be understood as a hierarchy of embellishment. Just as the expressive microtonal deviations, whether classified as in oriental music or freely improvised as in Western music, can be regarded as embellishments of the tones to which they are applied, so chromatic tones can be regarded as the embellishments of diatonic tones. Similarly the auxiliary diatonic tones can be regarded as embellishments of substantive diatonic tones, and so on, even to the sections some of which would then be considered as embellishments of others.

The essential point is that auxiliary tones, whether expressive deviants on the lowest architectonic level or whole sections on the highest level, are just as vital and important to musical communication as are the substantive tones toward which they move. Indeed, the importance of such tones is often indicated either by the names given to them or by the restrictions governing their use.

The Javanese scales, for example, "consist of one group of three and one group of two principal tones, separated by gaps of one tone. The tones that have been missed . . . are, as a matter of fact, not always completely eliminated; they may have a modest function as secondary tones." [57] What is of interest is the names given to these secondary tones. They are called *pamanis,* which comes from the word meaning "sweet" or "harmonious," or they are called *senggol nyimpang.* According to Coolsma's *Dictionary of the Sundanese Language,* the word *"senggol"* means "the modulation of the voice, trills, turns, etc. with which the singer ornaments the tune," [58] while *nyimpang* comes from the word meaning to step aside, to evade, to deviate. In this case the relationship between ornamental and auxiliary tones is absolutely clear. So, too, is the relationship between the several names given to these auxiliary notes.

The situation in Chinese and Japanese music is quite similar. Here the two tendency tones filling in the basically pentatonic structure "kept a transitional, auxiliary character and had not even the privilege of individual names: the Chinese called them by the name of the note directly above with the epithet *pièn,* which means 'on the way to,' 'becoming.' " [59] The names of these active tones indicate their tendency toward other tones, while their affective power is indicated by the fact that they were not permitted in palace or temple music because "far from soothing the passions [they] filled the soul with sensual lust." [60]

From all of this it seems clear that comparative musicologists who treat auxiliary notes as unimportant and incidental have misunderstood their function in the total musical process. The error is serious because an understanding and adequate description of style depends upon the recognition and examination of the relationship between the structural tones and the tendency tones belonging to the style.

Such misconceptions occur in part because musicologists and ethnologists have too often been concerned with the collection and classification of scales or with simple-minded statistical compilations. "In the study of folk music there has been perhaps a little too much preoccupation with scales and intervals, which are merely the raw material of melody, at the expense of studying tonality." [61] Even this admirable statement reveals a curious distortion of the facts, for scales are not the raw materials of melodies. It is just the other way round: melodies are the materials from which scales are abstracted. Scales are simply the tones of melodies arranged in a linear order of pitch succession. They are not usually present in the minds of the musicians, who think rather in terms of melodies directly.

CHROMATICISM

Almost all of the tonal systems that have been used in music, whether Western, Eastern, folk, or primitive, are essentially and basically diatonic.[62] Chromaticism is almost by definition an alteration of, an interpolation in, or deviation from this basic diatonic organization.

However, not every alteration of a diatonic organization results in a feeling of chromaticism, in a sense of deviation. Where several different and alternative modes of tonal organization are possible within a given musical style or style system or where such modes are themselves subject to transposition according to the rules of operation prevalent in the style, the alteration of one tonal group may well be interpreted by the listener as constituting a change or a transposition of mode rather than as being a chromatic passage. Of course, it is possible that the alterations involved in such mode changes or transpositions may at first be interpreted as chromaticism and only later be understood for what they really are. In other words, the hypothetical meaning and the evident meaning of the alterations may be different.

The interpretation of any alteration in the basic diatonic structure established at the outset of a piece will be governed by the operation of the law of Prägnanz as it functions within the particular cultural stylistic context; that is, the change will be interpreted in the simplest way possible within the style system. If it is simpler to consider the alteration as a change of mode, the listener practiced in the style will adopt this interpretation. While if it is easier to regard the alteration as a deviation from a single mode, as a chromatic modification or deviation, this will be the interpretation made by the listener.

Obviously the listener's understanding of such alterations is partly a function of their relative duration. If the alteration is only temporary, then it will probably be understood as a deviation. While if the alteration of a tone within the tonal structure persists for some time, then the alteration will be understood as constituting a change of mode or a transposition.

The distinction between chromaticism as a temporary phenomenon and the expressive pitch deviations discussed above is not an easy one to draw. The microtonal intervals which so often accompany the embellishments in oriental music could have been considered under the subject of chromaticism. Or, as previously stated, chromaticism may be viewed as a type of embellishment. Both types of pitch alteration or interpolation delay, block, or inhibit the arrival of the expected, normal diatonic tones of the given mode. Both perform an expressive function. The difference would appear to be one of standardization. The microtonal intervals employed in oriental music, though more consciously introduced and controlled than those introduced by performers in the West or those used by primitive and folk musicians, are not themselves really standardized, and the intervals as such appear to have been given no theoretical codification.[63]

It seems unnecessary to prove that in Western music chromaticism represents a deviation from the normal diatonic modes. Its treatment both in theory and practice is ample indication of its exceptional and unusual character. The special nature of chromaticism is evident whether we consider the construction of musical instruments, which are all essentially built to perform diatonic music; the prescriptions as to the use of *musica falsa;* the extreme emotions which chromaticism has been used to express; or the rules which Leopold Mozart and C. P. E. Bach set forth for the performance of chromatic notes.[64]

The affective aesthetic power of chromaticism not only arises because chromatic alterations delay or block the expected motion to the normal diatonic tones but also because uniformity of progression, if persistent, tends, as we have seen (see pp. 164 f.), to create ambiguity and hence affective tension. Moreover, ambiguity leads, particularly in the realm of harmonic progression, to a general tonal instability.

A particularly interesting instance of the coincidence of ambiguity, affect, and a quasi-chromatic device is to be found in the jazz "blue note." The aesthetic affect of this tone is generally acknowledged. Its ambiguity and relationship to chromaticism are made evident in the following: "The outstanding quality of the blue notes is their ambiguity. . . . This harmonic succession strongly suggests the ambiguity of the melodic note which, now a lowered third degree of the scale, now a raised second degree, produces either a leading tone to the major third, or a 'blue' minor third within the major scale." [65] Finally, it is important to bear in mind that chromaticism, though considered here as an independent variable, is in practice used in connection with other supporting types of deviation; e.g., rhythmic delays and irregularities, delays in the filling of structural gaps, weakly articulated melodic structures, and the various other means of affective aesthetic communication discussed in earlier chapters.

Instances of the connection between chromaticism and emotional communication are so common in the history of music since the Renaissance that any musician or music lover can easily cite a host of examples for himself. Only a few examples will be referred to in this study.

The most striking evidence of the connection between chromaticism and affect is to be found in music written to a text—music in which the emotional nature of the music is, as it were, warranted and specified by the text. Such is the case with the Renaissance Netherlands motet and the Italian madrigal.

Chromaticism always represents the extraordinary. . . . Again and again we find chromatic treatment given to such highly emotional concepts as crying, lamenting, mourning, moaning, inconsolability, shrouding one's head, breaking down, and so forth.
In the Italian madrigal the same concepts find expression through the medium of chromaticism. There they represent man as entangled in his earthly passions, while in the music of the Netherlands they symbolize the devout believer struggling with the burden of sorrow which God has laid upon him to test his faith.[66]

About fifty years later, just at the beginning of the baroque period, we find this relationship between chromaticism and affective experience neatly illustrated in the book of *Chromatic Tunes* (1606) by John Daniel (Example 84).[67] One might cite almost countless examples in baroque music of the relationship between chromaticism and affect (both in our sense of the term "affect" and in the eighteenth-century sense). Two particularly famous pieces illustrate this relationship clearly: namely, "Dido's Lament" from Purcell's *Dido and Aeneas* and the "Crucifixus" of Bach's Mass in B-Minor.

chro—ma—tic tunes most like my pas—sions sound

EXAMPLE 84

Chromaticism in Western music is not exclusively or even predominantly a melodic phenomenon;⁶⁸ it is also a harmonic phenomenon. As such it is capable of arousing affective aesthetic experience, not only because it may delay or alter the expected diatonic progressions which are the norms of tonal harmony, but also because it tends to create ambiguity and uncertainty as to harmonic direction. Chromatic passages of considerable duration, passages which are often modulatory, appear to be ambiguous because they obscure the feeling of tonal center, because the ultimate end of the progression cannot be envisaged or because more than one tonal center is indicated (see pp. 171 ff.). Such ambiguity creates suspense and uncertainty which, as we have seen, are powerful forces in the shaping of affective experience.

This relationship between suspense and uncertainty, on the one hand, and chromatic progressions and modulations, on the other, has been well understood and fully exploited by opera composers of all periods. For instance, John Brown, writing in the early eighteenth century, observes in his *Letters upon the Poetry and Music of the Italian Opera* that:

They [Italian composers] must, in the first place, have observed, that all those passages in which the mind of the speaker is agitated by a rapid succession of various emotions, are, from their nature, incompatible with any particular strain, or length of melody. . . . But, whilst the Italians conceive such passages to be incompatible with that regularity of measure, and that unity of strain which is essential to air, they felt, however, that they were of all others the most proper subject for musical expression: And, accordingly, both poet and musician seem, by mutual consent, to have bestowed on such passages their chief study; and the musician, in particular, never fails to exert on them his highest and most brilliant powers. . . . It is in this species of song that the finest effects of the chromatic, and, as far as our system of musical intervals is susceptible of it, even of the enharmonic scale, are peculiarly felt; and it is here also that the powers of modulation are most happily, because most properly, employed. . . .[69]

Donna Anna's confusion and agitation upon discovering the body of her father provides a fairly typical instance of the use of chromaticism to create a feeling of uncertainty and suspense (Example 85). Notice that not only are the progressions chromatic, but they

EXAMPLE 85

are also sequential, which heightens the element of suspense, since the ultimate goal of the passage is in doubt. Also observe that the passage extensively employs one of the most effective ornaments, the appoggiatura.

In the instrumental music of the classical period chromaticism is employed with great effectiveness but not, generally speaking, in the construction of themes and melodies. These tend to be diatonic—with, of course, some notable exceptions. Rather chromaticism finds its place in the bridge passages and development sections where, contrasting with the more regular and normal progressions of the theme groups, it combines with other types of deviation to create suspense and uncertainty. In this music chromaticism becomes one of the basic organizing forces of the total form. The level of chromaticism is no longer fairly constant throughout a piece. Instead, the generally normative, diatonic motion of the theme group is contrasted with the intensity of suspense to which chromaticism makes an important contribution.

Since this is not a history of chromaticism, it seems unnecessary to trace its progress up to the present. Suffice it to point out that in the nineteenth century chromaticism becomes an almost indispensable resource of composers, and one can find it at work on all levels of the musical organization—in the melodies, their harmonization, and in the construction of the musical periods, sections, and total structures. Indeed, it can be argued that its extravagant and prodigal use served, in the last analysis, to weaken and destroy its effectiveness because it tended to become normative within the style.

THE MINOR MODE IN WESTERN MUSIC

The theoretical and psychological basis for the affective power of the minor mode in Western music has puzzled and perplexed so many excellent musicologists and psychologists that it may seem rash to propose another answer here. But there are two good reasons for doing so. First, any theory which purports to explain the basis for the affective response to music must take account of and attempt to unravel this mystery. And second, the fact that the hypothesis under consideration leads to a satisfactory solution of the riddle of the minor mode, without recourse to any of the Pythagorean mysteries, is in itself strong evidence in support of the theory advanced in this study.

The theoretical attempts to solve the enigma of the minor mode have ranged all the way from Reimann's theory, which contends that the minor triad is built upon the inverted overtone structure of the major triad, to that of a psychologist who considers that since the minor triad is a "lowering" of the major one it clearly represents a castration complex and hence arouses feelings of anxiety.[70] Theorists with an acoustical bias have attempted to show that the minor triad is more dissonant than the major.

Each of these accounts, aside from being fairly farfetched, involves significant difficulties. Reimann's theory, for instance, not only provides no explanation of the psychic mechanism whereby the minor triad is sensed as the inversion of the major but also fails to relate such inversion to general affective processes. Above all, such theories seem implausible because they ignore both the facts of music history and those of comparative musicology.

The acousticians fail to convince because, though it might be possible to relate dissonance to affective experience (see p. 229), the minor triad is not more acoustically dissonant than the major one, at least not at its closed position (Example 86).

EXAMPLE 86

Eventually all these theories are faced with the single overwhelming fact that the minor triad has no peculiarly affective significance, carries no sad connotations in non-Western music, in folk music, or in the music of primitives.[71] This would seem to indicate, as Heinlein has pointed out,[72] that like most musical responses the one to the minor mode is not natural or universal but learned.[73]

This statement requires some qualification. For the minor mode as we know it did not exist before the Renaissance and "assumed universal importance only with the advent of baroque music." [74] It would be a grave mistake, though one commonly made, to confuse the minor mode as it has existed since the Renaissance with those church modes which happen to have a minor third. Nor is it entirely accurate to say that the affective response to the minor mode must of necessity be a learned response merely because no such response is attached to folk music or primitive music having a minor triad. For the minor mode in Western music is not the same mode as the melodic constructs of non-Western music, folk music, or primitive music which happen to employ a minor third above the tonic or keynote.

Here, then, we come to the great stumbling block of almost all theorists, musicologists, and psychologists. They have regarded the vertical organization of the minor triad as itself constituting the essential and peculiar feature of the minor mode. Yet the very name, "minor mode," indicates that what is involved is not a single, isolated structure (the triad) within the style system but rather a special system of tonal relationships within the style as a whole, i.e., a mode.

Melodically the minor mode differs from most other modes in that it is quasi-chromatic and changeable, appearing in several different versions, while other modes, whether the major mode of Western music, the modes of oriental music, or those of folk music and primitive music, are essentially diatonic and stable. This can be illustrated simply by comparing the number of tones available in most modes with those available in the minor mode. For instance, the major mode of Western music (Example 87, *A*) uses the same seven tones, whether ascending or descending, as does the primitive African scale (*B*) given by Hornbostel,[75] while the Japanese *Hirajoshi* scale (*C*) given by Sachs,[76] contains only five tones, ascending or descending. The minor mode, on the other hand, ap-

EXAMPLE 87

pears in three basic versions: the melodic minor ascending (Example 88, *A*), the natural minor descending (*B*), and the harmonic minor as well as in various permutations and combinations of these. If the commonly used phrygian (lowered) second of the scale, a tone imported from another mode, is included in the repertory of tones furnished by the variants of the mode given in *A* and *B*, all but two of the twelve tones of the chromatic scale are present and available in the minor mode (*C*).

EXAMPLE 88

Sometimes melodies in the minor mode are markedly chromatic. The theme of Bach's *Musical Offering*, for instance, employs eleven tones of the chromatic scale in what is, to all intents and purposes, a strict linear order (Example 89). In such cases the relationship between the minor mode and the affective quality attributed to it is not hard to establish. (The relationship between uniformity, ambiguity, and chromaticism has already been discussed in chapter v.)

EXAMPLE 89

But not all melodies or even a majority of the melodies written in the minor mode employ all of the tones available. Nor are the tones used generally arranged in linear (scalar) succession. Though in the minor mode, the opening melody of Brahms's Sonata in D Minor for Violin and Piano (Example 90) involves practically no chromaticism. Nevertheless, the affective quality of the minor mode makes itself felt even in such diatonic minor melodies. There are

EXAMPLE 90

several reasons for this. First, the minor mode is always potentially chromatic, and the listener practiced in the perception of and response to this music is well aware of the ever present possibility of chromaticism. Second, the tendencies of tones as they approach substantive tones is stronger in minor than in major. For the two most important substantive tones each have an additional "leading tone" in the minor; i.e., the fifth can be approached from a half step above and the tonic can be approached through the phrygian second. Furthermore, the tendency of the third toward the tonic is stronger in minor than in major because of its proximity to the second and hence to the tonic. The proximity of these tendency tones to substantive tones in the minor mode makes a delay in the arrival of a substantive tone particularly intensely felt. Third, while the probability of a particular succession of tones is greater in minor as we approach substantive tones, it is considerably weaker as we depart from substantive tones. For the very fact that the minor mode possesses a richer repertory of tones means that the probability of the occurrence of any particular given tone is weaker, the more so because the tones in the repertory tend to be used as alternatives for one another—i.e., either B or B-flat, A or A-flat, etc., may, for instance, be used in the key of C minor to follow some substantive tone. In other words, the minor mode is by its very nature more ambiguous than modes with a more limited repertory of tones.

From a harmonic point of view, the minor mode is both more ambiguous and less stable than the major mode. It is more ambiguous because the repertory of possible vertical combinations is much greater in minor than in major and, consequently, the probability of any particular progression of harmonies is smaller. While the tonic chord in the major mode can, with varying degrees of probability, move to any one of six triads (Example 91, *A*), the tonic chord in the minor mode can move to any one of at least thirteen different triads (*B*), not counting the chromatically altered chords so common in minor. Furthermore, in the major mode only one of the triads, the one built upon the seventh degree of the scale (marked with a cross in Example 91), is itself ambiguous. But in the minor mode four such ambiguous triads are possible. The diminished or augmented triads (marked with a cross in Example 91) are ambiguous

EXAMPLE 91

because their uniform construction enables them to imply several equiprobable resolutions (see pp. 166 ff.). In short, because their uniform construction leaves them without a root or focal point, they can easily swerve into new and sometimes remote tonal spheres. This instability of the triadic unit is complemented by the fact that in its natural form, i.e., without the raised leading tone, the minor mode as a total system lacks stability in that it tends to gravitate toward the key of the relative major. And this tendency is perhaps a sign of the basic harmonic normality of the major mode.

This analysis also accounts for the practice, common in recent

Western music, of moving from the major mode to the minor mode at the beginning of bridge passages, episodes, development sections (see Examples 37 and 63). Similarly it explains the practice of employing the minor mode for introductions to pieces which are in major (see Example 73). For since the minor mode tends to be chromatic and ambiguous, it provides a natural and convenient way of moving from the stable processes of the theme groups to the more irregular and uncertain progressions of the moving passages.

The interrelationship between affectivity, melodic and harmonic chromaticism, and the minor mode is not simply a theoretical or an accidental correspondence. It is a historical fact. The connection between them is not only a logical one but, as the following passage makes clear, a genetic one as well.

The desire for ever more vivid expression brought about increased use of chromaticism; a trend away from constructivism toward free designs dependent upon the changing content of the text; and the suggestion of dramatic recitative. The last of these, with its approach to monody through the predominance of the top voice and, incidentally, to the major-minor system, thus went hand in hand with much the same kind of chordal writing and lightly imitative counterpoint that are found in other music of the period.[77]

The minor mode is not only associated with intense feeling in general but with the delineation of sadness, suffering, and anguish in particular. This association, which as we have seen is also connected with chromaticism in general, appears to arise out of two different though related facts: (1) States of calm contentment and gentle joy are taken to be the normal human emotional states and are hence associated with the more normative musical progressions, i.e., the diatonic melodies of the major mode and the regular progressions of major harmony. Anguish, misery, and other extreme states of affectivity are deviants and become associated with the more forceful departures of chromaticism and its modal representative, i.e., the minor mode. (2) Marked or complex chromatic motions common in the minor mode—melodic lines which move conjunctly by semitones or disjunctly by unusual skips and uncommon harmonic progressions—have tended to be accompanied by tempi which were slower than those which accompanied more diatonic music. This was, of course, particularly true of the earlier use of chromaticism during the Renaissance and the baroque period. This coincidence of chromaticism and its modal representative with slower tempi can be explained at least in part on technical grounds. For not only are the instruments constructed with the diatonic norm in view so that it is more difficult to play chromatic passages rapidly, but musical training, both instrumental and vocal, is based upon the normality and simplicity of diatonic progression. Even after three centuries of the major-minor system Heinlein found that in a random sampling of some twenty-five hundred compositions for beginners only 7 per cent were in minor and almost all of these had descriptive titles of some sort. "It is," he writes, "a difficult matter to obtain a composition in the minor mode written for children that does not have a title related to the weird, the mysterious, the sad and the gloomy." [78]

Thus the association between the minor mode and emotional states depicting sadness and suffering is a product of the deviant, unstable character of the mode and of the association of sadness and suffering with the slower tempi that tend to accompany the chromaticism prevalent in the minor mode. Of course, there are numerous exceptions to this association, as a glance at the literature of the past century shows.

Although the affective qualities of the minor mode depend primarily upon its quasi-chromatic modal characteristics, the minor triad as such seems to have a peculiar power. This is particularly striking where the same melody is played first in the major and then in the minor, as, for instance, in the middle section of Chopin's Waltz in A Minor, Op. 34, No. 2. But it is not actually the triad per se which has this affective power. For it has been shown that the character of the triad depends upon and can be changed by training and musical context. Indeed, once a modal norm has been established within a given work, the reverse progression, from minor to major, can also create a powerful effect—as it does in the first movement of Schubert's String Quartet in A Minor. In so far as the minor triad in and of itself is an affective force it is so because it has become through association the sign and herald of the mode as a whole and all that the mode implies by way of chromaticism, modulation, and suspense.

Finally, it is clear that none of the foregoing discussion is meant to imply that all chromatic pieces are in the minor mode. The connection is common but by no means necessary.

CONSONANCE AND DISSONANCE

The role of dissonance in arousing affect or in depicting emotional states is evident in the practice of composers and in the writings of theorists and critics. Vincenzo Galilei, for instance, writes:

. . . In setting to music a sonnet, canzone, romanzo, madrigal, or other poem in which occurs a line saying, for example:

Bitter heart and savage, and cruel will,

which is the first line of one of the sonnets of Petrarch they [composers] have caused many sevenths, fourths, seconds, and major sixths to be sung between the parts and by means of these have made a rough, harsh, and unpleasant sound in the ears of the listeners.[79]

The specification of emotional states indicated in this quotation depends not only upon the use of dissonance but also upon conventional association.

Other writers treat dissonance in more general terms. C. P. E. Bach, for example, says that ". . . in general it can be said that dissonances are played loudly and consonances softly, since the former rouse our emotions and the latter quiet them." [80] Dissonance is also considered from a more purely aesthetic viewpoint. Zarlino, for instance, points out that while a composition is made up primarily of consonances, dissonance adds beauty and elegance to the work and makes the consonance which follows more acceptable and sweet. In fact, if compositions were "made up entirely of consonances, although beautiful sounds and good effects would issue from them, they would still be somehow imperfect, both as sound and composition, seeing that . . . they would lack the great elegance that dissonance affords." [81]

The aesthetic affective pleasure of dissonance in relation to consonance is not confined to Western music but has been noted in connection with oriental and primitive music as well. This is made clear, for instance, in the observations made by Rear Admiral D'Entrecasteaux about music in the Friendly Islands:

. . . She, the Queen, was there giving a vocal concert in which the Futtafaihe sang and beat time, which all the musicians followed with greatest exactness. Some performed their part in it by accompanying, with different modulations, the simple melody of the others. We now and then remarked some discordant notes, with which, however, the ear of these people seemed much gratified.[82]

Acousticians and psychologists from Pythagoras to Révécz have attempted to explain and account for the phenomena of consonance and dissonance on acoustical psychological grounds, but as yet no tenable, unobjectionable theory has been advanced.[83] For consonance and dissonance are not primarily acoustical phenomena, rather they are human mental phenomena and as such they depend for their definition upon the psychological laws governing human perception, upon the context in which the perception arises, and upon the learned response patterns which are part of this context. The case is well stated by Cazden:

Though much effort has been wasted in philosophical blind-alleys, studies of the psychology of musical perception have produced important negative results regarding consonance and dissonance. The naive view that by some occult process mathematical ratios are consciously transferred to musical perception has been rejected. Fusion or 'unitariness of tonal impression,' has been found to produce no fixed order of preference for intervals, with the remarkable exception of the octave. It has been discovered that individual judgments of consonance can be enormously modified by training. Perceptions of consonance by adult standards do not seem generally valid for children below the age of twelve or thirteen, a strong indication that they are learned responses.

In musical harmony the critical determinant of consonance and dissonance is expectation of movement. . . . A consonant interval is one which sounds stable and complete in itself, which does not produce a feeling of necessary movement to other tones. A dissonant interval causes a restless expectation of resolution, or movement to a consonant interval. . . . Context is the determining factor.

The resolution of intervals does not have a natural basis; it is a common response acquired by all individuals within a culture-area.[84]

It would undoubtedly simplify matters considerably if one could adopt such a completely cultural theory of consonance without reservations. Yet, in spite of recognizing the social and cultural nature of musical experience and the importance of context in the perception of and response to consonance and dissonance, viewpoints such as this, reacting to the absolutism prevalent for two thousand years, go too far. Such an exclusively cultural position is not only faced with the remarkable fact that the octave is a focal point in the music of all cultures but with the tendency for the fifth or fourth to become substantive tones and restful, consonant intervals.

For in this admittedly social art there is one constant: the nature of human thinking, the tendency to organize the stimuli presented to the mind by the senses in the simplest possible way. To put the matter in Gestalt terms: because of the way in which sounds combine, the learned responses of the listener, and the context in which an interval appears, a consonance forms a stable, total entity, while a dissonance forms a less stable, a less satisfactory, though not less necessary, Gestalt. On this basis it would be expected that if the octave is a simpler, more unified shape, then it would naturally tend to be more constant in changes of stimulation than other intervals would. Less well-integrated intervallic shapes, such as the third, sixth or second, would, on the other hand, presumably be more subject to changes in the cultural environment. Thus once we leave the octave, and perhaps the fifth and fourth, cultural factors (such as the accidents attendant upon the construction of instruments or the discoveries made in playful artistic deviation) play an increasingly important role in the development of the style system.

Why the octave is perceived as a particularly stable, well-shaped Gestalt and why the fifth and fourth tend, as demonstrated by their very frequent appearance in widely different cultures, to become normative intervals requires further study. The important point here is that the modes of human perception and intellection must be taken into account if an adequate theory of consonance and dissonance is to be developed.

It is evident, no matter what theory we adopt, that consonance "represents the element of normalcy and repose, [dissonance] the no less important element of irregularity and disturbance." [85] Dissonances, in short, are tendencies. This being the case, it is not difficult to see that dissonance derives its affective power, its elegance, as Zarlino puts it, from the fact that it is a deviant, delaying the arrival of an expected norm, the consonance appropriate in the particular stylistic, musical context. [86]

VII

The Evidence: Simultaneous and Successive Deviation

The musical processes examined so far—expressive deviations in pitch and rhythm, ornamentation, delays in the expected tonal succession, chromaticism, and so forth—have, generally speaking, been confined to a single melodic line or, as in the case of harmony, to a group of voices which were rhythmically more or less simultaneous. Moreover, in these processes the norms involved have been, on the whole, those which are given in the culture and style rather than those which, though rooted in tradition, are established by the composer-performer within the context of the work itself. This chapter considers the relationship of "simultaneous deviation" and "successive deviation" to affective aesthetic responses. The term "simultaneous deviation" denotes those musical situations in which two or more voices are "played off" against one another, either rhythmically, melodically, or both. The term "successive deviation" denotes those musical situations in which a norm established within the work itself (e.g., a melodic or rhythmic pattern) is repeated with either embellishments or major modifications. Of course, successive deviation may also include simultaneous deviation.

These processes are still, in a broad sense of the term, types of ornamentation, i.e., they are rhythmic and melodic embellishments of a basic structural plan. Although they differ in means rather than in kind from the processes already discussed, it is clear that simultaneous variation is more closely allied to what we normally call ornamentation, while successive variation is more closely related to what we normally think of as "form."

Simultaneous Deviation

Simultaneous deviation is very common in the Far East. In this type of deviation, which is often a kind of heterophony, the norm itself is presented together with one or more deviants which ornament it, modify its melodic outlines, and play with its rhythmic structure. Such heterophony is common in both accompanied songs and large orchestra pieces. Both musicians and musical ethnologists point out that this interplay between a basic melodic, rhythmic and metric structure and its simultaneous elaboration in the accompanying parts is an important source of aesthetic pleasure.

From a rhythmic and metric point of view the elaborating part plays around the chief melodic voice, now anticipating its notes, now coinciding with them, and now falling behind them. The deviating voice breaks up the longer tones into ornate filigrees and generally elaborates the rhythm and meter. Thus in Javanese poetry we find the statement that "the rebab part was characterized by the peculiarity that it now anticipated the melody, now coincided again with the other instruments." [1] Sachs notes that

. . . nearly all East Asiatic accompaniment depends on shifted phrases, on canonlike anticipation and retardation. The singer displays a rich ornamental realization of some melodic pattern, and the player, having this same pattern in mind, gives the singer all the freedom required and carefully tries to follow. His notes come in correct—though not pedantically precise—order, but are delayed when the voice unexpectedly restrains its ornaments and are ahead when the singer dwells upon a phrase. [2]

The basic metric structure is regular in most of this music. Kunst refers to the "quadratic structure" underlying the singer's ornamentation and Eta Harich-Schneider notes essentially the same thing with regard to Japanese court music. [3] Example 92 is a very simple illustration of this type of rhythmic and melodic displacement. [4]

In the course of such deviations clashes often occur between the notes of the structural voice and those of the ornamenting voice. To these dissonances must be added those which occur because of embellishments, the slight pitch waverings and glissandi so dear to the style of the Orient, and those which result from outright modifications and changes in the tones of the melody. In this latter category fall the *meri-kari* of Japanese court music, which Harich-Schneider describes as "the lowering and raising of the pitch observed in the parts of the vocalist, flute, and oboe-like reed while the rest of the instruments proceed in the unaltered intervals indicated in the partbooks."[5]

EXAMPLE 92 [*]

These wavering altered tones, which sound so weird and unusual to Western ears, are considered by the Japanese to be particularly expressive. This is what we should expect. For such deviations, delaying the arrival of substantive tones and inhibiting the normative coincidence of patterns, would, according to the present analysis, give rise to affect.

In the orchestras of Japan and Java simultaneous deviation is often very elaborate and complex. In Java, for example, one group of instruments, the single row *bonangs,* carry the nuclear theme and occasionally add a modest ornament, while other, higher instruments paraphrase this basic theme: "Now they anticipate it, now they analyze it into smaller values or imitate it at the octave. Then again they syncopate it. . . ."[6] In Kunst's words they "play around" with the theme. It is this play of simultaneous variations against one another which creates the motion from tension to release and affords to the trained listener a high degree of aesthetic pleasure.

In the Far East drumming generally serves to reinforce the important beats in an essentially four-square meter. But in India the drum not only articulates the meter of the singer's melody but frequently varies it by means of cross rhythms and cross meters. Fox Strang-

[*] Reprint permission granted by *The Musical Quarterly* and G. Schirmer, Inc., copyright owners.

ways quotes one Indian drummer as saying that "The beat (with the left hand) is like the seam of my coat—that must be there; the other notes (with the right hand) are like the embroidery I may put according to my own fancy over the seam!" [7]

Cross-rhythm drumming in India, in some parts of Indonesia, and in Africa is often extremely complex. Its function is to add tension and interest by creating subtle counter rhythms and meters to those of the melodic line. Beginning with a coincidence of beats, the drummer will play in what we would call 3/8 time, while the instrumentalist plays his melody, which is in 3/2 time, as, for instance, in Example 93.[8]

EXAMPLE 93 *

Notice that at the beginning the melodic instrument plays a measure of $4 + 4 + 2 + 2$ or $3 \times 4 = 12$, while the drum plays four groups of three, equalling twelve. They come out together at the beginning of the third measure, at a point of metric coincidence or "consonance," as Sachs puts it. Later the drum plays in units of eight $(3 + 3 + 2)$, while the melody continues in twelve $(4 + 4 + 2 + 2)$. Here the metric consonance takes place only after two measures: i.e., in the melody $2 \times 12 = 24$, while in the drum $3 \times 8 = 24$.

The crossing of the rhythm and meter serves not only to create tension within the line but also to articulate a simple type of over-all strophic form. That is, the melody remains constant; but the rhythm and meter which accompany each statement of the tune modify it, giving rise to a series of variations.

This is a fairly simple example of an extremely complex practice and theory.[9] Such crossing affords great delight to the Indian audience, particularly when it involves intricate deviations from the

* The example is given by permission of The Clarendon Press, Oxford, publishers.

standard pattern or the introduction of new ones. In all this there is a strong element of play. "The singer and drummer like to play hide and seek with each other; and the audience watch the contest with amusement." [10]

The same type of contest is described in some detail by Sargeant and Lahiri:

It often happens among Indian Musicians that a *vina* player and a drummer will engage in a friendly contest to see which can confuse the other into losing track of the *sam* [the structural beat]. The *vina* player will improvise a melody. The drummer, to whom the melody is of course unfamiliar, must first discover where the *sam* is. Having discovered it he starts his drumming. For a while everything runs smoothly. Then the syncopation and cross rhythm become very complex. The *vina* player uses all sorts of ruses to disguise the *sam*. . . . The drummer will meanwhile seek to confuse his opponent by insisting on his cross rhythms as though they were the true basic meter, playing meters of seven, or five against the latter's four or three and so on. Each one strives with might and main to retain his equilibrium. Eventually one or the other misses the *sam* and is worsted.[11]

The relationship of such contests to the creation and conquest of difficulties, to the process of play, is clear. And play is, as we have seen (p. 70), but one of the ways of looking at the affective aesthetic musical experience. There are, moreover, obvious similarities between this account of musical experience and those given by Raguenet, Glarean, and Dance (see p. 208). Indeed Sargeant and Lahiri themselves point out the resemblance between the experiences of Hindu music and jazz.

This type of syncopation, which is very much like that employed by Jazz players in their "breaks," except that it is infinitely more complicated, is an essential part of the technique of *gath*. The *vina* player delights in apparently losing himself in the most abstruse counter-rhythms, leaving the listener with a sense of utter bewilderment, only to issue forth triumphantly at the *sam* again without a hair's breadth of inaccuracy, and with a sparkle of obvious satisfaction. The effect, to one who is accustomed to this idiom of expression, is that of being hurled through chaos, and then suddenly landing right side up on terra firma again with no bones broken and a feeling of intense relief.[12]

Not all Indian music has a drum accompaniment. But even in unaccompanied music an underlying beat, against which the singer or instrumentalist performs intricate rhythmic and metric deviations, is presupposed. This can be seen in an example taken from Sargeant's article (see Example 94). The *astai* or "at home" is the main theme and the *tans* are short sections of varied rhythmic and metric material which are always of a certain length and metric structure. The metric structure or *tala* upon which the *tan* is built consists in this case of four beats arranged thus: 1 – 2 – 3 – 0 (not sounded). This metric structure is repeated four times during each statement of the *astai* and five times during the particular *tan* given in this example. The all-important *sam* or structural guide beat falls on the second beat of the *tala,* on the first important beat of the *astai,* and

EXAMPLE 94 °

on the first beat of the *tan*. In this passage the *vina* player must constantly keep this basic underlying organization in mind while playing meters of 3/8, 4/8, 5/8, and 4/4 against it. Similarly the audience must keep track of the *tala*. Notice that in the *tan* given in this example the performer plays with our expectations by playing a "false" *sam*, a device very similar to the so-called false recapitula-

° Reprint permission granted by *The Musical Quarterly* and G. Schirmer, Inc., copyright owners.

tion in sonata form. What happens is that the performer plays the melodic pattern which indicates a return to the *astai* but because the pattern occurs on the wrong beat, on 1 instead of 2, which is the *sam,* the return is "false." Only when the relationship between the *tala* and the melody is correct does the *astai* really return. Thus by raising our expectations, disappointing them, and finally satisfying them, the composer-performer molds an exciting and moving experience.

Not all oriental music, of course, has such a complex and intricate rhythmic metric organization. For instance, in the preludes, which so often precede more stable, traditional forms, the rhythmic-metric structure is free, almost rhapsodic. This is true of the *netori* of Japanese court music, the Indian *ālāpa,* the Arabian *taqsīm,* and the Indonesian *bebuka.*

Unfortunately little of the extensive research done in the field of primitive music is of value for this study. First, because the primitives themselves do not make musical creation a self-conscious endeavor, they have neither a theory of music nor even a crude "aesthetic" which might serve to connect their musical practices to their responses. It seems clear that on the most primitive level music is, on the one hand so intimately connected with ritual and magic that its aesthetic content is severely restricted and, on the other hand, that it is so closely associated with bodily effort that its shape and organization are to a considerable degree products of the physical activities connected with ritual, labor, or expressive behavior. And second, because music ethnologists have tended to collect and classify tunes and instruments, compile statistics, and concern themselves with the sociology of primitive music, the aesthetic meaning, if any, which music has for the primitive musician or listener, has for the most part been ignored.

However, African music, which can be called primitive only with great misgivings, has reached a very high state of development. It is especially complex and subtle in its rhythmic organization.

The very essence of African music is to *cross the rhythms.* This does not mean syncopation. On the whole African music is *not* based on syncopation. To put it in its simplest terms, what we mean by 'crossing the rhythms' is that if, say, two Africans are drumming in triple time and at the same speed (e.g. in 3/8 time where a dotted crochet equals 140) the main beat of the bar of No. 2 drum will fall either on the second beat of the bar of No. 1 drum or on the third, but *never* on the first. This is absolutely fundamental to African music. In actual practice, in a large ensemble, some instruments and singers do actually make their main-beats coincide. But this is only *duplication* of a rhythm and it is possible only because some other performers are already crossing the beat.[18]

If we look at an example of this, the whole process becomes quite clear and its complexities apparent.[14] In the following, three drums —the *Nzupe-nzupe*, the *Cibitiku*, and the *Kambape*—play an intro-duction known as *sefa*. The *Nzupe-nzupe* (*N*) begins alone beating a 3/8 group, as in Example 95.

EXAMPLE 95 °

Then the *Cibitiku* (*C*) also beating a 3/8 pattern comes in in such a way that the first beat of his pattern coincides with the last beat of the *N* drum (Example 96).

EXAMPLE 96

This forms the foundation which runs not only through *sefa* but through the following song and dance as well.

The *Kambape* (*K*) plays eighths which are equal in value to those played by the other drums, but they form a group of 2/4 notes rather than one of 3/8. This gives us the total pattern for the introduction (Example 97). Notice that, although the main beats of all three never coincide, the *C* and *K* drums do arrive at a coinci-dence at every twelfth eighth note.

The *sefa* continues until the leader of the dance gives a signal for the beginning of the song and dance. On the last playing of the

EXAMPLE 97

sefa, the K drum lengthens his beat from a quarter note to a dotted quarter in order to prepare for the rhythm which he will play during the song and dance. The song and dance enter in 12/8, which is really composed of $8 \times 3/16 = 24/16$. We now have four different patterns going on simultaneously in such a way that the main beats of three of the figures correspond every twelfth eighth note (see Example 98). Later in the song the organization becomes even more complex because the rhythm of the K drum changes when the chorus enters.

EXAMPLE 98

It is clear that the organization of this and other African pieces bears a strong resemblance to certain types of Indian and Indonesian music. We find here the same movement from complication of rhythm and meter to greater unity and coincidence that was found in Indian and other oriental music. And it is interesting to note that

Jones, like Sachs, though evidently quite independently of him, makes an analogy between the role of the temporal organization in African music and the role of harmony in Western music.

All this rhythm-crossing is the spice of life to the African. It is his real harmony. He is intoxicated by this rhythmic harmony, or rhythmic polyphony, just as we react to chordal harmony. It is this remarkable interplay of main-beats that causes him irresistibly, when he hears the drums, to start moving his feet, his arms, his whole body. This to him is real music.[15]

Hornbostel implies much the same sort of thing when he writes that: "The combination of binary and ternary time is characteristic of African metre in general. The principal division is two-fold: a period breaks up into question and answer, tension and relaxation, arsis and thesis. . . ."[16]

Richard Waterman's discussion of off-beat rhythms in African music confirms directly or by implication many of the observations made in this study. Waterman begins by observing that in order for there to be "off-beating," a series of regularly recurring pulses, a normative beat, must become established in the mind of the listener. This beat, which Waterman calls the "metronome sense," is primarily mental: "The regular recurrence of rhythmic awareness involves expectancy."[17] The off-beats are deviants from this normative pulse. They must be irregular or else they too will become normative; for "complete 'off-beating' has the same effect as complete lack of off-beat patterns; it is in this sense meaningless."[18] And, finally, the following statement, which cannot fail to recall those of Raguenet, Glarean, Dance, and Sargeant, relates the process of off-beating to the overcoming of difficulties, to uncertainty, and through these to affective aesthetic experience: "The off-beat phrasing of accents, then, must threaten, but never completely destroy, the orientation of the listener's subjective metronome."[19]

Simultaneous variation is not common in most folk music, which is essentially "soloistic." But in jazz it is of the essence. In jazz we find the same use of a basic beat against which counter rhythms and opposing metric patterns are played as we saw in Indian music. The procedures of jazz are very similar to the technique of *gath*: the main melody, the jazz tune, corresponds to the *astai*, and a "break" in jazz corresponds to a *tan* in the technique of *gath*. The tune or *astai* alternates with the "breaks" or *tans* against the background of a recurring pattern. In jazz this background, which is both metric and harmonic, is called a "riff." In India this background, which is metric, is called the *tala* or *tintal*. As was the case with *gath* technique, suspense and uncertainty play an important part in the response to jazz.

> The break, then, is a temporary lapse from the rigors of strict structure, in which logic is momentarily suspended and improvisatory chaos reigns. Its effect is to heighten the element of suspense and unrest. The listener is thrown for the moment on unmapped confusing ground. The basic rhythm ceases to offer its familiar thumping landmarks. The solo dangles dizzily without hope of support, and then, just as the listener has about abandoned hope of reorienting himself, the fundamental rhythm resumes its orderly way, and a feeling of relief ensues.
>
> In this process the fundamental rhythm is not really destroyed. The perceptive listener holds in his mind a continuation of its regular pulse even though the orchestra has stopped marking it. . . . The situation during the silent pulses is one that challenges the listener to hold his bearings. If he has any sort of rhythmic sense he will not be content to lose himself.[20]

In spite of the similarity between the processes described in this quotation and those discussed by Waterman, the procedures of jazz are somewhat different from those existing in African music. In jazz a clear and quite regular norm (the tune) is generally established before any rhythmic elaboration takes place. This makes the break a clear deviation from a norm. Thus the expectation of a return to regularity is a basic organizing principle in this music. In this respect jazz is, in a sense, more like Hindu music in which the *astai* alternates with the *tan*. In most African music tension operates within the "phrase" and is the organizing, articulating principle of the phrase. But tension does not perform an over-all organizing function, save in the sense that it creates a type of variation form. In other words, the level of tension is relatively constant between parts, though not within them.

Simultaneous melodic deviation is present in African music as it is in Japanese and Javanese music. The Chopi musicians of Portuguese East Africa play a heterophonic type of music on xylophones which is very similar to that of Java. After the composer-performer has developed a tune and its accompaniment, the other players join in with their own versions of the tune. Hugh Tracey reported that he heard "at least four variations on the basic melody in the front rank alone." [21] Hornbostel [22] gives a particularly interesting example in which the flute, which performs the main deviations, plays a fifth higher than the fundamental melodic line which is carried by the chorus. Speaking of the flute part, Hornbostel notes that: ". . . it follows the vocal part only half way and even there not strictly, indulging in playful deviations; then instead of going on to the second half, it repeats the first one, thus transforming the tune into an ostinato." [23] A wind instrument follows the tune in so far as its restricted repertory of tones will allow—performing slight deviations either of necessity or design—while a horn plays a drone on the tonic, apparently employing a counter rhythm in duple meter against the triple meter of the main parts.

Simultaneous deviation in the form of cross meters has not been common in Western music since the Renaissance, that is, until the twentieth century. Because a harmony must, almost by definition, be perceived as a single entity rather than an interplay between independent coexisting entities, the rise of tonal harmony meant an ever increasing emphasis upon vertical simultaneity, upon a co-incidence of main beats.

However, before the rise of tonal harmony, there was a considerable amount of metric and rhythmic crossing in Western music. The beginning of Convert's chanson, "Se Mieulx ne Vient" (Copenhagen MS, Thott 291[8]), for instance, provides a rather simple illustration of what was often a very complex practice in the fifteenth century (Example 99).[24] The presence of crossing—of the opposition of

EXAMPLE 99

6/8 and 3/4 meters and subsequently of $3 \times 2/4$ against 3/4 plus 6/8—is obvious in this example. Since unfortunately the significance of such metric crossing was not discussed in the theoretical or critical writings of the fifteenth century, we have nothing that relates these metric procedures to affective aesthetic experience. But one cannot help feeling that this music moves through increasing complexity to a metric "consonance" on the B and G.

We find only a few examples of metric crossing between the Renaissance and the twentieth century (see, for instance, Example 37). This does not mean that the resources of rhythm were not utilized during this period. Metric organization and deviation took other forms, e.g., the delays, anticipations, gaps, and incompleteness, whether of the main melodic line or of the over-all vertical organization, which were discussed at some length in chapter iv.

The twentieth century has from its very beginning sought and found inspiration in the resources of rhythm and meter. This, coupled with a tendency toward a more linear style of composition, has led to more frequent use of cross meters, as, for instance in Example 100 from the "Seconda Parte" of Bartók's Third String Quar-

EXAMPLE 100 °

tet. Here, as can clearly be seen from the abstract of the rhythmic pattern given in Example 101, the 6/8 and 3/8 meters of the cello

EXAMPLE 101

° Copyright 1929 by Universal-Edition. Copyright assigned 1939 to Boosey & Hawkes, Ltd. Used by permission.

and viola are played off against the 3/4 meter of the first violin, which is itself "crossed" by that of the second violin.

What in terms of contemporary style in general and that of Bartók in particular is the significance of such rhythmic crossing? Does it represent "a breathing in and out" of the phrase? Do we feel a motion from tension to expected release? In this case, at least, it appears that the rhythmic crossing is a norm of the movement; for not only does the *modus operandi* illustrated above continue for some time but rhythmic crossing is present almost at the outset of the movement, where Bartók indicates the coincidence of two separate meters by his notation.

We cannot as yet generalize about the use of simultaneous rhythmic deviation in contemporary music. The norms of the new style have not yet clearly emerged; and it is entirely possible that when they do, simultaneous metric deviation will be found to be a norm of the new style. At present we can determine the intended effect of cross rhythms only by the normative or deviant character of other devices used concurrently with them.

Successive Deviation

Every piece of music establishes norms—the melodies, rhythmic figures, instrumental groups, harmonic progressions, etc., created by the composer within the specific stylistic context—which are peculiar to that particular work. Such intra-opus norms may embody the stylistic norms upon which they depend or they may themselves be deviations from those norms. The "Tristan" motive, for instance, is replete with deviations from the diatonic norm which it presupposes and involves significant modifications of the normal simultaneity of harmonic progression. Thus the basic materials presented by a particular work may at times be said to involve successive deviation from the outset, in the sense that the materials embody deviations from the norms of the stylistic universe of discourse which is always prior to any particular work.

Often the stylistic universe of discourse contains alternative norms, as for example where several melodic or rhythmic modes are more or less equally normative within a style. When this is the case, the particular mode to be used may be rehearsed in a kind of prelude in order to establish the particular norm in the minds of the composer and listener alike. This is one of the main functions of the Indian *ālāpa*, the Arabian *maqām*, the Indonesian *bebuka*, the preludes to more sophisticated primitive music,[25] and the toccatas, fantasias, and introductions found in the music of the West.[26] The importance and significance of such "preluding"—a practice found in almost every type of music—lie in the fact that they support by implication the hypothesis that the process of deviation from habit-expected norms is one of the basic forces shaping and articulating musical experience. For in all the statements about such "preludes" it is made clear that the preludes serve to establish the norms with which the main piece will operate and from which it will, in one way or another, deviate. The norms thus established facilitate the perception and response to later deviations and are therefore a necessary condition for the arousal of affect and objectified meaning.[27]

That such introductions involve considerable melodic and rhythmic freedom and that they do not as a rule present well-shaped, substantive patterns leads one to speculate whether they do not perform a formal function, arousing tension and expectation. There are several reasons for supposing that they do so. In the first place, in the particular cultural context the audience knows that the *ālāpa, netori, sefa,* etc., is not the real piece but is only a precursor of the main event, which more often than not is known to involve dancing, singing, or both. And it is only natural to suppose that the listeners look forward to and expect the real piece. Second, as we have seen, a stimulus series which is not as well shaped as might be expected within the given stylistic context arouses an expectation of better articulation and more palpable patterns.

Once such a prelude or introduction has been presented, the norms of rhythm, melody, and harmony specific to the particular work are usually presented. These are generally speaking not only relatively well structured in and of themselves but seem especially so because they have been preceded by the more weakly articulated patterns of the introduction. These norms then become the basis for subsequent deviations.

Unfortunately both music theorists and ethnologists have mainly been concerned with stylistic descriptions and tabulations rather than with aesthetic effect. They have thus tended to discuss the process and significance of successive deviation only in the broadest terms. They simply tell us that the folk singer, the primitive musician, and the oriental composer do vary their materials in an elaborate and more or less conscious way, and they then describe and illustrate the processes involved. But of the affective aesthetic meaning of these processes to the artists we hear comparatively little.

Almost all writings about oriental music stress the presence of variation in this music and acknowledge its importance in the several styles considered. Although the greatest variations (deviations) from inter-opus norms generally occur toward the middle of a song or instrumental piece, exact repetition even at the beginning or end is almost unknown. Very often, moreover, one gets the impression that, as in folk music, the real norm is not actually presented by the composer-performer but rather exists in the minds and habit responses of the musicians and the audience. In other words, the opening motives are themselves "variations"—deviations from a cultural stylistic ideal type.

The problem in dealing with this material is one of interpretation. The facts are quite clear. Even a cursory glance at this Japanese song, given in Example 102, reveals the presence of successive deviation (variation) between the three verses quoted.[28]

EXAMPLE 102 °

° Reprint permission granted by the Harvard University Press, publishers.

To Western ears it seems clear that such successive deviation—the displacement of the rhythm and meter and the variation in the tone order—constitutes an affective aesthetic intensification; but in the absence of precise testimony from those whose habit responses are attuned to this style, such an interpretation might easily involve a misunderstanding of the meaning of the passage.

Though it is difficult to find written evidence to directly support interpretations of the affective aesthetic significance of such deviations, it is possible to utilize other indirect, corroborative evidence. For different types and levels of deviation tend to appear in concert, supporting one another in the evocation of the affective aesthetic experience. Expressive pitch deviations, for instance, are usually employed in coincidence with marked ornamentation, as in the music of India. Discontinuity of melodic and rhythmic patterns and the weakening of shape, are usually accompanied by chromatic sequences or ambiguity, as in Western music. In like manner it seems generally true that successive deviation tends to involve increased ornamentation, an intensification of simultaneous deviation, etc. And it is reasonable to suppose that since successive deviation is commonly associated with other types of deviation, which can be shown to have an affective aesthetic function, successive deviation itself performs a similar function.

The process and effect of successive deviation is especially clear in the music of India. In the following south Indian piece (Example 103), the *pallavi* (the south Indian term for *astai*) meaning "germ" or "sprout" consists of a three-measure melody (*A*), a conjunctive measure (*x*), and a repetition of the three-measure tune (*A'*).[29] It is clear that only slight modifications of the tune occur in the first total repetition (1); the most important of these, for present purposes, being the fact that the tone D occurs in the first measure instead of in the second. But in the second repetition of the tune (2) the opening measure of the first variation (*a''*) is expanded into five measures. This prolongation performs an aesthetic function, not only by deviating from the inter-opus norm established in the earlier statements of the *pallavi*, but also because it serves to delay the arrival of the expected substantive tone C, which is repeatedly implied by the descending scales g-f-e and f-e-d. It also seems probable that the first, extended half of the *pallavi* should be considered as tending toward the unextended, normative second half, thus creating a hierarchy of tendencies. In the third variation (3) the first measure of the theme is expanded still further (to nine measures), partly through the addition of an upbeat which delays the arrival of the opening motive. Such successive deviations are related by Strangways to affect and aesthetic play.[30]

EXAMPLE 103 °

In Jewish and Byzantine chant of the Near East successive deviation consists more in the arrangement of brief melodic formulas, and the ornamentation of these, than in variation of the type found in Indian or Far Eastern music.[31]

The examination of the structure of the melodies has made it clear that they are all built up of a limited number of formulas, short groups of notes that are significant of the mode, the echos of the melody.

The fact that the vast number of Byzantine melodies can be reduced to a limited number of archetypes may lead to a wrong judgment of the creative qualities of Byzantine composers. . . . The melodic archetypes he had to use and combine were to his mind the *apēchēma,* the echo of

° By permission of The Clarendon Press, Oxford.

the divine hymns. The work of the composer consisted in giving the melodies a new frame by linking them together.[32]

Elsewhere Wellesz relates this type of successive deviation to aesthetic pleasure.

The advantage of this kind of technique is obvious. The congregation heard the well-known musical phrases in every new Sticheron, but arranged in a different way, and connected by new transitional passages. They must have taken pleasure in hearing musical phrases which were familiar but were linked together in any unexpected way, just as a modern audience takes pleasure in the recurrence of the themes in a movement of a symphony.[33]

The pleasure taken in the adroit introduction of new melodies and new motives seems to be more than supposition on Wellesz' part. Idelsohn notes that the process of skilfully introducing a new melody to vary the chant is considered "the highest art" among Yemenite singers.[34]

This type of composition is characteristic not only of Near Eastern chant but of a good deal of the folk music of all countries. "In all folksongs, in the art of the German Meistersinger, in Luther's chorales, in Calvin's Psalter, and way back in Gregorian chant, the mosaic is quite obvious."[35]

As was the case in oriental music, the artistic performance of even a single verse of a folk song, in a sense, involves successive deviation. For the folk song, as distinguished from any particular realization of it, is an ideal type which exists as a norm (not an average) in the minds of the singer and listener alike; and the folk singer's performance is, if not an embellishment, at least a deviation from this ideal type. To put the matter somewhat differently: the normative ideal type is never actually performed but exists only in the collective consciousness of the group, in tradition.

Yet the folk singer is often aware of what is tune and what is embellishment. In an interesting article on folk song variants Helen Roberts discusses this whole process together with its aesthetic affective significance.

Working in Jamaica, Roberts found that the folk singers themselves recognize the difference between the fundamental substratum of the oral material handed down to them and their own creative actualization of that material. Parts of songs may be repeated *ad libitum*, and this process of freely repeating a part is given special semantic recognition: it is called "doubling." It is in doubling that the most freedom of embellishment is permitted. The natives find particular pleasure in these improvisations and report that such repetitions "mek it sweet." [36] Not only is the singer permitted freedom with respect to repetition, but he also has considerable latitude with regard to the order of the several phrases of the song. One singer told Roberts: "You can change it aroun', you know, an' sing about the akee in de middle or at de en'." [37]

Embellishments also receive recognition as facets of artistic expression. The more noteworthy deviations are referred to as "flourishes." According to Roberts, the technique of embellishment, of flourishing, has reached a level of consciousness which "almost amounts to extemporaneous composition." [38]

Evidence that such songs are indeed a kind of ideal type is furnished by the fact that the natives themselves believe that the thread of the song is all one needs to maintain the identity of a song. This process of variation is often more noticeable in the performance of instrumental music where the presence of a text does not act either as a restraining, conserving influence or as a kind of "automatic" cause of slight deviation. One flute player heard by Roberts was a particularly accomplished musician, and her report of his performance is most interesting.

No one would have been more capable of playing a part over exactly, yet this he seldom seemed able to do. The urge to embellish and play with the tune was greater than any to reproduce it exactly. I would whistle the two versions to him and emphasize the differences, which he would readily perceive, but when asked which was correct he would laughingly reply that it made no difference if one had the thread. He said the flourishes were not the tune proper, which always, (or nearly always) remained the same, and so it did within limits that are rather difficult to define. [39]

The relationship between deviation and aesthetic pleasure (and aesthetic play) is emphasized throughout this article. According to Roberts, such folk musicians weave in "variations at every opportunity. The more clever, the more pleasure they give." [40] Changes in detail "were welcomed with delight and it was in these that the individual expressed his own self." [41]

Much of this material duplicates what has already been discussed in connection with ornamentation. For in the case of folk material, successive deviation is also successive embellishment. By way of illustration, Example 104 presents Bartók's transcription of two verses of a folk song together with what he has analyzed to be the basic structure underlying the elaborately embellished version which the singer actually presents. [42] In this example, at least, it seems quite clear that successive ornamentation is not a direct product of changes in text. The role of text changes in determining ornamentation is often overemphasized since it is almost as common to embellish and vary two verses which have precisely the same text

EXAMPLE 104 °

as it is to vary the ornaments applied to verses with different texts, though, of course, textural changes will intensify the tendency to vary ornamentation.

Real jazz, as most writers have recognized, is a kind of folk music involving both simultaneous and successive improvisation upon a basic ground plan. This ground plan is essentially harmonic, though the specific tune used as the basis for variation may also be an important departure point for embellishment and deviation.

Hot jazz melody is improvisatory, but its structure is held to a coherent formal pattern which restrains it from complete chaos. This coherent pattern is provided by the harmonic sequences of the underlying accompaniment. . . . It is the simple harmonic phrase . . . that provides the unifying influence in hot jazz improvisation. . . . This phrase is repeated over and over again, with occasional interpolations, perhaps,

° Given by permission of the Columbia University Press.

of similar chordic sequences, forming a sort of 'ostinato' on which melodic and rhythmic variations are built. . . . At each variation of the harmonic phrase a new melodic and rhythmic superstructure is improvised by the hot player.[43]

Here, too, the aesthetic effect of the music depends both upon the listener's awareness of the basic ground plan, which is the norm from which deviations are made, and upon his ability to compare the successive variations as they follow one another.

It is rather difficult to establish a relationship between successive deviation and affective responses in the realm of primitive music (see p. 239). Yet many observers have noted the fact that primitive musicians do derive aesthetic pleasure from music and particularly from the process of variation. Willard Rhodes, for instance, discusses the aesthetic play interest which singers of different American Indian tribes exhibited in each other's songs and especially in the same song performed by singers of different tribes.[44] The aesthetic importance of successive deviation in primitive music is also noted by Jones:

But it is quite wrong to think that the tunes are repeated over and over again with no variation at all. There is variation: it is frequent and it is subtle. A slight change here, an extra note there, make all the difference to those who know what they are listening to. . . . It is all a question of nuance: and it is only the practiced European listener who can perceive and enjoy this cunning compound of bold repetition and subtle variation.[45]

INDIRECT EVIDENCE

The evidence advanced in support of the hypothesis that musical meaning, whether affective or aesthetic, arises when a tendency to respond is inhibited is not confined to chapters vi and vii. These chapters present what might be called direct evidence. This material has consistently demonstrated the connection between the inhibition of tendencies (deviation) and the affective aesthetic response. And while this evidence is not exhaustive, it is clearly representative.

The central thesis of this book is also supported by less direct, though not less convincing or important, considerations. First, the very fact that it has been able to furnish a basis for the analysis of music of very different styles and different cultural levels is persuasive. For it indicates that the account presented has reached a workable level of generality.

Second, the hypothesis advanced has provided the basis for a reasonable and consistent account of many problems heretofore unsolved or ignored. For instance, it has led to a new and fruitful use of Gestalt concepts in aesthetic analysis; it has accounted for the affectivity of the minor mode in Western music without recourse to mathematical mysticism. Employing corollaries of the hypothesis we have been able to understand and explain processes previously merely described; for instance, the "filling in" of tonal systems (the tendency toward equidistance), the use of ornaments, and the introduction of new tones at the end of a musical pattern, and the function of poorly defined pattern processes.

Finally it is important to emphasize that a theory of music does not exist in a kind of splendid, irrelevant isolation. If it is to be fruitful, music theory must not only be internally consistent but it must also be consistent with and relevant to concepts and theories in other realms of thought. Thus it is significant that many of the concepts presented in this book have clear counterparts in the theory of games and in information theory. To cite only one instance of this: it seems possible to equate the inhibition of a tendency, which of necessity gives rise to uncertainty and an awareness of alternative consequents, with the concept of entropy in information theory.

A theory is valuable, not only for conclusions it reaches and the phenomena it explains, but also for the questions and discoveries to which it leads. If the ideas presented in this book can lead to new questions and through them to new answers, if they can lead to reformulations of old questions and through these to new methodologies, and if they can lead to a more fruitful analysis and criticism of music, this will be their best ultimate validation.

VIII

Note on Image Processes, Connotations, and Moods

Image Processes and Affective Experience

The affective experiences thus far discussed result from a direct interaction between a series of musical stimuli and an individual who understands the style of the work being heard. Because the forces shaping such an experience are exclusively musical, the form of the affective experience will be similar to the form of the musical work which brought it into being.

Not all affective experiences are as direct as this. Often music arouses affect through the mediation of conscious connotation or unconscious image processes. A sight, a sound, or a fragrance evokes half-forgotten thoughts of persons, places, and experiences; stirs up dreams "mixing memory with desire"; or awakens conscious connotations of referential things. These imaginings, whether conscious or unconscious, are the stimuli to which the affective response is really made. In short, music may give rise to images and trains of thought which, because of their relation to the inner life of the particular individual, may eventually culminate in affect.

But if such image processes are really unconscious, we can never know them.

. . . only feeling penetrates into awareness, a feeling aroused by something of which the subject is quite ignorant. Self-conscious minds seem to have a repugnance for such isolated disembodied mental phenomena: they are felt to be morbid and eerie. Consequently a process of rationalization is undertaken at once. Whatever is in the focus of attention at the moment when the affect arises is held to be the direct cause of it.[1]

256

Thus many affective experiences attributed directly to musical stimuli may in point of fact be the products of unconscious image processes. Because neither we nor the subject himself can know anything about such unconscious image processes any discussion of such an experience is clearly impossible.

Often, however, image processes are conscious. The listener is aware of the associations which he makes while listening. Conscious image processes may be either private, relating only to the peculiar experiences of a particular individual, or they may be collective, in the sense that they are common to a whole group of individuals within a culture. The image processes of a whole community will be referred to as connotations.

Private images, even when they are brought to consciousness without psychic distortion, are problematical because it is almost impossible to trace the relationships existing either between the musical stimulus and the image processes aroused or between the image processes and the resultant affect. The peculiar experience of an individual may, for example, cause a "happy" tune to be associated with images of a sad occasion.

Even where the original association appears to be relevant and appropriate to the character of the music being played, affective experience may be a result of the private meaning which the image has for the particular listener. For example, the image of a triumphal procession might within a given culture be relevant to the character of a piece of music; but the association might for private reasons arouse feelings of humiliation or defeat. Thus while the image itself is relevant to the music, the significance which it has for the particular individual is purely personal.

Image processes, whether private or collective, are tremendous temptations toward extramusical diversion. For an image, even though originally relevant to a particular passage, may itself initiate further image processes. The development and proliferation of these may, however, proceed without reference to the subsequent successions of musical stimuli. That is, one image may follow another, not because of the associations which obtain between the images and the progress of the music, but because of the associations in the mind of the listener between the images themselves.[2]

Neither the form nor the referential content of such experiences, however affective they may be, have any necessary relationship to the form and content of the musical work which presumably activated them. The real stimulus is not the progressive unfolding of the musical structure but the subjective content of the listener's mind.

Yet, in spite of the many and cogent objections which can be leveled against the relevance of such responses, it seems probable that conscious or unconscious image processes play a role of great importance in the musical affective experiences of many listeners. Indeed, it is often difficult for even the most disciplined and experienced listeners to escape the deepseated power of memory over affective experience.[3]

It should be noted in this connection that not only do memories frequently result in affective experience but affective experiences themselves tend to evoke memories and arouse image processes appropriate to the character of the affective experience, whether sad or gay, noble or tender, as determined by the objective situation. In other words, even the most purely musical affective experiences may give rise to image processes which, developing their own series of associations, may become independent of the musical succession itself.

Connotation

By connotations, as distinguished from image processes, are meant those associations which are shared in common by a group of individuals within the culture. Connotations are the result of the associations made between some aspect of the musical organization and extramusical experience. Since they are interpersonal, not only must the mechanism of association be common to the given cultural group, but the concept or image must have the same significance for all the members of the group. The concept must be one that is to some extent standardized in cultural thinking; it must be a class concept that has the same meaning for, and produces the same attitudes in, all the members of the group. In the West, for example, death is usually depicted by slow tempi and low ranges, while in certain African tribes it is portrayed in frenzied musical activity; yet this results from difference in attitudes toward death rather than from differences in the associative processes of the human mind. The particular way in which a connotation is realized or represented in music cannot be understood apart from the beliefs and attitudes of the culture in question.

Some connotations are entirely traditional. Association is by contiguity; i.e., some aspect of the musical materials and their organization becomes linked, by dint of repetition, to a referential image. Certain instruments become associated with special concepts and states of mind. The organ, for example, is associated for Western listeners with the church and through this with piety and religious beliefs and attitudes. The gong is linked by contiguity to the Orient and often connotes the mysterious and the exotic. In fact, even where this association does not seem intended, as in Varèse's *Ionisation,* it tends to modify our response to this music. Certain modes of tonal organization may awaken connotations. The pentatonic mode, for example, is used in the nineteenth century to represent things pastoral. Certain intervals may be used to indicate special concepts or states of mind. For instance, the diminished fifth was closely associated with expressions of grief and anguish during the baroque period. Or specific tunes may be employed to evoke concepts, memories, or image processes. This is a frequent device in the music of Charles Ives.

As a rule such associations are used in combination so that each reinforces the other. If the composer wishes to evoke connotations of piety and those connected with religious beliefs, he will not only employ the appropriate instrument but he will also use techniques of composition—modality, polyphony, and so forth—that have the same associations.

Notice that all these associations are intracultural. The gong will not have a special exotic meaning for the oriental in whose music it is common, though it may have other different associations for him. Nor will the pentatonic mode connote things pastoral to peoples who use this mode for all kinds of music, for cultivated art music as well as for folk music.

Because such associations are completely cultural and in no sense

necessary, they are subject to change. Old associations die and new
ones come into being. In Western music, for example, the harp is
no longer associated, as it was in the Middle Ages, with religious
subjects. Because of its use in French music of the late nineteenth
century, it is much more likely to be associated with a certain tender
vagueness.

A particular epoch may develop quite an elaborate system of connotations in which certain melodic, rhythmic, or harmonic practices
become signs of certain states of mind or are used to designate
specific emotional states. The composers of the baroque period developed such a system of connotations. Other composers, notably
Wagner, have invented their own systems of connotative symbols,
in which a specific melody, not just a more or less general figure,
indicates and symbolizes a specific idea, concept, or individual.

If our responses to such special systems of connotative or designative symbols are to be really effective, they must become habitual
and automatic. This requires time and repeated encounters with a
given association. We do not need to learn that an oboe is traditionally a pastoral instrument. By hearing it used in this context
time and time again, by reading about pipes and shepherds in literature, and by seeing such instruments depicted in paintings of Pan
or Marsyas, we gradually build up a set of powerful associations.
Once such an association has become firmly established, our response to it will be just as direct and forceful as if the response were
natural.

However important associations made by contiguity may be, they
constitute but a small fraction of the total group of connotations
evoked by music. Most of the connotations which music arouses are
based upon similarities which exist between our experience of the
materials of music and their organization, on the one hand, and our
experience of the non-musical world of concepts, images, objects,
qualities, and states of mind, on the other.

There is a great deal of evidence, some of it intercultural, which
indicates that our experience of musical stimuli is not a separate,
special category of experience but that it is continuous with and
similar to our experiences of other kinds of stimuli.

Both music and life are experienced as dynamic processes of growth and decay, activity and rest, tension and release. These processes are differentiated, not only by the course and shape of the motions involved in them, but also by the quality of the motion. For instance, a motion may be fast or slow, calm or violent, continuous or sporadic, precisely articulated or vague in outline. Almost all modes of experience, even those in which motion is not directly involved, are somehow associated qualitatively with activity. Spring, revolution, darkness, the pyramids, a circle—each, depending upon our current opinion of it, is experienced as having a characteristic motion. If connotations are to be aroused at all, there will be a tendency to associate the musical motion in question with a referential concept or image that is felt to exhibit a similar quality of motion.

The unity of perceptual experience, regardless of the particular sense employed, is also demonstrated by the fact that in experience even single musical tones tend to become associated with qualities generally attributed to non-aural modes of sense perception. This tendency is apparent not only in Western culture but in the cultures of the Orient and in many primitive cultures. In Western culture, for example, tones are characterized with respect to size (large or small), color value (light or dark), position (high or low), and tactile quality (rough or smooth, piercing or round). Furthermore, it should be noted that these qualities are interassociated among themselves; that is, volume is associated with position (e.g., a large object is generally associated with a low position), and both of these are associated with color.[4]

Through such visual and tactile qualities, which are themselves a part of almost all referential experience, tones become associated with our experience of the world. Thus the associations, if any, evoked by a low tone will be limited, though not defined, by the fact that in Western culture such tones are generally associated with dark colors, low position, large size, and slower motion.

Often referential experiences are themselves partly aural. A city, the wind, solitude, or the expressions of the human voice—all have a peculiar quality of sound which music can imitate with varying success. Such imitation will tend to awaken connotations similar in some respects at least to the experiences which originally conditioned the musical organization.

To what extent the associations arising from similarities between our experience of music and our experience of the non-musical world are products of cultural conditioning and to what extent they are in some sense natural is difficult to say. The many studies made by psychologists, although they present ample evidence of associative consistency within Western culture, throw little light upon the problem of the naturalness of these responses; for the subjects in such experiments have, almost without exception, already been saturated with the beliefs and attitudes of Western culture.

Evidence from primitive and non-Western cultures is not conclusive. Frequently the associations formed are ones which appear natural to us. But sometimes a connotation strikes us as odd or unusual. In the latter case, however, it must be remembered that the association evoked by a given musical passage depends upon the attitude of the culture toward the concept as well as upon the mechanism of association. In other words, although in a given culture one attitude toward an object or process will usually be dominant, others are possible. For example, although in our culture death is generally considered to be a solemn, fearful, and majestic summoner, it has also been viewed as an old friend or as the sardonic mocker of human pretensions. And obviously each of these attitudes would become associated with very different types of musical presentation.

This much, however, is clear: (1) In most cultures there is a powerful tendency to associate musical experience with extramusical experience. The many musical cosmologies of the Orient, the practice of most primitive cultures, and the writings and practices of many Western composers are striking evidence of this fact. (2) No particular connotation is an inevitable product of a given musical organization, since the association of a specific musical organization with a particular referential experience depends upon the beliefs and attitudes of the culture toward the experience. However, once the beliefs of the culture are understood, most associations appear to possess a certain naturalness because the experiences associated are in some sense similar. (3) No matter how natural a connotation may seem to be, it undoubtedly acquires force and immediacy through cultural experience.

Obviously a complex and subtle connotation is not defined by any single element of the sound organization. Taken individually any one aspect of the musical organization is a necessary but by no means a sufficient cause for defining a given connotation. For instance, while it would not be possible in Western culture to depict the joys of youth in the lowest ranges of the bassoon, high ranges alone would not assure such an association either. Other aspects of the musical organization, such as tempo, dynamics, rhythmic character, and texture, would have to play a part in defining such a connotation.   + Pitch.

But the degree of specificity attained in association, the degree to which a given musical disposition will evoke the same or similar connotations in all listeners within the cultural group, is not merely the function of the number of elements defining the connotation. All the elements of music are always present if there is any music at all. That is, there is always texture, whether it be that of a single melodic line or that of a complex polyphonic web; there is always dynamic level, whether it be that of a striking fortissimo or that of a mezzoforte.

The specificity of a connotation depends upon the divergence of the elements of sound from a neutral state. A tempo may be neither fast nor slow; a sound may be neither loud nor soft; a pitch may seem neither high nor low, relative either to over-all range or the range of a particular instrument or voice. From the standpoint of connotation these are neutral states. Connotation becomes specified only if some of the elements of sound diverge from such neutral states.

The elements of sound are interdependent with respect to neutrality and divergence. For instance, changes in pitch are generally accompanied by changes in dynamics, timbre, and sometimes tempo. The relationship is physical as well as psychological. If a 33⅓ r.p.m. phonograph record is played at 78 r.p.m., pitch will get higher, dynamics louder, and timbre more piercing. Thus it is possible to build one divergence upon another. For instance, if tempo is fast and pitches are high, very soft dynamics will be experienced as a divergence, not only from the neutral state of moderate loudness, but also from the "contingent neutrality" in which a rapid tempo and high pitches are generally accompanied by loud dynamics.

In general, the more markedly the elements of a sound pattern diverge from neutrality the more likely they are to evoke connotations and the more specific those connotations are liable to be. Note that this accounts for the fact that many musical works arouse a wide variety of connotations. For the connotations aroused by a piece of music which, on the whole, employs normal ranges, moderate tempi, and so forth will be determined more by the disposition and susceptibility of the particular listener than by the nature of the musical organization itself.

But even where the most complex disposition of the musical materials and the most effective deviations are presented in a piece of music, they function only as necessary causes for the particular connotative experience aroused.

In the first place, unlike literature or the plastic arts, which generally speaking cannot be understood apart from the designative symbols they employ, most musical experience is meaningful without any reference to the extramusical world. Whether a piece of music arouses connotations depends to a great extent upon the disposition and training of the individual listener and upon the presence of cues, either musical or extramusical, which tend to activate connotative responses.

In the second place, unlike verbal symbols or the iconic signs used in the plastic arts, musical sounds are not, save in a few isolated instances, explicit in their denotation. They limit and define the associations possible but, in the absence of either a specific musical symbolism such as Wagner's or a definite program furnished by the composer, they cannot particularize connotation. The musical materials and their organization are the necessary causes for a given connotation but, since no summation of necessary causes can ever amount to a sufficient cause, the sufficient cause of any connotation experienced must be supplied by the listener.

The fact that music cannot specify and particularize the connotations which it arouses has frequently been cited as a basic difficulty with any attempt to theorize about the connotative meanings of music. Yet from one point of view, this flexibility of connotation is a virtue. For it enables music to express what might be called the disembodied essence of myth, the essence of experiences which are central to and vital in human existence.

The human mind has an uncanny power of recognizing symbolic forms; and most readily, of course, will it seize upon those which are presented again and again without aberration. The eternal regularities of nature, the heavenly motions, the alternation of night and day on earth, the tides of the ocean, are the most insistent repetitious forms outside our own behavior patterns. . . . They are the most obvious metaphors to convey the dawning concepts of life-functions—birth, growth, decadence, and death.[5]

What music presents is not any given one of these metaphorical events but rather that which is common to all of them, that which enables them to become metaphors for one another. Music presents a generic event, a "connotative complex," which then becomes particularized in the experience of the individual listener.

Music does not, for example, present the concept or image of death itself. Rather it connotes that rich realm of experience in which death and darkness, night and cold, winter and sleep and silence are all combined and consolidated into a single connotative complex.

The interassociations which give rise to such a connotative complex are fundamental in human experience. They are found again and again, not only in the myths and legends of many cultures, but also in the several arts. For example, the connotative complex discussed above is made explicit in Shelley's *Ode to the West Wind:*

> O thou,
> Who chariotest to their dark wintry bed
> The winged seeds, where they lie cold and low
> Each like a corpse within its grave. . . .

Connotative complexes may be more and less specific. Additional divergences in timbre, dynamic level, and so forth may help to limit the quality of the complex. Association by contiguity or the imitation of actual sound processes heard in the extramusical world may also play a part in defining the extent of connotation. Finally, connotation may be specified by the presence of a text, a plot, or a program established by the composer.

Ultimately it is the listener who must make connotation concrete. In so doing the listener may draw upon his stock of culturally established images, including those derived from literature and mythology, or he may relate the connotative complex to his own particular and peculiar experiences. But in either case there is a causal connection between the musical materials and their organization and the connotations evoked. Had the musical organization been different, the connotation would also have been different.

Mood

Since, however, connotations are not necessary concomitants of musical experience (see p. 246), a potentially connotative passage may fail to evoke any concrete images whatsoever. Instead the listener may become aware of how the musical passage "feels" in relation to his own designative emotional experiences and the observed emotional behavior of others. The music may, in short, be experienced as mood or sentiment. For not only are connotations themselves intimately associated with moods, in the sense that youth or spring, for instance, are traditionally considered to be times of exuberant and carefree gaiety, but the same psychological and musical processes which arouse specific connotations also evoke definite, though perhaps less specific, mood responses.[6]

In a discussion of the communication of moods and sentiments two important considerations must be kept in mind.

1. The moods and sentiments with which music becomes associated are not those natural spontaneous emotional reactions, which, as noted in chapter i, are often diffuse and characterless. Rather music depicts those modes of behavior, conventionalized for the sake of more efficient communication, which were called "designative emotional behavior." In Western culture, for example, grief is communicated by a special type of behavior: physical gestures and motor behavior tend to minimal; facial expression reflects the cultural picture of sorrow; the range of vocal expression is confined

and often sporadic; weeping is customary; and dress too serves as a behavioral sign. It is this special, culturally sanctioned picture of grief which is communicated in Western music. But such designative emotional behavior is not the only possible way of denoting grief. Were the standardized expression of grief in Western culture different, were it, for instance, that of an incessant and violent wailing and moaning, then the "expression" of grief in Western music would be different.

This is important because it allows for and accounts for variation in mood expression between the music of different cultures. That is, different cultures may communicate moods and sentiments in very different ways, not because the psychological mechanism of association is different but because the behavior patterns denoting mood and emotional states are different.

2. Just as communicative behavior tends to become conventionalized for the sake of more efficient communication, so the musical communication of moods and sentiments tends to become standardized. Thus particular musical devices—melodic figure, harmonic progressions, or rhythmic relationships—become formulas which indicate a culturally codified mood or sentiment. For those who are familiar with them, such signs may be powerful factors in conditioning responses.

Association by contiguity plays a considerable role in the musical definition of mood. A melodic figure, a set of modal relationships, or a harmonic progression is experienced time and time again in conjunction with texts, programs, or extramusical experiences which either designate the mood directly or imply it. In oriental music, for instance, a particular mode or even a particular pitch may become associated with a specific sentiment or humour as well as with connotative concepts such as winter, night, and blackness. Once such associations become habitual, the presence of the proper musical stimulus will, as a rule, automatically evoke the customary mood response. In Western music of the baroque period, to cite only one example, melodic formulas, conventionalized for the sake of communication, attain precision and force through contiguity with texts and programs which fix their meanings within the culture and style.

Mood association by similarity depends upon a likeness between the individual's experiences of moods and his experience of music. Emotional behavior is a kind of composite gesture, a motion whose peculiar qualities are largely defined in terms of energy, direction, tension, continuity, and so forth. Since music also involves motions differentiated by the same qualities, "musical mood gestures" may be similar to behavioral mood gestures. In fact, because moods and sentiments attain their most precise articulation through vocal inflection, it is possible for music to imitate the sounds of emotional behavior with some precision. Finally, since motor behavior plays a considerable role in both designative emotional behavior and in musical experience, a similarity between the motor behavior of designative gestures and that of musical gestures will inforce the feeling of similarity between the two types of experience.

Like connotation, mood or sentiment depend for their definition upon divergence. If the elements of sound are neutral then the mood characterization, if any, will depend largely upon the disposition of the individual listener. That is, there will be no consistency in the responses of various listeners. But, and this is of paramount importance, the fact that the mood is indefinite does not mean that affect is not aroused. For a lack of divergence in the elements of sound does not preclude significant deviation in those dynamic processes which form our affective responses to music.

It was observed earlier that image processes, whether conscious or unconscious, and connotations often result in affective experience. Whether mood responses can eventuate in affect is doubtful. Merely because the musical designation of a mood or sentiment is comprehended by the listener does not mean that the listener responds affectively. It is perfectly possible to be aware of the meaning of behavior without responding as though the behavior were our own. But even an empathetic response to the materials delineating mood or sentiment does not require a resultant affective experience. We may sympathize with the mood of another individual without having an emotional experience ourselves. In fact, although such empathetic behavior may create a psycho-physiological condition in which affect is likely to arise, it is difficult to see what direct causal connection could exist between mood and affect. It appears more likely that mood eventuates in affect only through the mediation of image processes or connotations. That is, a mood arouses image processes already associated in the experience of the individual with the particular mood response, and these image processes are the stimuli which actually give rise to affect.[7]

The Role of Mood and Connotation in Affective Experience

Not only do mood and connotation frequently give rise to affect but they also color and modify the affective experiences evoked by the musical processes discussed in the preceding chapters. The converse of this is also true; namely, the character of the deviations embodied in a particular work play a part in conditioning our opinion of what, in general terms, its designative content is. If, for instance, we compare the first theme of the rondo of Haydn's Symphony No. 102, in B-flat, with the first theme of the rondo of Beethoven's "Waldstein" Sonata, it is clear that the designative character of each, the roguish and spirited playfulness of the Haydn and the flowing lyricism of the Beethoven, is a product not only of such factors as tempo, phrasing, accompaniment, melodic contour, and so forth but also of the fact that the theme of the Haydn rondo involves considerable irregularity, abruptness, and deception, while the theme of the Beethoven rondo is quite regular and forthright. Once the listener becomes aware of this difference in character, he is definitely prepared for different kinds of movements—for the witty and highly sophisticated surprises of the Haydn and the striking but not unexpected contrasts which mark the Beethoven.

It was stated in the first chapter that an affective experience is differentiated and characterized by the stimulus situation in which it occurs. Both the stimulus and the situation serve to differentiate musical experience from "real-life" experience.

Since musical affective stimuli are obviously different from the referential stimuli of real life, there will always be a generic difference between musical affective experience and the experiences of everyday life. From this point of view musical experience is unique.

However, in so far as music is able, through connotation, mood, or the use of a program or text, to designate situations similar to those existing in extramusical experience, such designations will tend to color and modify our musical affective experience. Our experience of a melody first played forte in a low range by a trombone and then immediately played pianissimo in a high range on the violin is not only shaped by the expectations aroused by the repetition, the changes in dynamics, range, and instrumentation but it is colored and qualified by the changes perceived in the designative character of the two passages.

Last but most important of all, because our understanding of the designative character of a passage may affect our interpretation and evaluation of its function within the total work, such understanding of designative meaning may play an important role in the actual shaping of our affective experience.

Connotation, Mood, and Aesthetic Theory

Reacting against the strong emphasis placed upon mood designation and connotation in nineteenth-century music, many critics, theorists, and psychologists have in recent years questioned the relevance and pertinence of the connotative and mood responses made to music.

The attack upon such referential musical experience has focused (1) upon the causal connection between the musical stimulus and the referential response, (2) upon the apparent disparity between the responses of different listeners, and (3) upon the lack of specificity in the responses made. The difficulty, writes Hanslick, is that "there is no *causal nexus* between a musical composition and the feelings it may excite, as the latter vary with our experience and impressibility." [8]

These objections are, however, without merit. In the first place, all significant responses to music, the affective and aesthetic as well as the designative and connotative, vary with our experience and impressibility. The response to style is a learned response, and both the appreciation of style and the ability to learn require intelligence and musical sensitivity. In the second place, though the causal nexus between music and referential experience is a necessary not a sufficient one, there is a causal nexus, as is evidenced not only by the practice of composers within a given style but also by the responses of listeners who have learned to understand the style.

While Hanslick's attack is directed largely against the belief that music communicates feelings, C. C. Pratt denies the possibility of connotation.

The shaping of these [tonal] mosaics may receive impetus from all sorts of objects and ideas and the composer, in his innocence, may believe that he has embodied his non-musical idea in sound. And a goodly number of still more innocent listeners may persuade themselves that they comprehend the composer's ideas. It requires, however, only the simplest sort of experiment to demonstrate the utter lack of correspondence between the idea which the composer may think he has represented and the interpretations which an unselected group of listeners, if asked to do so, will furnish. . . .[9]

The first difficulty with this argument lies in the phrase "unselected group of listeners." Of course, if they are unselected, if they have not learned the style, they will give very different responses. And this will also be true of their responses to embodied meaning. But connotations will vary even among those who do have the same cultural background and who are acquainted with the modes of association established within the style. However, this variation, though significant, is often not as wide as it seems at first glance. Because the modes of experience are continuous with one another and because experience itself can be expressed in a wide variety of metaphors, a connotative complex which has the same potential meaning for all listeners may be actualized differently in the experience of each. In other words, while it is true that on one level (that of specific meaning) the ideas entertained by various listeners are patently different, on another level (the level of symbolic and metaphorical meaning) the concepts entertained by the various listeners are very similar.

The difficulty with an aesthetic of music based upon connotative and mood responses is not that the associations between music and referential experience are fortuitous or that there is no causal connection between music and feelings. The difficulty is that, in the absence of a specific referential framework, there is no causal nexus between successive connotations or moods. In literature or in life, successive experiences are apparently causally connected by the sequence of events which take place between them. A depressing experience is followed by a joyful one, and the change is understood in the light of the events connecting them. But though music can present the experiences themselves, if only metaphorically, it cannot stipulate the causal connection between them. There is no logical reason, either musical or extramusical, for any particular succession of connotations or moods.[10]

Confirmation for this argument can be found in the practice of composers of instrumental music who, realizing that the difficulty with referential music lies in the lack of a causal connection between successive moods or connotations, have sought to correct this weakness by using descriptive programs. Although a program does serve to specify connotation, its main function is not to designate mood or arouse connotation. Music can as a rule accomplish this more effectively than a program can. What the program does is to provide the causal connection between the successive moods or connotations presented in the music.[11]

Seen in this light, the program is not the mere whim of the composer, an unnecessary and superfluous addition to meanings already inherent in the music, nor is it an attempt to depict moods and connotations. Its function is to connect them. The great disadvantage of a program lies in the fact that it is a powerful temptation toward extramusical diversion.

Notes

NOTES TO CHAPTER I

1. Norman Cazden, "Musical Consonance and Dissonance: A Cultural Criterion," *Journal of Aesthetics*, IV (1945), 3–11.

2. Paul R. Farnsworth, "Sacred Cows in the Psychology of Music," *Journal of Aesthetics*, VII (1948), 48–51.

3. Susanne K. Langer, *Philosophy in a New Key* (New York: Mentor Book Co., 1951).

4. *Ibid.*, p. 171.

5. H. P. Weld, "An Experimental Study in Musical Enjoyment," *American Journal of Psychology*, XXIII (1912), 283.

6. C. S. Myers, "Individual Differences in Listening to Music," in *The Effects of Music*, ed. Max Schoen (New York: Harcourt, Brace & Co., 1927), p. 14.

7. See H. D. Aiken, "The Aesthetic Relevance of Belief," *Journal of Aesthetics*, IX (1950), 301–15.

8. James L. Mursell, *The Psychology of Music* (New York: W. W. Norton & Co., Inc., 1937), pp. 27–28.

9. *Ibid.*, p. 37.

10. David Rapaport, *Emotions and Memory* (New York: International Universities Press Inc., 1950), p. 21.

11. John Dewey, "The Theory of Emotion," *Psychological Review*, I (1894), 553–69; II (1895), 13–32.

12. R. P. Angier, "The Conflict Theory of Emotions," *American Journal of Psychology*, XXXIX (1927), 390–401.

13. J. T. MacCurdy, *The Psychology of Emotion* (New York: Harcourt, Brace & Co., 1925), p. 475.

14. For MacCurdy the term "instinct" includes learned habit responses. See p. 24 of this study.

15. Notice that this analysis makes apparent the great significance of Aiken's contention that our beliefs as to the nature of aesthetic experience lead to the suppression of overt responses; for such inhibiting of overt behavior tends to intensify the affective response.

16. F. Paulhan, *The Laws of Feeling*, trans. C. K. Ogden (New York: Harcourt, Brace & Co., 1930), p. 19.

17. *Ibid.*, p. 123.

18. The term affective or emotional "state" will henceforth be used to designate those aspects of emotional experience which have been given names and which are in one way or another fairly standardized in a broad sense.

19. See Robert S. Woodworth, "How Emotions Are Identified and Classified," in *Feelings and Emotions: The Wittenberg Symposium,* ed. M. L. Reymert (Worcester, Mass.: Clark University Press, 1928), p. 224.

20. Ernst Cassirer, *An Essay on Man: An Introduction to a Philosophy of Human Culture* (New York: Doubleday & Co., 1953), p. 190. This admirable statement like so many of its kind suffers at the end from an irritating vagueness in which an intangible "the dynamic process of life itself" is substituted for a definite account of how and why the emotions of art are not comparable to any single state of emotion. It is for a solution to this problem that we are searching in the present discussion of emotional differentiation.

21. C. Landis, "Studies in Emotional Reactions: II, General Behavior and Facial Expression," *Journal of Comparative Psychology,* IV (1924), 496.

22. Donald O. Hebb, *The Organization of Behavior* (New York: John Wiley & Sons, 1952), p. 258.

23. *Ibid.,* p. 232.

24. This statement must be qualified by the reservation that in so far as it can designate or represent extramusical stimuli, music can be said to evoke such affective states as are normally connected with the situations represented.

25. It is also clear that since the world of emotions is not composed of a series of separate compartments, a given listener may feel that a purely musical emotion is comparable or analogous to affects experienced in real life.

26. The term "emotional expression" is misleading in that it implies that such behavior is the direct, necessary expression of affect.

27. Though not within the province of this study, it can, I believe, be shown that similar aspects of experience are involved in musical and other designation. Both, for example, utilize the generality of motion (fast or slow, continuous or interrupted, smooth or disjunct, intense or weak) in such designation. And musical designation, though probably in some respects natural, is, like designative behavior, in the last analysis a product of culture and learning rather than a product of nature. See also pp. 261 f.

28. See John Dewey, *Art As Experience* (New York: Minton, Balch & Co., 1934), pp. 35, 56.

29. MacCurdy, *op. cit.,* p. 556.

30. John Dewey, *Intelligence in the Modern World,* ed. J. Ratner ("Modern Library" [New York: Random House, 1939]), p. 733.

31. MacCurdy, *op. cit.*, p. 556.

32. Aiken, *op. cit.*, p. 313; also see Arthur D. Bissell, *The Role of Expectation in Music* (New Haven: Yale University Press, 1921), p. vii; and Hugo Riemann, *Catechism of Musical Aesthetics,* trans. H. Bewerung (London: Augener & Co., n.d.), p. 29.

33. Aiken, *op. cit.*, p. 305.

34. If this takes place, the listener may shift his attention to another aspect of the musical materials, or he may simply abandon the attempt to make sense of the music altogether.

35. Thus the designation of mood and character, whether accomplished in purely musical terms or with the aid of a program or text, is important not only for its own sake, as a source of enjoyment, but also because, as part of the stimulus situation, it is necessary for the proper understanding of the musical processes in progress.

36. Both these aspects of the process of expectation are discussed in the following chapters, where much of the preceding discussion is treated in more detail.

37. Eduard Hanslick, *The Beautiful in Music,* trans. E. Cohen (London: Novello, Ewer & Co., 1901), p. 135. The difficulty with this statement is that Hanslick confuses intellectual satisfaction with intellectual activity. For although intellectual activity, in the sense of mental awareness and cognition, may, as we shall see, be unconscious, intellectual satisfaction implies a self-conscious awareness of the activity taking place.

38. Dewey, *Art As Experience,* p. 59; also see *Intelligence in the Modern World,* pp. 755 ff. Robert Penn Warren writes to much the same effect: ". . . a poem, to be good, must earn itself. It is a motion toward a point of rest, but if it is not a resisted motion, it is a motion of no consequence" ("Pure and Impure Poetry," *Kenyon Review,* V [1943], 251).

39. It is clear that the terms "norm" and "deviation" are being used in a very broad and general sense. Deviation includes all delays and inhibitions which give rise to expectation within the context of the particular style in question.

40. Morris R. Cohen, *A Preface to Logic* (New York: Henry Holt & Co., 1944), p. 47.

41. See George H. Mead, *Mind, Self, and Society* (Chicago: University of Chicago Press, 1934), p. 76.

42. Thus Pratt, while maintaining that the ideas aroused in association with music "have little to do with the intrinsic nature of musical sound" (C. C. Pratt, "Music and Meaning," *Proceedings of the Music Teacher's National Association,* Series XXXVII [1942], p. 113), does contend that "music *sounds* the way emotions *feel*" (*Ibid.,* p. 117); a statement which seems to be a disguised form of referentialism.

Incidentally though Pratt's first statement is undoubtedly true, its implications are not. For while our associations may have nothing to do with the intrinsic nature of sound, whatever that may be, they do have something to do with our experience of sound. See pp. 261 f. of this study.

43. The term "stimulus" as used here includes any tone or combination of tones which are marked off as a unitary event which is related to other musical events. It is, to use Mead's terminology, "a musical gesture." Or, in the terminology used in chap. ii of this study, it is a "sound term." In this sense, a single tone, a phrase, or a whole composition may be considered to be a gesture, a stimulus, or a sound term. In other words, meaning must be considered as being architectonic as well as consecutive.

44. Of course, it may have designative meaning. The more difficult it is to grasp the embodied meaning of a work, the greater the tendency to search for designative meanings.

45. Notice, too, that the final tones of a piece, conditioned by all that has gone before, lead us to expect silence and that it is this expectation which makes them meaningful.

46. Note that hypothetical meanings as well as the other kinds of meaning are architectonic. If we are set to listen to a Haydn rondo, then the idea we have of Haydn rondos is, in a sense, the hypothetical meaning of that particular rondo; it is what we envisage and what points to the impinging stimulus.

47. Bertrand Russell, *Selected Papers* ("Modern Library," [New York: Random House, n.d.]), p. 358.

48. Mead, *op. cit.*, p. 194.

49. Mead, *op. cit.*, pp. 42–75.

50. *Ibid.*, p. 47.

51. Of course, if the composer is developing a relatively new style, as many contemporary composers have tried to do, the imagined listener may correspond to no listener who actually exists. He is rather one whom the composer hopes to create as his style becomes part of the general style, part of the listening public's stock of habit responses.

52. Leopold Mozart, *Versuch einer gründlichen Violinschule*, quoted in *Source Readings in Music History*, ed. Oliver Strunk (New York: W. W. Norton & Co., Inc., 1950), p. 602.

53. Generally speaking this study is not concerned with the creative act but rather with the experience which the art work brings into being. This aspect of the composer's creative life is discussed because it clearly concerns the problem of aesthetic experience. Obviously many other mental processes and attitudes which have not been touched upon are involved in the act of composition. One of these is dealt with on pp. 69 f., but most of them are left to the speculations of others.

54. Cassirer, *op. cit.*, p. 191.

NOTES TO CHAPTER II

1. Edward Sapir, "Language," *Encyclopedia of the Social Sciences,* IX (New York: Macmillan Co., 1934), 157.

2. I know of only one study, that of Arthur D. Bissell (*The Role of Expectations in Music* [New Haven: Yale University Press, 1921]), which deals explicitly with the subject of expectations, and this study is by no means exhaustive.

3. Similarly any compound or serial term established in accordance with (*c*) in turn enters into probability relationships with other terms of the system and other compound terms.

4. A. H. Fox Strangways, *The Music of Hindostan* (London: Oxford University Press, 1914), p. 18.

5. See Felix Salzer, *Structural Hearing* (New York: Charles Boni, 1952), pp. 182–83.

6. C. P. E. Bach, *Essay on the True Art of Playing Keyboard Instruments,* trans. William Mitchell (New York: W. W. Norton & Co., Inc., 1949), p. 84. The relation of ornamentation to deviation and delay is discussed in chap. vi, p. 204 of this book.

7. Curt Sachs, *The Rise of Music in the Ancient World, East and West* (New York: W. W. Norton & Co., Inc., 1943), p. 37.

8. Hindemith's objection to the concept that chords are susceptible of various interpretations is unfortunate; first, because the chords which he cites are not necessarily ambiguous and, second, because ambiguity may function as an important affective aesthetic device. See Paul Hindemith, *Craft of Musical Composition,* trans. Arthur Mendel (New York: Associated Music Publishers Inc., 1942), pp. 90 ff.

9. Salzer, *op. cit.,* pp. 19–20.

10. Henry D. Aiken, "The Aesthetic Relevance of Belief," *Journal of Aesthetics,* IX (1950), 305–6. Aiken includes under the term "belief" the habits, dispositions, and attitudes which the listener and composer bring to the work of art.

11. Walter Piston, *Harmony* (New York: W. W. Norton & Co., Inc., 1941), p. 17.

12. Strangways, *op. cit.,* p. 150.

13. *Ibid.,* p. 128.

14. See, for instance, Frances Densmore, *Pawnee Music* (Smithsonian Institution, Bureau of American Ethnology, Bulletin 93, [1929]), pp. 120 ff.

15. As Ernest Nagel notes: "An estimate of a probability which is made simply on the basis of unanalyzed samples or trials is not likely to be a safe basis for prediction. If nothing is known concerning the mechanism of a situation under investigation, the relative frequencies

obtained from samples may be poor guides to the character of the indefinitely large population from which they are drawn" (Ernest Nagel, *Principles of the Theory of Probability,* "International Encyclopedia of Unified Science," Vol. I, No. 6 [Chicago: University of Chicago Press, 1939], p. 59).

16. Henry D. Aiken, "The Concept of Relevance in Aesthetics," *Journal of Aesthetics,* VI (1947–48), 159.

17. Hugo Riemann, *Catechism of Musical Aesthetics,* trans. H. Bewerung (London: Augener & Co., n.d.), p. 31.

18. George Herzog, "A Comparison of Pueblo and Pima Musical Styles," *Journal of American Folklore,* XLIX, No. 194, 286.

19. Many acoustical and psychological theories have been advanced to explain why certain sound complexes tend to become normative in some style systems. But a satisfactory explanation cannot be found either in the physics of sound or the pleasure-displeasure reactions of listeners. It lies in the nature of human mental processes (see p. 231).

20. Herzog, *op. cit.,* pp. 290, 308–9. The relationship between ornamental or decorative tones and the affective aesthetic response is discussed in chap. vi.

21. Egon Wellesz, *A History of Byzantine Music and Hymnography* (London: Oxford University Press, 1949), pp. 207–8.

22. Winthrop Sargeant, *Jazz: Hot and Hybrid* (New York: E. P. Dutton & Co., 1946), pp. 156–57.

23. Igor Stravinsky, *Chronicle of My Life* (London: Victor Gollancz Ltd., 1936), pp. 185–86.

24. As a rule these self-imposed resistances and difficulties have been limited to the exigencies of the communicative process (see pp. 40 f.). But at times the composer's concern with the creation and the conquest of self-imposed tasks has been in part intrapersonal. In the rhythmic structure of much late gothic and early Renaissance music and in the permutations of the tone-row in some twentieth-century music, the composer often seems to manipulate and play with the musical material, not for the sake of any aesthetic effect it may have upon the listener, but rather for the pleasure he derives from the feeling of power and command over the materials of his art.

Of course, such works do communicate on the interpersonal level. But the special craft secrets in which the composer has taken obvious delight are not apparent to the uninitiate. To appreciate this aspect of the composition, the listener must actively take the attitude of the composer. He must self-consciously solve the riddle of the music, enjoying the intricacies of its masterful manipulations in a manner similar to that of the composer.

25. Karl Groos, *The Play of Man,* trans. E. L. Baldwin (New York: D. Appleton & Co., 1901), p. 8.

26. Even if the act of listening is not directly intentional, in the sense of being planned beforehand, once the decision to listen, to pay attention, is made, preparatory sets will be brought into play.

27. Ernst Kris, *Psychoanalytic Explorations in Art* (New York: International Universities Press, 1952), p. 42.

28. This belief appears to have its roots in the seriousness of play, on the one hand, and in the significance and power attributed to art, through its ancient relation to ritual, magic, and religion, on the other. In spite of the secularization of art, this feeling of its significant seriousness remained.

29. K. Koffka, *Principles of Gestalt Psychology* (New York: Harcourt, Brace & Co., 1935), p. 173.

30. James L. Mursell, *The Psychology of Music* (New York: W. W. Norton & Co., Inc., 1937), p. 37.

31. B. Pasquarelli, "Experimental Investigation of the Body-Mind Continuum in Affective States," *Journal of Nervous and Mental Diseases,* CXIII (1951), 512.

32. Part of this behavior probably results from the fact that "absolute silence makes us uncomfortable, and, when it is lasting, conveys to the mind a special quality of emotion" (Groos, *op. cit.,* p. 21; also see Donald O. Hebb, *The Organization of Behavior* [New York: John Wiley & Sons, Inc., 1952], p. 252).

33. Notice, for example, that such common criticisms of modern painting as "my little brother could have done that" are not primarily statements of aesthetic value, though this is implied, but rather statements about belief.

34. Mere numbers are not the criteria for all members of the listening public. There are those groups who prefer to be exclusive, who are in the know as to what the "right" music is. Here belief functions in inverse ratio to general opinion.

35. David Riesman, *The Lonely Crowd* (New York: Doubleday & Co., 1953).

36. Koffka, *op. cit.,* p. 206.

37. *Ibid.,* p. 19.

38. Otto Ortmann, "On the Melodic Relativity of Tones," *Psychological Monographs,* Vol. XXXV, No. 1 (1926).

39. O. H. Mowrer, "Preparatory Set Expectancy: Further Evidence of Its Central Locus," *Journal of Experimental Psychology,* XXVIII (1941), 116–33.

40. Bach, *op. cit.,* p. 152. For the psychological viewpoint see P. E. Vernon, "The Apprehension and Cognition of Music," *Proceedings of the Music Association,* LIX (1933), p. 66.

41. Stravinsky, *op. cit.,* p. 122.

42. *Ibid.,* pp. 122–23.

43. Mursell, *op. cit.,* p. 162.

44. Curt Sachs, *Rhythm and Tempo* (New York: W. W. Norton & Co., Inc., 1953), p. 38.

NOTES TO CHAPTER III

1. George H. Mead, *Mind, Self, and Society* (Chicago: University of Chicago Press, 1952), p. 25.

2. Donald O. Hebb, *The Organization of Behavior* (New York: John Wiley & Sons, Inc., 1952), p. 35.

3. *Ibid.*, p. 58.

4. This example is similar to one quoted in Curt Sachs, *The Rise of Music in the Ancient World, East and West* (New York: W. W. Norton & Co., Inc., 1943), p. 125.

5. K. Koffka, *Principles of Gestalt Psychology* (New York: Harcourt, Brace & Co., 1935), p. 303, and chap. x.

6. *Ibid.*, p. 110.

7. *Ibid.*, p. 109.

8. *Ibid.*, p. 143.

9. *Ibid.*, p. 305.

10. Max Wertheimer, *Productive Thinking* (New York: Harper & Bros., 1945), pp. 193, 197.

11. Koffka, *op. cit.*, p. 499.

12. *Ibid.*, p. 109.

13. See *ibid.*, p. 507.

14. *Ibid.*, p. 473.

15. *Ibid.*, p. 476.

16. *Ibid.*, pp. 335, 338, 618–23.

17. *Ibid.*, pp. 608–9.

18. *Ibid.*, p. 175.

19. These observations point up a basic fallacy in the work of Helmholtz, Wundt, and Stumpf, all of whom isolate sensation from its aesthetic context and make pleasure-displeasure reactions the basis for a "psychology of music." On this point see Susanne K. Langer, *Philosophy in a New Key* (New York: Mentor Books, 1951), p. 171.

20. Koffka, *op. cit.*, pp. 302–3.

21. For other examples of this see J. S. Bach, *Well-tempered Clavier*, Vol. I, Preludes 1 and 2.

22. R. B. Stetson, "A Motor Theory of Rhythm and Discrete Succession," *Psychological Review*, XII (1905), 250–70, 293–350.

23. *Ibid.*, p. 308.

24. H. Woodrow, "A Quantitative Study of Rhythm," *Archives of Psychology*, XIV (1909), 1–66.

25. This should be kept in mind because there is always a tremendous temptation to specify and classify, to regard the groupings as clear and

definite. But there are many cases in which the real significance of the rhythmic organization lies precisely in its elusive ambiguity.

26. Curt Sachs, *Rhythm and Tempo* (New York: W. W. Norton & Co., Inc., 1953), pp. 16 f. Actually Sachs probably means meter; and if this is the case, his argument is more plausible. However, even here it may well be that the establishment of a metric pulse on the level of the phrase will persist, furnishing the composer with the possibility of creative deviation. For a discussion of meter see pp. 115 f.

27. Also see discussion of the fifth movement of Beethoven's String Quartet in C-Minor, pp. 145 ff.

28. See almost any piece of Schubert or Brahms, for example.

29. This is worthy of note because it seems to indicate that even our tendency to respond to music in a motor way is, in the last analysis, a learned response. This is also indicated by the experimental literature on the subject (see James L. Mursell, *The Psychology of Music* [New York: W. W. Norton & Co., Inc., 1937], pp. 153–54). Furthermore, it emphasizes the cultural character of even such seemingly basic responses as the motor response and the necessity of bringing the proper attitudes into play.

30. The quotation is not complete in all parts but presents the essential elements necessary for the present analysis. It may be found in the miniature score (published by J. & W. Chester, London) from two measures before No. 8 to two measures after No. 9.

31. This sense of progressive and continuing harmonic motion is made possible because (as Example 40 shows) there is no real dominant preparation, no pause on the dominant; rather the music rushes headlong into the melodic-rhythmic recapitulation.

NOTES TO CHAPTER IV

1. A. H. Fox Strangways, *The Music of Hindostan* (London: Oxford University Press, 1914), p. 329.

2. H. J. Watt, "Functions of the Size of Interval in the Songs of Schubert and of the Chippewa and Teton Sioux Indians," *British Journal of Psychology*, XIV (1923–24), 370–86.

3. *Grove's Dictionary of Music and Musicians*, ed. H. D. Colles (New York: Macmillan Co., 1936), III, 577.

4. See, for instance, Knud Jeppesen, *Counterpoint*, trans. Glen Haydon (New York: Prentice-Hall, Inc., 1939), pp. 85–86.

5. Winthrop Sargeant, "Types of Quechua Melody," *Musical Quarterly*, XX (1934), p. 239. The importance of the process of ornamentation is discussed in chap. vi of this book.

6. Joseph Yasser, *A Theory of Evolving Tonality* (American Library of Musicology, 1934).

7. J. Kunst, *Music in Java* (The Hague: Martinus Nijhoff, 1949), p. 53.

Actually it is the sléndro scale which added new tones to achieve equidistance. The nine-tone scale first referred to is a variation of the seventoned pélog scale. But the addition of the two tones would not have made the pélog equidistant; temperament was required for this.

8. Hugh Tracey, *Chopi Musicians: Their Music, Poetry, and Instruments* (International African Institute; Oxford: Oxford University Press, 1948). It is possible that this scale is an import from India; that it is derived from the scale referred to in the quotation from Kunst.

9. Curt Sachs, *The Rise of Music in the Ancient World, East and West* (New York: W. W. Norton & Co., Inc., 1943), pp. 283 f.

10. Eduard Hanslick, *The Beautiful in Music,* trans. G. Cohen (London: Novello, Ewer & Co.), pp. 48–49. Hanslick's contention that this melody might just as well express joy is probably justified; but this does not mean, as he implies, that the passage is not affective. It only means that since Gluck knew that he could depend upon the text to characterize the affect, it was unnecessary for the music to do so.

11. K. Koffka, *Principles of Gestalt Psychology* (New York: Harcourt, Brace & Co., 1935), p. 414.

12. In this connection it is important to realize that the context which determines the effect of repetition is cultural as well as purely musical. For instance, while exact repetition will generally be viewed as wasted effort by the Westerner, it may seem efficacious and productive to people of other cultures: "To us, for whom time is a motion on a space, unvarying repetition seems to scatter its force along a row of units of that space, and be wasted. To the Hopi, for whom time is not a motion but a 'getting later' of everything that has ever been done, unvarying repetition is not wasted but accumulated. It is storing up an invisible change that holds over into later events" (Benjamin Lee Whorf, *Collected Papers on Metalinguistics* [Department of State, Washington, D.C., 1952], p. 39).

13. James L. Mursell, "Psychology and the Problem of Scale," *Musical Quarterly,* XXXII (1946), 568.

14. P. R. Farnsworth, "The Effect of Repetitions on Ending Preferences in Melodies," *American Journal of Psychology,* XXXVII (1926), 116–22; and "Ending Preferences in Two Musical Situations," *ibid.,* 237–40. It is also important to remember that a particular listener may have learned to understand several different styles.

15. W. V. Bingham, "Studies in Melody," *Psychological Review: Monograph, Supplement,* L (1910).

16. Arthur D. Bissell, *The Role of Expectation in Music* (New Haven: Yale University Press, 1921), p. 19.

17. See James L. Mursell, *op. cit.,* p. 569; and Bingham, *op. cit.,* p. 86.

18. Paul Hindemith, *Craft of Musical Composition,* Vol. I, trans. Arthur Mendel (New York: Associated Music Publishers Inc., 1945), pp. 220–23.

19. Note that this is the case partly because of the intra-opus procedures set up thus far. That is, it is partly a result of the fact that the previous cadences in measures 10, 18, and 24 have all been deceptive.

20. Bingham, *op. cit.*, p. 33.

21. Sachs, *op. cit.*, pp. 30–44.

22. For a further discussion of successive comparison see chap. vii.

23. Obviously the fact that a greater time span is involved in the case of return plays a role in minimizing differences; for details which might be noticed if juxtaposed will often be lost if there is considerable separation.

NOTES TO CHAPTER V

1. It is interesting to observe that the Gestalt nature of melodic shapes is confirmed by the experience of many collectors of primitive and folk music, who have found that native singers often are unable to break off in the middle of a song and then continue from the same place. The singers have to go back to the beginning of the song and sing the total melody (the whole shape), which is not simply an aggregation of its parts. See, for instance, J. C. Anderson, "Maori Music with Its Polynesian Background" (Polynesian Society, Memoire 10 [1932–34]), p. 95; or Helen H. Roberts, "A Study of Folk Song Variants," *Journal of American Folklore*, XXXVIII (1925), 60.

2. K. Koffka, *Principles of Gestalt Psychology* (New York: Harcourt, Brace & Co., 1935), p. 126.

3. Also see the discussion of rhythmic incompleteness pp. 143 f.

4. The voices in such a series may be inverted so that the upper voice is the conjunct one and the lower voice the disjunct.

5. Of course, salient differentiation between harmonies is only a necessary cause, not a sufficient one, for the apprehension of progression. Other factors also play an important part in the fixing of tonal relationships; e.g., the fact that the tone F in the subdominant harmony limits tonality on the "sharp" side, while the tone B in the dominant harmony limits tonality on the "flat" side.

6. Koffka, *op. cit.*, p. 191.

7. Within the context of a piece of music silence may appear to form a continuous ground; for then certain attributes already established as given in the work, such as the meter or even a repeated rhythmic group, are continued subjectively in the mind of the listener, even in the absence of any objective stimulation.

8. *Ibid.*, p. 197.

9. *Ibid.*, p. 206.

10. The importance of such trained attention is illustrated by the difficulty which unpracticed listeners usually have in following a pol-

yphonic texture or by the trouble which European trained musicians have in apprehending the intricate cross rhythms of African music (see p. 254). This again calls attention to the powerful influence which early musical practice, even of a rather elementary nature, has upon the responses of the listener in later life; for it seems very probable that a listener's apprehension of a polyphonic texture or of African cross rhythms is greatly facilitated by his own motor practice—that initially these complexities are perceived in terms of the listener-performer's own motor responses.

11. The converse of this will also tend to activate expectation, though not as strongly; i.e., textures which are abnormally thick, closely spaced, will be expected to become thinner, to separate.

12. See the discussion on pp. 184 ff. of the opening measures of Mozart's Piano Concerto in D Minor.

13. That this constitutes a deviation is shown by the fact that of the eight fugues in Handel's twelve Concerti this is the only one in which the polyphonic web is decisively broken.

14. Koffka, *op. cit.,* p. 192.

15. Notice that had this final texture been presented by itself, had there been no progressive weakening of the figure, it might well have been understood simply as a rather active ground.

NOTES TO CHAPTER VI

1. C. P. E. Bach, *An Essay on the True Art of Playing Keyboard Instruments,* trans. William J. Mitchell (New York: W. W. Norton & Co., Inc., 1949), p. 150; also see Sol Babitz, "A Problem of Rhythm in Baroque Music," *Musical Quarterly,* XXXVIII (1952), 533–65.

2. Oliver Strunk, *Source Readings in Music History* (New York: W. W. Norton & Co., Inc., 1950), p. 607.

3. *Grove's Dictionary of Music and Musicians,* ed. H. C. Colles (New York: Macmillan Co., 1936), I, 635.

4. David D. Boyden, "The Violin and Its Technique in the 18th Century," *Musical Quarterly,* XXXVI (1950), 35–36.

5. Carl E. Seashore, "Objective Analysis of the Musical Performance," *Studies in the Psychology of Music,* Vol. IV (Iowa City: University of Iowa Press, 1937), p. 26.

6. Milton Metfessel, *Phono-photography in Folk Music* (Chapel Hill: University of North Carolina Press, 1928), p. 11, 12; see the introduction by Carl E. Seashore. Notice that Seashore's word "flirtation" comes very close to the idea of play mentioned earlier in this study. Also see Raymond B. Stetson ("A Motor Theory of Rhythm and Discrete Succession," *Psychological Review,* XII [1905], 337), who notes that "aside

from such irregularities which the rhythm requires, there are various minor variations for the purpose of expression."

7. Carl E. Seashore, "A Base for the Approach to Quantitative Studies in the Aesthetics of Music," *American Journal of Psychology*, XXXIX (1927), 141–44.

8. Carl E. Seashore, *Psychology of Music* (New York: McGraw-Hill Book Co., Inc., 1938), p. 212.

9. George Herzog, "General Characteristics of Primitive Music" (abstract), *Bulletin of the American Musicological Society*, VII (1942), 24.

10. Frances Densmore, *Chippewa Music*, (Smithsonian Institution, Bureau of American Ethnology, Bulletin 45 [1910]), p. 4.

11. George Herzog, "Folk Song," *Dictionary of Folklore, Mythology and Legend* (New York: Funk & Wagnalls Co., 1949), p. 1041. Notice the juxtaposition of the words expressive and ornamental; the connection is not accidental.

12. Bela Bartók and Albert B. Lord, *Serbo-Croatian Folk Songs* (New York: Columbia University Press, 1951), p. 4. In addition to the experience of such singing, our acceptance of these particular deviations in this particular situation is probably abetted by our belief in their purposefulness.

13. R. H. van Gulik, *The Lore of the Chinese Lute: An Essay in Ch'in Ideology* (Tokyo: Sophia University, 1940), p. 75.

14. *Ibid.*, p. 77.

15. Japp Kunst, *Music in Java* (The Hague: Martinus Nijhoff, 1949), p. 59.

16. A. K. Coomaraswamy, *Figures of Speech or Figures of Thought* (London: Luzac & Co., 1946), p. 86.

17. Thus in the examples analyzed earlier in this study, e.g., the Hindemith example, p. 140, the basic outline gives the structural tones, and the other tones and progressions may be considered to be an ornamentation of this basic structural line.

18. Alain Danielou, *Northern Indian Music* (London: Christopher Johnson, 1949), p. 102. The quotation is from the *Nātya Shāstra,* a compilation of theoretical writings, which has been variously dated from the second century B.C. to the fourth century A.D.

19. Gustave Reese, *Music in the Middle Ages* (New York: W. W. Norton & Co., Inc., 1940), pp. 204 ff.

20. From Blanchet's *Art du Chant,* quoted in *Grove's Dictionary, op. cit.*, III, 769.

21. François Raguenet, "A Comparison Between the French and Italian Music" (anon. trans. *ca.* 1709), *Musical Quarterly*, XXXII (1946), 429.

22. Bach, *op. cit.*, p. 84.

23. *Ibid.*, p. 322.

24. Knud Jeppesen, *Counterpoint,* trans. Glen Haydon (New York: Prentice-Hall Inc., 1939), p. 147.

25. Wilfrid Mellers, *François Couperin* (London: Dennis Dobson Ltd., 1950), p. 305. Similar effects are very common in oriental music. See, for instance, Jan La Rue, "The Okinawan Notation System," *Journal of the American Musicological Society,* IV (1951), 30; or Danielou, *op. cit.,* pp. 104 ff.

26. Raguenet, *op. cit.,* pp. 417–18.

27. This quotation from Heinrich Glarean, *Dodecachordon,* Book III, chap. xxiv, is given in Oliver Strunk, *op. cit.,* pp. 222–23.

28. *Jazz Journal,* January, 1950, quoted in Rex Harris, *Jazz* (Harmondsworth, Middlesex: Penguin Books, 1952), p. 349.

29. Kunst, *op. cit.,* p. 401.

30. A. K. Coomaraswamy, "India Music," *Musical Quarterly,* III (1917), 165.

31. Sachs, *The Rise of Music in the Ancient World, East and West* (New York: W. W. Norton & Co., Inc., 1943), pp. 108, 143. For specific illustrations of such classifications see Danielou, *op. cit.,* pp. 104 ff.; and La Rue, *op. cit.,* pp. 31–32.

32. Kunst, *op. cit.,* p. 276.

33. *Ibid.,* pp. 333–34.

34. *Ibid.,* p. 277.

35. A. K. Coomaraswamy, *The Dance of Siva* (New York: The Sunrise Turn Inc., 1924), p. 76. For a very similar statement see A. H. Fox Strangways, *The Music of Hindostan* (London: Oxford University Press, 1914), p. 182.

36. *Op. cit.,* pp. 146–47.

37. See examples, *ibid.,* p. 188.

38. A. Z. Idelsohn, *Jewish Music* (New York: Tudor Publishing Co., 1948), pp. 98, 183.

39. Sachs, *op. cit.,* p. 83.

40. Percy Grainger, "The Impress of Personality in Unwritten Music," *Musical Quarterly,* I (1915), 422.

41. From the introduction to Bartók and Lord, *op. cit.,* pp. xii–xiii. The relation between abundant ornamentation and free or rubato tempo is by no means unique. Writing of music in the early baroque, Bukofzer notes that "the accumulation of intricate embellishments so strongly affected the rhythm that the music could no longer be performed in strict time" (Manfred F. Bukofzer, *Music in the Baroque Era* [New York: W. W. Norton & Co., Inc., 1947], p. 28).

42. Bartók and Lord, *op. cit.,* p. 74.

43. Phillips Barry, *Folk Music in America* ("American Folk Song Publications," No. 4, Works Progress Administration, Federal Theatre Project [New York: National Service Bureau, 1939]), p. 112. The phrase is a

quotation from an article by Robert W. Gordon, which appeared in the *New York Times* November 27, 1927.

44. Metfessel, *op. cit.,* p. 21.

45. *Ibid.,* p. 48.

46. Winthrop Sargeant, *Jazz: Hot and Hybrid* (New York: E. P. Dutton, 1946), p. 24. Of course, there need be no printed guide so long as the several players know the tune and plan.

47. Harris, *op. cit.,* pp. 62–63.

48. *Ibid.,* p. 155.

49. Richard A. Waterman, " 'Hot Rhythm' in Negro Music," *Journal of the American Musicological Society,* I (1948), 31.

50. This is emphasized by Willard Rhodes in his article, "Acculturation in North American Indian Music," *Selected Papers of the XXIXth International Congress of Americanists,* ed. Sol Tax (Chicago: University of Chicago Press, 1952), pp. 127–32; see in particular p. 130.

51. Ornamentation might itself be said to be a partial basis of musical style. Within a cultural area style is not so much a matter of fundamental tunes but of differences in ornamentation. Discussing the music of the Maoris of New Zealand, Anderson writes: "One tribe might adopt a melody from another tribe, and the outline would probably be unaltered, but the adventitious ornamentation of the melody might be varied—in fact, Sir Apirana Ngata has told me that any Maori familiar with their music could tell from the ornamentation what tribe was responsible for that particular form of the melody." J. C. Anderson, "Maori Music with Its Polynesian Background" (Polynesian Society, Memoire 10 [1932–34]), p. 191.

52. A. M. Jones, "African Music," *African Affairs,* XLVIII (1949), 295.

53. George Herzog, "Speech-Melody and Primitive Music," *Musical Quarterly,* XX (1934), 456.

54. Helen H. Roberts, "Melodic Composition and Scale Foundations in Primitive Music," *Journal of American Anthropology,* XXXIV (1932), 80.

55. Strangways, *op. cit.,* p. 19.

56. The expectations aroused by the active tones on any given architectonic level are not solely the product of the functions of the individual tones. For the expectations engendered by any given tone are not only a product of its function and position in the tonal system but are also a result of the tones which have preceded it. It is likewise clear that the rhythmic placement of tones affects their degree of activity or rest.

57. Kunst, *op. cit.,* p. 51.

58. *Ibid.,* p. 51, n. 3.

59. Sachs, *op. cit.,* p. 134.

60. *Ibid.,* p. 133.

61. Herzog, "Folk Song," *op. cit.*, p. 1043.

62. Indeed, the author knows of no tonal system that is not diatonic. The twelve-tone system of Schoenberg and his followers is no exception to this rule because it is intentionally and explicitly non-tonal. The tempered five-tone sléndro scale of Malaya, a seeming exception, appears, in origin at least, to have been diatonic and it seems possible that it is still heard as such (Sachs, *op. cit.*, pp. 130–31).

63. Such embellishing pitch deviations are not, it must be emphasized, to be confused with the microtonal elements, e.g., the śruti in Indian music, which find a place in the theoretical foundation for the various modes and *rāgas* of Indian or Arabian music; see Strangways, *op. cit.*, chap. iv.

64. Strunk, *op. cit.*, pp. 602 f.; and Bach, *op. cit.*, p. 163.

65. Otto Gombosi, "The Pedigree of the Blues," *Proceedings of the Music Teachers, National Association,* Series XL (1946), p. 385.

66. Edward E. Lowinsky, *Secret Chromatic Art in the Netherlands Motet,* trans. Carl Buchman (New York: Columbia University Press, 1946), p. 79.

67. The example is taken from *Grove's Dictionary*, I, 645.

68. Indeed, it is important to realize that melodic chromaticism which occurs over a static harmony and only on unaccented beats, as, for instance, in the opening melody of Debussy's *Afternoon of a Faun,* is really a rapidly passing "effect" which may have only a minimal embodied meaning and give rise to but little affective response since it inhibits or delays no important tendencies. However, such passages may give rise to important designative meanings and, as is pointed out in chap. viii, may arouse affect through them.

69. John Brown, *Letters upon the Poetry and Music of the Italian Opera* (Edinburgh: Bell and Bradfute, 1789), pp. 12–16.

70. A. Montani, "Psychoanalysis of Music," *Psychoanalytic Review,* XXXII (1945), 225–27.

71. See Herzog, "Folk Song," *op. cit.*; and Barry, *op. cit.*, Introduction.

72. C. P. Heinlein, "The Affective Characters of the Major and Minor Modes in Music," *Journal of Comparative Psychology,* VIII (1928), 101–42.

73. Nevertheless, the influence of the minor mode in Western music and on Western listeners has been a very powerful one, as even a cursory glance at the literature will show. See, for example, Kate Hevner, "The Affective Character of the Major and Minor Modes in Music," *American Journal of Psychology,* XLVII (1935), 103–18.

74. Bukofzer, *op. cit.*, p. 287.

75. Erich M. von Hornbostel, "African Negro Music," *Africa,* I (1928), 16.

76. Sachs, *op. cit.*, p. 125.

77. Gustave Reese, *Music in the Renaissance* (New York: W. W. Norton & Co., Inc., 1954), p. 400. It seems possible that the minor mode is not only a deviation from the norm of the diatonic but also from a deeply rooted feeling for major, which is present in the West. See Sachs, *op. cit.*, pp. 295–311; also see George Herzog, "Some Primitive Layers in European Folk Music," *Bulletin of the American Musicological Society*, IX (1947), p. 13. If it is true that our modern major mode is a primordial norm in Western musical culture, then the minor mode is, so to speak, a doubt deviant: it deviates both from the intercultural norm of diatonicism and from the norm of major, which is specific to European culture.

78. Heinlein, *op. cit.*, pp. 136–37.

79. Vincenzo Galilei, *Dialogo della musica antica e della moderna*, quoted in Strunk, *op. cit.*, pp. 315–16.

80. Bach, *op. cit.*, p. 163.

81. Gioseffe Zarlino, *Istituzioni armoniche*, Book III, quoted in Strunk, *op. cit.*, p. 232.

82. Anderson, *op. cit.*, p. 63.

83. This literature need not be reviewed here since it is admirably summarized in an article by M. Guernesey, "The Role of Consonance and Dissonance in Music," *American Journal of Psychology*, XL (1928), 173–204.

84. Norman Cazden, "Musical Consonance and Dissonance: A Cultural Criterion," *Journal of Aesthetics*, IV (1945), 4–5. This general position is supported by several authors. Guernesey, *op. cit.*, concludes that consonance is "an aesthetic description, totally dynamic in nature, and is not a scientifically determinable constant" and that its perception depends upon training, environment, and musical context. The importance of context is also emphasized by P. A. D. Gardner and R. W. Pickford, "Relation between Dissonance and Context," *Nature*, CLII (1943), p. 358. The importance of cultural factors in the perception of consonance is stressed in an article by R. W. Lundin, "Toward a Cultural Theory of Consonance," *Journal of Psychology*, XXIII (1947), 45–49.

85. Willi Apel, *Harvard Dictionary of Music* (Cambridge, Mass.: Harvard University Press, 1945), p. 18.

86. Nor is it difficult to account for the fact that the dissonance norm has constantly risen in Western culture. For it seems likely that when a vertical combination of sound has been heard often enough as a unit, it achieves the status of an independent, unified Gestalt, complete in itself. It becomes a norm and ceases to perform its affective aesthetic function adequately. Therefore, the composer, seeking for aesthetic effect and expression and wishing to explore less common paths, will tend to treat what was formerly a deviant as a norm and use that which was formerly unused or forbidden as a deviant.

NOTES TO CHAPTER VII

1. Japp Kunst, *Music in Java* (The Hague: Martinus Nijhoff, 1949), p. 59.

2. Curt Sachs, *The Rise of Music in the Ancient World, East and West* (New York: W. W. Norton & Co., Inc., 1943), p. 145.

3. Eta Harich-Schneider, "The Present Condition of Japanese Court Music," *Musical Quarterly*, XXXIX (1953), 58.

4. E. Cunningham, "The Japanese Ko-uta and Ha-uta," *Musical Quarterly*, XXXIV (1948), 71.

5. Harich-Schneider, *op. cit.*, p. 53.

6. Kunst, *op. cit.*, p. 157.

7. A. H. Fox Strangways, *The Music of Hindostan* (London: Oxford University Press, 1914), p. 226.

8. *Ibid.*, p. 238.

9. Curt Sachs, *Rhythm and Tempo* (New York: W. W. Norton & Co., Inc., 1953), chap. vi.

10. Strangways, *op. cit.*, p. 233.

11. Winthrop Sargeant and Lahiri, "A Study of East Indian Rhythm," *Musical Quarterly*, XVII (1931), 435–36.

12. *Ibid.*, p. 434.

13. A. M. Jones, "African Music," *African Affairs*, XLVIII (1949), 294.

14. All of these examples are taken from A. M. Jones, "African Music: The Mganda Dance," *African Studies*, IV (1945), 180–88; also see A. M. Jones, "The Study of African Musical Rhythm," *Bantu Studies*, XI (1937), 295–320; and R. Brandel, "Music of the Giants and the Pygmies of the Belgian Congo," *Journal of the American Musicological Society*, V (1952), 16–28.

15. Jones, "African Music," *op. cit.*, p. 294. Also see A. M. Jones, *African Music in Northern Rhodesia and Some Other Places* ("Occasional Papers of the Rhodes-Livingston Museum" [Oxford University Press, 1949]), pp. 20, 78.

16. Erich M. von Hornbostel, "African Negro Music," *Africa*, I (1928), 52.

17. Richard Alan Waterman, "African Influence on the Music of the Americas," *Selected Papers of the XXIXth International Congress of Americanists*, ed. Sol Tax (Chicago: University of Chicago Press, 1952), p. 213.

18. *Ibid.*, p. 213.

19. *Ibid.*, p. 214.

20. Winthrop Sargeant, *Jazz: Hot and Hybrid* (New York: E. P. Dutton, 1946), pp. 238–39.

21. Hugh Tracey, *Chopi Musicians: Their Music, Poetry and Instru-

ments, International African Institute (London: Oxford University Press, 1948), p. 101.

22. Hornbostel, *op. cit.,* p. 48.

23. *Ibid.,* p. 47.

24. I am indebted to Professor Scott Goldthwaite, not only for calling my attention to this example of rhythmic crossing, but also for permitting me to use his transcription of the chanson. For a much more complex example from the early fifteenth century see A. T. Davidson and W. Apel, *Historical Anthology of Music* (Cambridge, Mass.: Harvard University Press, 1949), p. 51, No. 48a.

25. See Tracey, *op. cit.,* p. 91.

26. Such free preludes may eventually become more or less standardized within the style, may become fairly fixed forms which are themselves norms of the style.

27. Sachs, *The Rise of Music in the Ancient World,* pp. 191, 285, and 290; Strangways, *op. cit.,* p. 281; Harich-Schneider, *op. cit.,* p. 60; Jones, "African Music: The Mganda Dance," *op. cit.,* p. 185; and Kunst, *op. cit.,* pp. 310–11. Although these preludes may at times also serve as display pieces in which the individual performer may exhibit his ingenuity and virtuosity in improvising upon the mode, this is not their basic aesthetic function.

28. I have quoted only the beginnings, the verse parts, not the connecting material of a song given in Davidson and Apel, *op. cit.,* pp. 3–4. Note the presence of both successive and simultaneous deviation. Not only are the *koto* part and voice part varied melodically and rhythmically from verse to verse, but within each verse the accompaniment deviates from the song proper or vice versa.

29. Strangways, *op. cit.,* pp. 282–83.

30. *Ibid.,* chap. xi.

31. A. Z. Idelsohn, *Jewish Music* (New York: Tudor Publishing Co., 1948), pp. 24–25.

32. Egon Wellesz, "Words and Music in Byzantine Liturgy," *Musical Quarterly,* XXXIII (1947), 306–7.

33. Egon Wellesz, *Byzantine Music and Hymnography* (London: Oxford University Press, 1949), p. 286.

34. Idelsohn, *op. cit.,* p. 370.

35. Sachs, *The Rise of Music in the Ancient World,* p. 84.

36. Helen H. Roberts, "A Study of Folk Song Variants Based on Field Work in Jamaica," *Journal of American Folklore,* XXXVIII (1925), p. 155.

37. *Ibid.,* p. 168.

38. *Ibid.,* p. 158.

39. *Ibid.,* p. 167.

40. *Ibid.,* p. 167.

41. *Ibid.*, p. 215.

42. Bela Bartók and Albert B. Lord, *Serbo-Croatian Folk Songs* (New York: Columbia University Press, 1951), pp. 114–15.

43. Sargeant, *Jazz: Hot and Hybrid*, pp. 156–57. The use of a common ground bass, a common harmonic sequence, can also be found in Western art music of the sixteenth and seventeenth centuries; for the relationship between these basses and those found in hot jazz see Otto Gombosi, "The Pedigree of the Blues," *Proceedings of the Music Teachers National Association*, Series XL (1946), 382–89.

44. Willard Rhodes, "Acculturation in North American Indian Music," *Selected Papers of the XXIXth International Congress of Americanists*, ed. Sol Tax (Chicago: University of Chicago Press, 1952), p. 130.

45. Jones, "African Music," *op. cit.*, pp. 292–93; also see Tracey, *op. cit.*, pp. 91 f.

NOTES TO CHAPTER VIII

1. J. T. MacCurdy, *The Psychology of Emotion* (New York: Harcourt, Brace & Co., 1925), p. 568.

2. One of the dangers of descriptive program notes and poetic criticism is that they tend to initiate such image processes, which later develop without reference to the music itself.

3. For a detailed discussion of the relationship between memory and affect see David Rapaport, *Emotions and Memory* (New York: International University Press, 1950).

4. After citing some interesting experiments dealing with the intersensory character of experience, Koffka observes that "we must, in accordance with our theory, conclude that perceptual space is *one* and that it can be filled with objects of different sense modalities . . ." (K. Koffka, *Principles of Gestalt Psychology* [New York: International University Press, 1952], p. 303).

5. Susanne K. Langer, *Philosophy in a New Key* (New York: Mentor Books, 1951), p. 155.

6. Probably one of the fundamental conditions for the existence of any connotative complex is the presence of a single-mood response which is common to all of its components. Indeed, connotation and sentiment are so inextricably united that every connotative experience is to some extent a mood experience as well.

7. Because the chain of responses usually takes place with such rapidity that there is no noticeable delay between the initial perception of mood and the final affective experience, the mediating stimulus is less likely to be a connotative reference involving some sort of conscious cognition or re-evaluation of the original stimulus, i.e., the music.

8. Eduard Hanslick, *The Beautiful in Music,* trans. Gustav Cohen (London: Novello, Ewer & Co., 1891), p. 25.

9. C. C. Pratt, "Structural vs. Expressive Form in Music," *Journal of Psychology,* V (1938), p. 150.

10. The need for variety is undoubtedly a reason for a change of mood or connotation, but it does not provide a rationale for the order of change. However, once a particular succession has been established in a composition, we may expect a return of the succession or, if one of the parts does return, we may expect the other parts to return in their established order. But this does not account for the order of the original succession.

11. It is, of course, possible for a rationale of mood and connotative complex succession to become a feature of a particular style, for a set of mood orders to be established as part of a tradition. The opera composers, the librettists, and the theorists of the early eighteenth century were often concerned with this very problem, and rules were laid down for the sequence of moods. Were such an order to become a really well-known feature of the style, it would presumably not only establish a reasonable relationship between moods but would also have important effects upon the embodied meaning of musical experience.

Index

Accent: defined, 103 f.; distinguished from stress, 104; on rest, 149; stress on, may alter grouping, 104, 107 f.; *see also* Beat; Meter; Rhythm

Aesthetic belief; *see* Belief, aesthetic

Aesthetic experience: belief in special nature of, 73 f. (*see also* Belief, aesthetic); problematical in primitive music, 239; responses not overt in, 9, 74, 273 (n. 15); *see also* Affective experience; Meaning; Play

Affect: differentiation of, 16–20; distinguished from affective experience, 19; distinguished from mood, 7; meaning and, 39–40; subjective nature of, 12; 256; suppression of overt behavior intensifies, 9, 74; tendency inhibition creates, 15–16; *see also* Affective experience; Psychological theory of emotions; Suspense

Affective experience: basis of, in music, 31; belief in mental control modifies, 19 f.; characterized by stimulus situation, 19; conquest of difficulties an aspect of, 70; differentiation of, in music theory, 17, 20; expectation and, 23–25, 30–32 (*see also* Expectation); Hebb's account of, criticized, 19; image processes create, 256–58; inhibition and conflict create, 15, 16 f.; intellectual and, complementary, 39 (*see also* Meaning); MacCurdy's analysis of, 14 f.; mood and connotation color, 269 f. (*see also* Connotation; Mood); mood indirectly evokes, 268; necessarily differentiated, 19; non-referential character of, in music, 20; Paulhan's analysis of, 15; play and, 70 (*see also* Play); *sui generis* musical, 20; suspense creates, 27–29 (*see also* Suspense;

Uncertainty); *see also* Behavior, emotional; Philosophy of music

African music: deviation and ornamentation in, 214; differences of, from jazz, 243; heterophony in, 244; rhythmic structure of [Ex. 95–98], 239–42; tendency toward equidistance in, 133

Aiken, Henry D., on aesthetic beliefs, 9, 73 f.

Ambiguity: affect and, 16 (*see also* Suspense; Uncertainty); architectonic level modifies view of, 52; chromaticism and, 164, 218 f.; expectation and, 26, 51, 171; of formal function, 182–84; harmonic, 95, 166, 179–82; melodic, 163–67; metric, 144 f.; of minor mode, 266; mitigated by good shape, 174; nature of, 51–52; and probability, 52; rhythmic (*see* Rhythm); of texture, 192–95; *see also* Suspense; Uncertainty

Amphibrach rhythm; *see* Rhythm

Anapest rhythm; *see* Rhythm

Anxiety; *see* Suspense; Uncertainty

Appoggiatura: affective function of, 101, 210 f.; inhibits tendencies, 100 f., 207; *see also* Ornamentation

Architectonic levels: ambiguity on different, 52; completeness and closure on different, 130; deviation on different, 215 f.; meaning on different, interdependent, 47; melodic-harmonic uniformity on higher, 168; metric organization on different, 115 f.; ornamentation on different, 205; overemphasis on highest, 52 f.; rhythmic incompleteness on different, 144–48; rhythmic organization on different, 110–15

Art: academic, traditional, and deca-